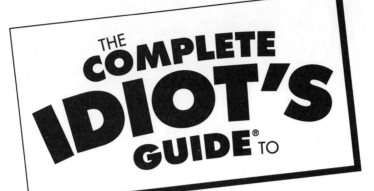

Crystals

D1592735

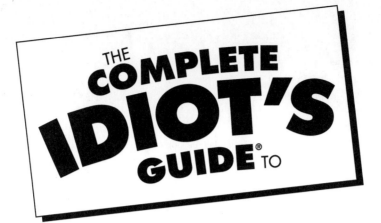

THE

COMPLETE
IDIOT'S
GUIDE® TO

Crystals

by Karen Ryan

ALPHA

A member of Penguin Group (USA) Inc.

ALPHA BOOKS

Published by the Penguin Group

Penguin Group (USA) Inc., 375 Hudson Street, New York, New York 10014, USA

Penguin Group (Canada), 90 Eglinton Avenue East, Suite 700, Toronto, Ontario M4P 2Y3, Canada (a division of Pearson Penguin Canada Inc.)

Penguin Books Ltd., 80 Strand, London WC2R 0RL, England

Penguin Ireland, 25 St. Stephen's Green, Dublin 2, Ireland (a division of Penguin Books Ltd.)

Penguin Group (Australia), 250 Camberwell Road, Camberwell, Victoria 3124, Australia (a division of Pearson Australia Group Pty. Ltd.)

Penguin Books India Pvt. Ltd., 11 Community Centre, Panchsheel Park, New Delhi—110 017, India

Penguin Group (NZ), 67 Apollo Drive, Rosedale, North Shore, Auckland 1311, New Zealand (a division of Pearson New Zealand Ltd.)

Penguin Books (South Africa) (Pty.) Ltd., 24 Sturdee Avenue, Rosebank, Johannesburg 2196, South Africa

Penguin Books Ltd., Registered Offices: 80 Strand, London WC2R 0RL, England

Copyright © 2010 by Karen Ryan

International Standard Book Number: 978-1-61564-020-1
Library of Congress Catalog Card Number: 2009943482

12 11 10   8 7 6 5 4 3 2 1

Interpretation of the printing code: The rightmost number of the first series of numbers is the year of the book's printing; the rightmost number of the second series of numbers is the number of the book's printing. For example, a printing code of 10-1 shows that the first printing occurred in 2010.

Printed in the United States of America

Note: This publication contains the opinions and ideas of its author. It is intended to provide helpful and informative material on the subject matter covered. It is sold with the understanding that the author and publisher are not engaged in rendering professional services in the book. If the reader requires personal assistance or advice, a competent professional should be consulted.

The author and publisher specifically disclaim any responsibility for any liability, loss, or risk, personal or otherwise, which is incurred as a consequence, directly or indirectly, of the use and application of any of the contents of this book.

Most Alpha books are available at special quantity discounts for bulk purchases for sales promotions, premiums, fund-raising, or educational use. Special books, or book excerpts, can also be created to fit specific needs.

For details, write: Special Markets, Alpha Books, 375 Hudson Street, New York, NY 10014.

Publisher: *Marie Butler-Knight*
Associate Publisher: *Mike Sanders*
Senior Managing Editor: *Billy Fields*
Executive Editor: *Randy Ladenheim-Gil*
Development Editor: *Lynn Northrup*
Senior Production Editor: *Janette Lynn*

Copy Editor: *Megan Wade*
Cover Designer: *William Thomas*
Book Designer: *Trina Wurst*
Indexer: *Julie Bess*
Layout: *Brian Massey*
Proofreader: *Laura Caddell*

Contents at a Glance

Contents

Part 2: Starting Your Crystal Collection

Introduction

For thousands of years, crystals have captivated the imagination of the rich and poor, the young and old, and inspired wonderful works of sacred art and regal ornamentation. But there's much, much more to these beauties than their dazzling display. Healing—physical, emotional, and spiritual—is possible through the energy these gemstones emit.

How many crystals are there, you might be wondering, and what, exactly, are they capable of? Suffice it to say that no matter what your need, no matter what your worry, no matter what your illness, there is a gemstone that can help ease it. Throughout this book, I discuss different conditions and suggest crystals that are appropriate for healing. The resources at the back of the book will also be helpful if you are interested in a particular crystal.

Crystal therapy really centers on energy—the energy of the gemstone and the energy of your subtle body, or *chakras* (concepts I discuss in detail in the middle chapters of the book). When these two force fields interact (providing the crystal in question is appropriate for the area it's laid upon or near), the healing that can occur is nothing short of amazing.

To focus that energy for healing, crystal healers rely on clients to have an open mind, a willingness to meditate, and a belief that they *can* be healed. But whether you're a true believer already or a skeptical seeker, I hope that you will try the methods in this book with an open mind. What do you have to lose?

How to Use This Book

This book is divided into five parts:

Part 1, "All About Crystals," covers the ins and outs of gemstones, including the history of some of the most famous gemstones in the world; the scientific properties of crystals (that is, why they work in healing *and* in certain small appliances!); and more metaphysical issues, such as subtle body energies and sacred healing. This part ends with a beginner's buying guide to help you determine which crystals you absolutely need, and how crystals "speak" to you.

Part 2, "Starting Your Crystal Collection," shares some basic handling techniques, such as cleansing and charging crystals, and how to use them in some everyday environments.

Part 3, "Healing Properties of Crystals for Body, Mind, and Spirit," discusses which crystals you might use for specific health conditions. Information is also included on how to choose crystals for every member of your family.

Part 4, "Crystal Healing Techniques," goes deeper into crystal healing and actually spells out the healing practices you can use for yourself and for friends and loved ones. Here's where you learn to become a crystal healer.

Part 5, "Personal Development," leaves you with some extra information to build on, such as the benefits of taking courses on crystal healing, and advanced meditation techniques.

You'll also find three helpful appendixes: an A-to-Z crystal guide; a glossary of terms used throughout the book; and a list of books for further reading.

Extras

As you read about crystal energy and healing, you'll notice boxes of text designed to give you extra information:

def•i•ni•tion

Here's where you'll find explanations of crystal healing terms that might be unfamiliar to you.

Yellow Flag

Pay extra attention to these cautions and caveats concerning the use of gemstones.

Gem of an Idea

Check these boxes for creative uses, tips, and ideas for starting, maintaining, and caring for your crystal collection.

Crystal Clear

Check these boxes for additional ideas, thoughts, or historical information related to the topic at hand.

Acknowledgments

There are always helpers from the friendship corner of my bagua who come forward when needed. I am grateful for the assistance of Jevan, for reviewing technical components of the book; and to Joanne, for trying the crystal exercises, which completely surprised her with the results!

My three Lhasa Apso doggies ensured that I got frequent breaks to dole out biscuits about every 20 minutes. Their "babysitter," Cynthia, was also encouraging, leaving notes for me to read and inquiring how the book was coming along.

Thank you to Jacky Sach, Lynn Northrup, and Randy Ladenheim-Gil for their encouragement in bringing this book forward for readers with an interest in crystals. For helping with the style of the book, I am grateful to Shelly Hagen for her keen abilities to unravel the tight spots.

Lastly, I want to thank the people who asked about the power of crystals because they are the ones this book is for. Without their curiosity and sincere interest, this book would not have been written. For those already using crystals, remember, there is always room for more crystals in your collection!

Trademarks

All terms mentioned in this book that are known to be or are suspected of being trademarks or service marks have been appropriately capitalized. Alpha Books and Penguin Group (USA) Inc. cannot attest to the accuracy of this information. Use of a term in this book should not be regarded as affecting the validity of any trademark or service mark.

Crystal Therapy System (CTS) is a proprietary name of Karen Ryan and the Crystal Alchemy Academy.

Part 1

All About Crystals

Some of the most famous diamonds and gemstones are more accessible to us today than ever before. You can visit a museum or a castle to see the largest natural crystals ever found, cut and polished to perfection. Such perfection can inspire us to become flawless like a priceless jewel.

Although their beauty can be blinding, it is also important to know about the science behind crystals. Technological changes during the past century have provided a solid foundation for studying these nuggets from the earth, and the cross-over from science to sacred science is helping a new generation of crystal healers understand the science behind connecting with the energy of crystals. Crystal healing is examined and explained as a therapy for those pursuing self-transformation and healing.

Knowing about the basic subtle energies of the human body will always be a large component of crystal healing. Crystals have amazing influence on subtle energies, including auras, chakras, meridians, and even more subtle spiritual energies. Part 1 gives you a great general overview of where crystals have been, where they are now, and where they are headed!

Chapter 1

Crystals 101

In This Chapter

- How crystals inspire the imagination
- Dynasty gemstones
- Gemstone myths and superstitions
- Create a gemstone from yourself

There is no question that crystals are alluring. They catch our eyes and draw us in for a closer look. Why, even people who don't know the true power of crystals are taken in by their pure physical beauty—but as they (and you) will soon learn, there is much, much more to these sparkling stones than meets the eye!

Crystals come in all sorts of shapes, sizes, and colors—and as if there wasn't enough variety already, the earth continuously provides new crystals. With a new "crop" constantly growing, we have a lot of material to explore and experiment with. But before we get too far ahead of ourselves, let's take a look at where crystals come from ….

What's in a Word?

The word *crystal* comes from the Greek word *krustallos*, meaning "ice," no doubt because a clear quartz crystal has similar characteristics as an ice cube—it's colorless, transparent, and cold to the touch. (But it won't keep your soda cold, so keep it in your hand or on a chain around your neck, and not in your drink!)

def•i•ni•tion

A **crystal** is a solid material comprised of two molecules of silicon dioxide and one molecule of oxygen. The different shapes of crystals are due to differences in molecular bonding. Crystals also have electrical properties.

Crystals are some of the most visually inspiring materials on Earth. Think about it. Literature often refers to the understanding of an idea, a voice, or a concept as being "crystal clear." A lake can be crystal clear, meaning that you can look down to the bottom. A glass of water is also crystal clear, meaning that it is colorless, you can see through it, and that there aren't nasty little bits floating around inside. Ideas are "crystallized" when thoughts are transformed from uncertainty into perpetual clarity.

When we use these phrases, we imagine the twinkle and sparkle of tiny little gemstones, providing a light through the darkness or an entirely new way of seeing things. And as you read through this book, you'll learn that that's really what crystal power is all about!

Crystals Fit for a King

Although there is a resurgence in holistic health interests and the use of crystals, we're hardly the first generation to have discovered this natural resource. In fact, the use of crystals goes back thousands of years. Perhaps you've heard of an ancient Egyptian king named Tut? Well, when the noted archaeologist Howard Carter opened the boy-king's tomb back in the 1920s, he unearthed magnificent inlayed gemstone jewelry laid inside the tomb and an extraordinary sarcophagus (coffin) richly decorated with lapis lazuli and gold. (Lapis lazuli is a dark blue stone known to promote a clear mind and provide spiritual protection—a wise choice for the casket of a king on his way to the next world.)

Now this was obviously a wonderful archaeological find, but Tut was not the only king or leader to be draped in the richness of gemstones.

British Crown Jewels

You knew this one was coming! The British royal family has the Imperial State Crown, perhaps the most recognizable of all the British royal jewelry. There are over 3,000 diamonds and 3 very important jewels set into the crown: At the top is St. Edward's Sapphire, set in the Maltese Cross. Below the sapphire is the 170-carat Black Prince's Ruby, which is actually a crystal called spinel. Below the ruby is the second Cullinan Diamond, the fourth-largest polished diamond in the world. The State Crown is used at coronations and at the annual opening of the British Parliament, where it arrives in its own stage coach before being worn by the reigning monarch. The crown represents the sovereignty of the monarch but no longer represents the divine right to rule over its people. The history of Britain is as rich as its jewels!

Crystal Clear

There is often confusion between a spinel and a ruby. Both are deep red and vibrant crystals, and both were actually identified as rubies until the eighteenth century, when science clarified that ruby was from a material called *corundum*. Aluminium oxide may combine with magnesia to form spinel, or it may form as the mineral corundum.

The Pope's Ring

Amethyst has long been the principle gemstone in the ring given to cardinals who serve just below the pope in the Catholic church. A cardinal's ring is usually made from gold, and the amethyst is carved with the diocesan seal. The ring is now made in an oval shape to represent the traditional Christian fish symbol but without the tail lines. The carved gemstone also doubles as a wax seal for use on official documents.

That's all well and good, you're thinking, but why amethyst? Well, it's regarded as a mystical symbol of modesty, humility, and innocence. The color is actually a blend of red and blue—this mixture reflects the blood of Christ and the blue robe of the Madonna. The deep purple color is also used as a symbol of authority to signify the power of the wearer as a man of God.

Amethyst is respected not only in the Papal offices, but also among the British royals. Amethyst is also highly regarded as the national gemstone of Scotland and is often used for weaponry and decorative pins. Amethyst also has significant healing qualities; you'll learn why it's called a Master Healer in Chapter 10.

Crystal Clear

A Greek myth tells the tale of a nymph named Amethyst who fell in love with the young shepherd Sirikos. As Amethyst's rejected lover, the wine god Dionysus was furious. However, before he could cause trouble, the goddess Artemis turned Amethyst into clear quartz to protect her. Dionysus, apparently feeling remorseful, poured wine over the crystal to restore Amethyst, turning the crystal to a violet color.

Crystals Make the World Go 'Round

Other dynasties have also enjoyed flaunting their treasures from the earth. For example:

♦ Catherine the Great of Russia had an enormous collection of jewelry, including the second-largest spinel in the world, weighing 398.72 *carats!*

♦ Part of the collection of the Imperial Crown Jewels of Iran includes the Diamond of Darya—e Noor (Sea of Light), one of the largest and rarest pale-pink diamonds in the world, weighing in at 186 carats.

♦ The Golden Jubilee Diamond is part of the Crown Jewels of Thailand and weighs in at a whopping 545.67 carats—that's the record-holder for the largest cut diamond in the world.

def•i•ni•tion

A **carat** is the standard measurement for gems. One carat is equivalent to 200 milligrams.

All right, so these jewels are lovely, awe-inspiring, and coveted, but what significance do they play in the real world? In other words, if we never get to see or wear these beauties, is there still something to be learned from them? You bet there is! These perfect jewels teach us about perfecting ourselves through self-transformation. These gemstones didn't just appear in a crown or a ring one day—they came from the earth in roughest form, only to achieve the highest status. This is also possible of all of us if we seek spiritual, emotional, and/or physical healing. Our life's work is to transform our souls into a perfect jewel.

Crystal Folklore

Crystals have inspired terrific stories from the beginning of time. For instance, one folktale held that if a young woman placed a moonstone in her mouth and looked at the moon over her shoulder in a mirror, she would see the face of the man she would marry. Farmers would tie agates to their plows to provide for an abundant crop. Green stones were thought to be gifts from the Gods providing good luck.

Crystals obviously capture the imagination and the attention of people from every socioeconomic status, from the peasant right on up to the leaders of various countries. But crystal fascination doesn't stop there. Just about every culture attributes some healing or magical properties to crystals.

The Hope Diamond

This amazing jewel fluoresces with a unique reddish color when exposed to ultra-violet light. Originally from India, the gemstone was 115 carats, but by the time it reached King Louis XIV of France, it was recut to 67 carats and worn as a pendant. During the French Revolution, the pendant was stolen and the diamond was not recovered at that time. In fact, it wasn't until 2005 that this now-45-carat blue diamond was acknowledged to be part of the stolen French Blue Crown Jewels.

By 1839, the diamond ended up in the Henry Philip Hope family collection of gems, giving it its name. The noted jeweler Harry Winston purchased the stone in 1949 and donated the jewel to the Smithsonian in 1958 by mailing it in a plain brown paper bag. Why would he do such a thing? Well, perhaps because the diamond is rumored to be cursed. Legend has it that anyone associated with it tends to live a short life.

The Hope Diamond is on display at one of the finest gem and mineral collections of the world, the Smithsonian's National Museum of Natural History. When you see such a beautiful crystal, you'll know why humans have chased after it!

The Regent Diamond

The Regent Diamond from India was originally known as the Pitt Diamond, named after Thomas Pitt, who sent the 410-carat stone to England to have it cut. The result was a cushion-shaped diamond of 140 carats. It was sold in 1717 to the Duke of Orleans, the regent of France, and used by French royalty in a number of settings, including:

- Set in the crown of Louis XV
- Used as a hair ornament for Queen Marie, Louis's wife
- Designed for Marie Antoinette's hat
- Set into the hilt of Napoleon Bonaparte's sword

After Napoleon's death, his widow Marie Louisa returned with the fabulous jewel to Austria. Her father later returned it to the French Crown Jewels where it remains in the French Royal Treasury at the Louvre. Although there isn't a specific curse or tale associated with the diamond, it has no doubt absorbed the energy of those who have procured it over the years (which would make for some very interesting stories if you could hold that gemstone and listen to its story!). You'll learn about cleansing negative energy from crystals in Chapter 7.

A Sapphire Story

How about a little story about St. Edward's Sapphire, which is set in the British Imperial State Crown? The sapphire was first used in the coronation ring of Edward the Confessor in 1042. Edward was a pious man and is credited with founding Westminster Abbey in 1065. The story goes that Edward was asked by a beggar for food. As kings don't usually walk around with change jingling in their pockets, Edward had nothing to give the beggar. However, in an act of generosity, Edward removed his ring and gave it to the man.

Years later, some pilgrims from Britain traveled to the Holy Lands and in Syria, a storm came upon them. They were approached by an old man who led them to food and lodgings and asked about their country of origin and the name of their king. The next day, the pilgrims sought out the old man to thank him for his assistance. When they met up with him, the old man said that he was John the Evangelist and handed them the sapphire ring that had been given to him by Edward years earlier when he wore the guise of a beggar! He also said that he would see Edward in paradise in six months' time.

When the pilgrims returned to England, they gave the ring back to Edward along with John the Evangelist's message. Exactly six months later, Edward died and was buried with the ring, his crown, and other regalia in Westminster Abbey. He was canonized by Pope Alexander III in 1161.

When a building project at the Abbey in 1269 required Edward's tomb to be relocated, they discovered Edward's body was in immaculate condition and from that time forth, he was referred to as St. Edward. The sapphire and the items were venerated, and it was thought that divine authority originated with these objects. Thus, this crystal sits on top of the most famous of all the British crowns, even above the monarch who wears the crown. No doubt, that sapphire truly holds divine energy.

Opal's Bad Rap

Opals have amazing sparkle and brilliant flashes of color caused by *diffraction*. They were once thought to help make the wearer invisible, prevent hair color from diminishing, and help ward off lightning strikes and disease. Opals seem to offer innocence to the wearer and were often presented to young, chaste girls to enhance their appeal to suitors.

def•i•ni•tion

Diffraction happens when a light passes through an obstacle and the rays of light are deflected or broken up and scattered into parallel slits or fringes of light. The result is an array or irregular patchwork quilt of color.

Most people are impressed with the colorful patchwork display of iridescent light that plays across the opal's surface. But again, there's more to the story. There are many myths associating bad luck with opals. In one story, a noted and well-loved British author of the early nineteenth century, Sir Walter Scott, wrote a trilogy called *Anne of Geierstein*. Lady Hermione, the heroine in the story, was accused of being a demon. When a drop of holy water fell on her opal, the stunning gemstone lost its sparkle. Hermione became ill and took to her bed. The next day, all that was found of her and the gemstone were ashes.

Now if people had read the complete trilogy, they would have discovered in the third book that the change in the opal's color was caused by poison and that it had been a warning to the heroine that something was very much amiss. Unfortunately (for Scott and opal dealers), not everyone read the third book and the public understood only that opals were omens of bad luck! How bad was it? The opal market crashed and remained at a depressed state for over 50 years until a new, vibrant black opal from Australia stirred up interest once again.

Crystal Clear

I like to look at opals in an entirely different way. When I see them, I get a sense of joy. The brilliant-colored light dances to an inner cosmic tune. Opals are all like children wanting to play and enjoy life, each one with its own personality!

Another superstition states that opals should be worn by a person only if it is that person's birthstone. In truth, the jewelry industry set up a birthstone for each month, probably for economic reasons.

Real or Fake?

Is there a difference between a lab-grown synthetic gemstone and one that is natural from the earth? Of course there is, but most of us would have trouble discerning between the two. Even some trained gemologists have trouble telling the difference.

Natural crystals have the best healing powers; a manufactured gem just can't get this kind of work done. However, there are some legitimate reasons for using lab-grown crystals. For instance, what if you need a perfect crystal for your state-of-the-art laser and you can't wait around for a few thousand years? Just turn to the synthetic gem industry!

Lab-Grown Crystals

It's hard to believe that perfect crystals can be grown under lab conditions. When you think of the fact that it takes the earth several hundreds of thousands of years to produce large quantities of all kinds of crystals, it makes you wonder: How could the production time be mimicked and shortened? And why do we need science and engineering inventions to create more gemstones?

Well, first of all, even though crystals from the earth are lovely and unique, nature is not flawless. Crystals come in different shapes and colors with different chemical compositions. No two are identical. When you are looking for a reliable product for use in manufacturing delicate instrumentation (such as watches or lasers), you can't leave it to chance that the earth will provide literally tons of exactly what you need, exactly when you need it.

So one of the advantages of lab-grown crystals is that they are flawless. There are no inclusions, no impurities or unseen structural weaknesses that could cause a fissure or breakage. The clarity and color are consistent throughout the crystal.

All right, but let's take one step back and talk about lab-growing conditions so we can appreciate what a crystal growing in the earth must go through over a significantly longer period of time. Synthetic quartz is grown using a hydrothermal process in a pressure cooker called an *autoclave*, which can produce over 20,000 psi (pounds per square inch, a measurement of pressure) under extreme heat and steam. Crushed silica is put at the bottom of the autoclave; at the top of the chamber, metallic seed plates are attached to natural quartz crystal. The plates are electromagnetically charged with positive and negative polarity wires attached between the natural crystal and the plates. The growth of the seed crystals is stimulated by the *piezoelectric* activity of the natural quartz crystal under heat and pressure and will take on the energy characteristics and six-sided signature structure from the natural quartz crystal.

def•i•ni•tion

Piezoelectric refers to the ability to generate energy in response to pressure.

At 300° Celsius, the crushed silica at the bottom of the autoclave dissolves and, in the rising steam, condenses and crystallizes onto the seed plates. The crystal can grow at different rates—for instance, it can take three or more weeks to grow a crystal of 150mm, it can take one or two months for a crystal weighing up to 1 kg, and a ruby or sapphire for use in a NASA laser may take one to two years!

Even if you are not a science lover, I hope you can appreciate how crystals—manmade and natural—begin and the intense pressure they experience before they appear in our hands, watches, lasers, chakras, and spiritual toolkits.

Crystals in a Class by Themselves

We all swoon over Swarovski crystals, used to encrust throw pillows, create lovely figurines and jewelry, and basically dazzle us all into a state of contentment. When we see something as lovely as the rainbow light these crystals throw off, all seems right with the world.

Well, here's a shocker: The composition of Swarovski crystal is glass—they are not made from natural rock crystal! Swarovski crystal, like other types of manmade glass crystals, use lead to give it weight. Lead also provides that wonderful clarity and brilliance that a diamond has. A Swarovski crystal is not a rhinestone, in that no reflective backing is used to enhance the brilliance or reflected light. The glass is molded and cut.

It should be noted that glass "crystal" is not natural rock "crystal," so glass does not contain the beneficial scientific elements that natural rock crystal has. In fact, some people consider the vibration of lead to be detrimental to one's health. So don't try to use your Swarovski crystals in your healing sessions. You'll get nowhere fast!

That's not to say that there are no benefits to glass crystals. Indeed, a nice, showy piece can bring happiness to both the wearer and admirers of the piece. It's like carrying a little rainbow wherever you go. And if you have one of these beautifully formed crystals as a table piece or other stationary object, just put it in the sun and a lot of happiness instantly radiates in the room. Place many throughout your house to remind you of your spiritual path, to enhance the feng shui in your house (more on this in Chapter 5), and to create beauty and joy in your home. Although there are no real physical healing benefits from these "crystals" themselves, there are emotional and spiritual benefits to be gained from the beauty they provide.

> **Yellow Flag** _____
>
> Rock crystal is composed of natural quartz crystal. Lead crystal is nothing more than glass with up to 35 percent lead oxide to increase the "sparkle"; it does not contain the same crystal structure as a true crystal. The U.S. Department of Agriculture warns that using lead crystal for serving food contains a potential health hazard because the lead can leach into the food.

Crystal Remains

It is not unusual to learn that the physical remains of very spiritually devoted followers of a religious faith have been enshrined and are venerated. The viewing of relics help a follower to develop a deeper faith, a sense of validation, and a belief in the teachings of their faith.

It might sound a bit more unusual to learn that there are ways to memorialize a loved one—such as turning their remains into a diamond. (Yes, I am telling you that you can actually be a diamond one of these fine days!)

> **Crystal Clear** _____
>
> The remains of hair taken from the most extraordinary King of Pop, Michael Jackson, after the filming of a disastrous commercial will be used to produce a small quantity of diamonds.

LifeGems is a company that takes the cremated remains of a loved one and creates a high-quality diamond from them. Molecularly, these gems have the same characteristics as a natural gemstone. But you actually don't have to wait until death parts you—a living gem can also be made from your own hair and that of your beloved. (Talk about a unique anniversary gift!)

Spiritually Speaking

Crystalline energy is being understood in a new way and is coming in under a different mind set, one of spiritualized or sacred science. When crystals are used in healing, is it science or spirituality, or both? There is a fine line between what we know as healing through medicine and science and what we term *spiritual healing*.

Now more than ever, we need the power of crystals to help us move past the boundaries and limitations of day-to-day living. As more and more people learn about and become involved with crystals, especially through science and technology, these gemstones are starting to generate new interest.

Healing practices and meditation are becoming more widely supported and accepted by the Western medical community. Crystals can help in these processes, so there's a real tie-in between accepted scientific research and the more metaphysical aspects of healing. I'm looking forward to seeing where science and medicine take crystal power! Stay tuned to Part 3 to learn about the many different aspects of crystal energy healing.

The Least You Need to Know

- Crystals have been used for centuries for spiritual, economic, and healing purposes.
- Some of the most powerful dynasties in the world hold and revere the largest crystals known to man.
- Lab-grown crystals may be molecularly similar to natural gemstones, but they lack the healing qualities of those grown in the earth.
- You can create a diamond from the cremated remains of a loved one, or from your own hair.
- Science and Western medicine are beginning to bring the real powers of crystals to light.

The Science of Crystals

In This Chapter

- The difference between minerals, rocks, crystals, and gems
- Crystal enhancement
- Examining the scientific properties of crystals
- How crystals are used in the cosmetics industry and in computer technology

Learning the differences between minerals, rocks, crystals, and gems is part and parcel of the discussion we'll be having in this book because, although all these things come from the earth, they are not interchangeable—especially when it comes to their energetic properties. Understanding crystalline structures and their properties will prepare you for the greater discovery of crystal healing.

In this chapter, you'll see how crystals relate to and, in many cases, enhance the world around us. For example, you will learn how the science of crystals is applied in computer technology. These same principles or characteristics of crystals used in technological applications are also used in crystal healing. This might just lead you to ask the question: Is there nothing that crystal power can't do?

Gifts from the Earth

We use several words to describe that rock-hard stuff that comes from the earth—that which forms mountains, glitters in rings, and regulates the time in our watches and electrical pulses in our computers. We know these substances as minerals, rocks, crystals, and gems. Are they all the same, or at least related to each other, or are these separate entities, free and clear from one another? Let's get down to the details of what makes each group unique.

Minerals

When you were growing up, you were probably told to take your vitamins, but did you also learn to take your minerals? Did you know that minerals are crystals, too?

def•i•ni•tion

A repeating pattern of atoms, molecules, or ions extending in three spatial directions to form a structure is known as **crystalline**, a crystalline solid, or a crystal. The process of forming a crystal-line structure or crystal is called crystallization.

A mineral must be solid and must have a *crystalline* structure. Minerals are formed from geologic processes such as volcanic activity. They have a recognizable element or chemical composition. The study of the structure, chemistry, and properties of minerals is called *mineralogy*.

Some examples of minerals are magnetite, barite, gypsum, and halite.

There are several important minerals that your body needs to function well, including copper, a trace mineral used in the formation of hemoglobin to keep bones and nerves healthy. Your veggies simply absorbed the nutrient from the earth!

Rocks

We seem to name anything that's hard, found on the ground, and looks like a stone a *rock*. That's often the case as rocks are formed on the surface through a process called the *rock cycle*. A rock ends up as an aggregate of minerals and does not necessarily have a specific chemical compound.

Rock has the ability to transform and crystallize into another form. This is how crystals are made. This ability to transform is a characteristic of the ongoing processes on our planet. Our Earth really does have the ability to renew its own resources—and does so on a regular basis by moving through the transformation rock cycle.

There are three rock classifications:

♦ **Igneous rock**—This has solidified from a molten state when magma reaches the earth's surface and hardens. Examples are granite, obsidian, and basalt.

♦ **Sedimentary rock**—This consists of compressed particles on the surface of the earth. Layers of rock are formed, such as limestone or shale, which sometimes traps fossils.

♦ **Metamorphic rock**—This is formed when existing rock undergoes dynamic changes from heat, pressure, and chemical activity. Marble is a metamorphic rock formed from limestone, recrystallizing the original calcite under heat and pressure. Other examples include quartz, kyanite, and garnet.

Quartz is crystal that can be formed from any of the three classifications but is principally formed of silica, the most common mineral found on Earth. One important note about silica: Think of all the beaches and lake and ocean bottoms where there is sand. It's all silica! As minute silica particles are floating freely in the air throughout the world, your body also makes use of silica in forming hair and nails and strengthening cells. So your body is already partly crystallized!

Crystals

A crystal is a structure composed of an orderly spatial arrangement of atoms. The crystal *lattice* provides a definition of its symmetry and geometric shape based on a three-dimensional axis system. This lattice is a structure that also holds the energy within the crystal used for healing.

def•i•ni•tion

A geometric arrangement or network of points in which a crystal grows is called a **lattice**. A lattice provides symmetry and definition for the crystal.

The following seven lattice systems form the basic structure of all crystals:

♦ **Isometric**—The basic structure of an isometric crystal is in the shape of a cube. Halite and pyrite are examples of a crystal with an isometric crystal lattice structure.

♦ **Tetragonal**—A tetragonal crystal structure is in the shape of a rectangle. An example of a crystal with a tetragonal crystal structure is rutile.

- **Orthorhombic**—Orthorhombic crystal structures are in the form of a rectangular prism with a rectangular base. Examples of crystals with an orthorhombic lattice are celestite and topaz.

- **Hexagonal**—Hexagonal crystals like aquamarine or emerald have a six-sided lattice structure.

- **Trigonal**—Clear quartz is an example of a crystal with a trigonal lattice, made of six sides with interlaced unit cells.

- **Monoclinic**—The lattice of a monoclinic crystal is a rectangular prism with a parallelogram as its base. An example is moonstone.

- **Triclinic**—The triclinic lattice is the least symmetric, with unequal vectors. Turquoise and rhodonite are examples of crystals with a triclinic lattice.

As you can see in the following illustration, there is also an amorphous lattice, in which the crystal holds no particular shape or distinguishable form. Opals are amorphous.

Note that for every lattice axis, there is a positive (+) and a negative (-) pole. That is because there are positive and negative ions that hold the structure together. Remember that these lattices are three-dimensional and give the crystal its crystalline structure as well as its ability to hold energy.

In his book *The Seven Secrets of Crystal Talismans* (Llewellyn Publications, 2008), Henry M. Mason details each of these crystal lattice systems for their power to attract, protect, and transform us.

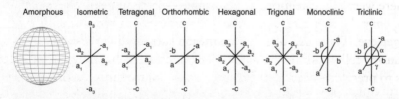

Crystal lattices chart. The internal structure of crystals to a specific pattern of atoms around an axis point is called a lattice, and can be used to uniquely identify a crystal.

As humans, we have a natural curiosity and want to know how things are put together. We don't really see the DNA that composes our human bodies or, for that matter, the crystalline formation of a crystal. Some of us don't need this deeper knowledge to use the power of a crystal, but some of us simply have to know what makes a crystal a crystal and what makes it tick! That's *crystallography*, or the study of the structure of crystals.

def•i•ni•tion

> **Crystallography** is the study of how crystals are actually formed, including their internal structures. **X-ray crystallography** is the study of a crystal's molecular structure by examining the light diffraction patterns made when x-rays are beamed through it.

Specialized techniques such as x-ray diffraction are used to determine crystalline structures under the study of *x-ray crystallography*. There is even more sophisticated science for studying the structure of crystals that includes mathematical macro-molecular models and geometric relationships. However, because we're going to focus on the healing aspects of crystals in this book, I'm going to leave the advanced formulaic work to other experts!

Crystallography is used in various earth sciences and biochemistry and has many industrial applications, such as developing timing and oscillating devices used in digital electronics and printed circuit boards.

Gems

A gemstone is a cut and polished mineral, crystal, or other valuable material, such as amber or pearl. (Throughout this book, when I talk about gemstones, I am referring to the crystal variety.)

At one time there were two categories of gemstones—precious gemstones such as diamond, ruby, emerald, sapphire, and topaz and semiprecious gemstones such as amethyst or tiger eye. There can be some confusion surrounding these terms because the jewelry industry follows trends in fashion and often a mineral moves from semi-precious status to precious or from precious to semiprecious status. Really, there is no difference between them in the jewelry trade—there are no half-precious gemstones. However, when selecting a gemstone, clarity, color, and style are very important. A transparent gemstone such as aquamarine should be flawless with no particles or cloudiness. The color should appear strong, intense, and vibrant. An opaque crystal such as turquoise should have a consistently even color tone.

Enhanced Appearances

When we hear the word *enhancement* these days, we often think of cosmetic proce-dures that make men and women look younger, thinner, larger, or more beautiful somehow. But the word *enhanced* can take on a negative connotation, too, such as in the case of performance-enhancing drugs in the world of sports. If things are enhanced by scientific means, should we think less of them? What about crystals? If they are enhanced, what happens to their structure and their potential for healing?

Irradiation

To enhance the beauty and other features of crystals, radiation is used to modify the color of some crystals. A crystal or gemstone subjected to radiation literally cooks and changes color from radioactivity passing through the gem. The source of radiation can come from gamma ray emissions, linear accelerators used to beam electrons, or nuclear reactors that pass neutrons and gamma rays through gems. The gems go through a cooling off period that usually lasts two weeks.

The most notable change is probably the transformation of clear quartz into smoky quartz. There is a story that during the 1940s the U.S. government conducted explosions of atomic devices in sealed caves in New Mexico. When the experimenters checked the caves after the explosions, the clear quartz crystals had turned black, absorbing the radiation. Recognizing that there was some commercial value to this oddity, the crystals were harvested and sold regardless of the level of irradiation or remaining radioactivity in the crystal.

The following crystals are often irradiated to enhance their value for the jewelry industry:

- **Amethyst**—Turns an intense purple.

- **Blue topaz**—Transforms into more intense blue or sometimes brown.

- **Clear quartz**—Darkens into the brown-black opaque smoky quartz called irradiated quartz.

- **Diamond**—The color changes can include yellow, orange, pink, brown, green, and blue hues. (A diamond irradiated in 1914 and donated to the British Museum still has not lost its radioactivity!)

- **Emerald**—The green color becomes more vibrant.

Yellow Flag _____

Ongoing exposure to radioactivity can be harmful to your health. However, brief exposure to irradiated gemstones with long-lived radioisotopes may have less health risks. Unfortunately, unless your gemstone is tested for the level of radioisotopes, you might not know what the health risk is. Despite regulations under the Nuclear Regulatory Commission (NRC), there appears to be little enforcement to ensure monitoring of residual radioactivity of imported reactor-irradiated jewelry, particularly those brilliant blue topaz gemstones.

Heating

Some crystals are simply heated and not irradiated to produce color enhancement. They include the following:

- **Aquamarine**—The greener color of this gemstone is removed, leaving a more desirable blue.

- **Carnelian**—Enriches the deep orange color.

- **Citrine**—Amethyst is heated into a brassy gold color. Much of what we know as citrine is actually heated amethyst. Through controlled heating of a gemstone, both citrine and amethyst combine into ametrine, one half of the stone is shaded citrine and the other half is amethyst.

- **Ruby**—Often rubies are found with cracks. Using borax or alumina powders and heating it to the melting point of corundum at 2050°C, the powders melt and fill in superficial fractures and pits that might have occurred naturally. Emeralds are often treated with fracture filling, too.

- **Tanzanite**—Tanzanite is usually heat treated at 300°C to 600°C, causing it to lose its yellow-brown hues and leaving behind the rich purple and blue with enhanced transparency.

- **Tiger eye**—Heating golden tiger eye can produce a red variety.

- **Topaz**—Turns an orange or brown topaz to a pink.

Although colors are made more vibrant in both processes, if you have a choice, it's probably safer to get gemstones that are heated and not irradiated.

Dyeing

What about coloring crystals? Although this is generally a safer practice than wearing irradiated stones, you might not be getting exactly what you expected. For example, howlite is dyed to look like turquoise. It is named turquisite and sold as an inexpensive alternative to its pricier doppelganger. If you are wearing turquoise simply for fashion reasons, the howlite is a fine substitute. However, if you're expecting to get healing properties from turquoise, this imposter will not fit the bill!

> **Gem of an Idea**
>
> If you want to check your turquoise-colored gemstone, scratch a hidden area with a steel knife or look down into the hole of a bead or a crack on the surface to see if any white area is showing. Obviously, you would not want to do this testing on an item you enjoy for fear of ruining it.

Other crystals are subject to dyeing as they are being processed and prepared for market. Black onyx, for example, is permanently dyed in normal processing. Colored oils are used to dye emeralds and rubies. Examine emeralds in diffused transmitted lighting and look for color concentrated around fractures. Some green-colored oils fluoresce a greenish yellow. On transparent-colored gemstones, dye can be visible in cracks that are darker than the rest of the stone. Sometimes dye appears as a residue that rubs off or as white patches.

Rose quartz stones are commonly dyed to enhance the pink color. You may notice when wearing a necklace made of rose quartz that chips will slowly fade after a while. Submerge the necklace string in warm water and the dye will rinse off.

Lapis lazuli is an aggregate of minerals that include white calcite and pyrite. The white calcite can take a dye to create a more uniform blue. You can test the surface of a gemstone using a swab dipped in acetone to see whether any blue dye is removed.

All the irradiation, heating, and various other enhancement techniques used to beautify a gemstone do not change the underlying crystal lattice. Still, if you want an authentic experience with a crystal that has no residual chemical, radiation, or other foreign substances to alter its vibrational rate, only an unaltered gem will do. Enhancement isn't bad if you're interested in a gem strictly for aesthetic purposes. But because you now know the difference, you'll probably want the genuine gemstone.

Scientific Properties of Crystals

There are a number of properties that all crystals have in common to varying degrees due to their unique compositions. The most important property is the crystal's ability to produce a piezoelectric effect, or the ability to generate energy in response to pressure.

When resting, the crystal lattice just sits inside the crystal maintaining its structure. As no stress is being applied, the crystal's positive and negative poles are evenly distributed and any energy stored is kept in a state of balance or equilibrium. Once disturbed by pressure, the piezoelectric effect separates energy from the lattice, generating a voltage. This release of crystal energy is what is used in crystal healing.

If you apply electricity to a quartz crystal, it will bend, sending out an energy wave. It will vibrate at a precise frequency, much like a tuning fork. Each crystal uniquely vibrates at a specific frequency when an electrical current is passed through it. The crystal will vibrate at 60 hertz (60 times per second) and can be used for different applications, such as keeping time.

When you hold a crystal in your hand and squeeze, the electrical shock isn't very strong. In fact, most people feel nothing. However, when pressure is applied with a mechanical device, 1 cubic centimeter of quartz can produce a whopping 12,000 volts! (By comparsion, a C battery is only 1.5 volts.) The release of energy from a quartz crystal has enough spark in the energy charge to ignite gas. Some appliances, such as gas stoves and barbecues, use piezo igniters. You can see this energy release for yourself by rubbing two quartz crystals together in a darkened room. Enough light energy will be released to see a flare of light but little heat energy will be produced.

Crystal Clear

It might sound odd, but there has been speculation that because New York City sits on top of piezoelectric rock, the underground optical network beneath the city is running on crystalline vibrations from its own bedrock.

Piezoelectricity was first discovered in 1880 by Jacques and Pierre Curie, and it led to the use of quartz resonators in sonars during World War I. The Curies discovered a reverse effect to crystals releasing their energy. A transducer sends an electrical signal to a crystal. This pulse causes the crystal to become slightly deformed; the resulting reflected energy wave can be used for determining the distance from one object to another.

Freaky Frequency

Here's something you might not have known about crystals: Their resonance can produce sound. Within the field of biomechanics, sonomicrometry—a means of measuring the distance between two piezoelectric crystals depending on the speed of acoustic signals traveling between them—has been used for studies of the human heart and with other muscles to measure changes in their lengths. Here's how it works: An electric signal is sent to a crystal planted in muscle tissue; the signal is then transformed into sound. This sound—in the form of an energy wave—passes through a special material that focuses the signal and is received by another crystal. The second crystal converts the sound into electricity, which is detected by a receiver.

The distance between the two crystals can be calculated based on the speed at which the sound moves between the crystals. Pretty cool, huh?

I have met only a few people who have actually heard these crystal tones subliminally and I have heard these tones inside my head occasionally. It is a bit like having earphones on in that the tones were in between my ears. If you haven't heard crystals sing yet, don't worry; most people haven't. The ring of crystal bowls is the closest you may come to hearing the natural tones of a crystal.

Now here's something else that might really get you thinking: Each crystal has a specific resonance or vibration and, when suitably charged, it can also emit a color vibration! Some people can even see a colored glow to crystals.

Mohs Scale of Hardness

Another property of crystals is their hardness, which depends on the strength of the chemical bond as well as spatial density of atoms with the crystal. A harder crystal can scratch a softer one. The *Mohs scale of hardness* was developed for use in the identification of crystals and consists of 10 classifications beginning with the softest (1) and graduating to level 10, which is the hardest. The exception is any liquid form of crystal, such as mercury. Gemstones used in jewelry making usually don't include gems softer than level 5 because they can crack or disintegrate with common wearing.

def•i•ni•tion

Mohs scale of hardness, named after F. Mohs, a German mineralogist (1773–1839), is a method used to determine the hardness and scratch resistance of a rock. A lower number on the scale indicates a softer stone.

Mohs Scale of Hardness

Hardness	Crystals	Characteristic of Hardness Level
1	Talc, graphite	Can be scratched with a fingernail (Moh 2.5) or a copper penny (Moh 3.5) or by any stone at a higher Moh level than itself
2	Gypsum, bismuth, lepidolite, chlorite	Can be scratched with a fingernail (Moh 2.5) or a copper penny (Moh 3.5) or by any stone at a higher Moh level than itself
3	Calcite, celestite, barite	Can be scratched using a steel knife (Moh 6.5) or glass (Moh 6) or by any stone at a higher Moh level than itself
4	Fluorite, malachite, platinum	Can be scratched using a steel knife (Moh 6.5) or glass (Moh 6) or by any stone at a higher Moh level than itself
5	Apatite, dioptase	Can be scratched using a steel knife (Moh 6.5) or glass (Moh 6) or by any stone at a higher Moh level than itself
6	Orthoclase, feldspar, pyrite, amazonite, hematite	Can be scratched using a steel knife (Moh 6.5) or glass (Moh 6) or by any stone at a higher Moh level than itself
7	Quartz, tourmaline, amethyst	Will scratch glass (Moh 5.5) and can be scratched by any stone at a higher Moh level than itself
8	Topaz, spinel	Will scratch glass (Moh 5.5) and can be scratched by any stone at a higher Moh level than itself
9	Corundum, ruby, sapphire	Will scratch glass (Moh 5.5) and can be scratched by any stone at a higher Moh level than itself
10	Diamond	Will scratch glass and all stones in Moh levels 1–9

Properties of Healing Crystals

By now you know that a crystal can interact with your own bioelectric energy fields and that a crystal in itself does nothing without a relationship to another energy source. Now let's take another step toward understanding the properties of crystals used for healing.

The scientific properties of crystals will always be there. The bridge to using these properties for healing is a combination of developing the consciousness to direct crystal energy for healing; the intent and compassion to heal; and the use of your breath as a carrier when charging, clearing, and programming crystals (you will learn about all these processes in upcoming chapters).

The following table offers more specifics about the properties of crystals and provides some additional information on techniques to use the properties listed.

11 Properties of Crystals Used for Healing

	Scientific Property	Definition
1	Piezoelectric energy charge and discharge	The ability to convert pressure into an electrical charge. Using the breath to charge the crystal energetically, the energy loops from the crystal back to you until a maximum energy charge is reached. Then the energy can be discharged according to the programming in the crystal and as directed by the intent (the thought pattern) of the crystal holder.
2	Resonant oscillator/ frequency regulator	The ability to maintain sound or a wave of energy at a precise frequency. It has the ability to maintain a specific vibrational frequency or tone that is maintained at a regular, consistent, and precise vibration. When placed close to an erratic energy signal, the crystal regulates the vibrational frequency.
3	Programmable memory	The ability to store and retrieve information and to repeat a set of instructions. Using the breath to pulse the intent or program into the matrix of the crystal.
4	Polarity	The ability to hold positive, negative, and neutral electrical frequencies. When a person is in contact with the crystal, these polar frequencies are activated.

	Scientific Property	Definition
5	Electrical battery	The ability to store the energy of positive or negative charge in the crystal's precise internal structure. The crystal can discharge the electrical impulse coherently through the crystal according to the thought patterns of the crystal holder, to preprogrammed intent, or incoherently without focus.
6	Amplify	The ability to take a pattern of energy and increase its charge into a more intense and coherent energy. Crystals can amplify programming as well as the energy of other energy sources, including other crystals.
7	Broadcast	The ability to send out energy patterns or information to be received by others, including other crystals. The effect is similar to a radionic transmission and is useful in distant healing.
8	Penetrate	The ability to transmit crystalline energy through any substance. When crystals are placed on the body, energy passes through layers of clothing and skin/bone. This ability applies in distance healing, where energy can be sent and received at a considerable distance.
9	Project	The ability to discharge and transmit its own stored energy at any distance. A programmed set of instructions could be sent out as a continuous signal provided there is sufficient energy in the "battery" or proximity to other sources.
10	Duplicate energy	The ability to resonate another like object at the same frequency. The crystal can discharge an energy pattern that can be inherited as an exact duplicate by another like energy source such as water or another type of crystal.
11	Conductor	The ability to receive energy through itself with or without altering the energy pattern or program. As used in radio sets or with healing, the crystal is a carrier or pipeline of energy. Its original matrix/mission is not altered.

Three other properties that all crystals share are:

♦ A crystal has the ability to regrow after it's removed from its matrix or if it's chipped.

♦ A crystal can clear out retained energy through applied cleansing processes such as using salt water, which discharges negative ions.

♦ Crystals can be recharged using energy from other crystals, ultraviolet light, and other subtle energy sources compatible with its matrix.

Crystals Converted to Practical Uses

It's kind of nice to know that crystals are all around us. Some very smart scientists have discovered how to use crystals in some very surprising and yet incredibly practical and familiar ways. So if you think you're brand-new to the crystal world, you probably aren't. Chances are, you've been using them without even knowing it!

Cosmetics

One of the earliest uses of minerals and crystals was in the cosmetic area. In ancient Egypt, recipes for eye paint included kohl, a refined soot often containing lead, powered lapis lazuli, honey, and ochre. To obtain green pigment for eye paint, malachite, ore of copper, and silvery Galena were used. (Galena is lead sulfide and poses as much a health risk today as it did then.) Water was mixed with the powders and extracted from tube-shaped containers using a moistened stick to apply the paste to the eyelids.

Yellow Flag

Recently there has been a resurgence of more natural-source cosmetics using minerals such as titanium dioxide, zinc oxide, and mica. However, the use of lead-contamination found in kohl, lipsticks, and other cosmetics in Middle Eastern and South Asian countries shows a prevalence of anemia in the population from lead poisoning. The cosmetic market in North America is somewhat more strictly regulated under the U.S. Food and Drug Administration (FDA), but there are still campaigns to alert consumers to potential hazardous substances from imports. Remember to read the labels and select brands you can trust.

Computer Technology

The semiconductor industry uses a variety of silicon to create a material that has an electrical resistance. The lattice of a crystal can be easily modified by adding impurities while the crystal is being formulated in a lab environment for different uses.

If you apply electricity to quartz, it vibrates at a precise frequency, much like a tuning fork. The optimum shape to sustain the vibration was found to be a quartz bar. Thin sheets of quartz are used in delicate instruments requiring an accurate frequency such as radio transmitters, radio receivers, and computers. In fact, you can use crystals every day to balance out the energy of all kinds of appliances—you will learn more about this in Chapter 19.

The Least You Need to Know

- Minerals, rocks, crystals, and gems all come from the earth. All have crystalline structures.

- Crystals can be enhanced using dye or irradiation techniques. Dye is generally considered safe; there is some question as to the safety of certain irradiated gemstones.

- The frequency and energetic field emitted by a crystal can be measured—and both can be quite strong.

- Computers, conductors, and cosmetics all contain crystals, so you're probably basking in crystal energy without even knowing it!

Metaphysical Mysteries

In This Chapter

- ◆ Science, metaphysics, and mysticism

- ◆ Platonic solids and sacred geometry

- ◆ Karma and your perception of illness

- ◆ Meditating does a body and brain good!

- ◆ How the power of intent affects your healing time

Although many things in this world have a scientific explanation, many things do not. Who can say how a person at death's door bounces back and makes a recovery, for example? Sometimes we just have to take a leap of faith and believe in something that goes beyond our normal experience.

In this chapter, we explore metaphysics, mysticism, and sacred healing. Now these might seem like heavy concepts to those of you who are new to them, but I assure you that all you need to benefit from the information here is an open mind and a willingness to learn!

Crystal Energy: Myth, Mystery, or More?

Scientists and doctors often want predictable results that can be repeated with consistency before they will declare a theory or healing process "valid." However, many things exist that science can't regulate or explain, such as the spirituality present in all things. Therefore, science and Western medicine have traditionally pushed alternative modes of healing off to the side.

Fortunately, we are now entering an age in which the spiritualization of science and medicine is emerging and beginning to accept the wholeness of the ecological system, the concept of *Gaia*, and the cosmos. In this shift in thinking, the thin line between knowledge about a predictable outcome and *metaphysics*, the study of what exists, is challenged by a new order of *mysticism*, the pursuit of knowledge about the ultimate truth.

def•i•ni•tion

> **Gaia** is a concept stating that the organisms of the biosphere (Earth) regulate the planet to the benefit of the whole. For example, rocks, soil, plants, and the atmosphere all work in harmony. **Metaphysics** is a philosophical inquiry into the nature of reality and the relationships between things. **Mysticism** is the awareness of an absolute reality or spiritual truth through direct experience or communion with an ultimate source such as God.

Open Up and Learn Something New

Speaking of truth …

We grow up being told that empirical evidence is the only truth. And yet, as we grow older, many of us will find that not everything can be analyzed, charted, or even necessarily explained. Often, we don't know what to do with these experiences because they don't match with what we've learned to accept as "truth" in the past. It's a shame that so many people push the unexplained aside and miss out on some of the great mysteries of life—including healing energy—because they're told that if they can't see it, it isn't real.

Twentieth-century mythologist Joseph Campbell said we haven't moved much beyond a thirteenth-century mind—in other words, we're still unable to open up and process new information for fear of being seen as different from others. When we encounter experiences outside the known range of our expectations with no science to back us up with explanations, we become terrified! Breaking through the past inhibitions and artificial boundaries is a task that takes time, but it is possible and desirable if you want to change your health or your outlook on life. The result is a level of wholeness of being that provides a sense of peace and harmony where healing can occur.

Keep this in mind as you continue through this book. Nothing extraordinary can take place without a belief that it is possible. And nothing new can take place in a mind that is closed to opportunities.

There for the Taking

Without a concept in the wholeness of all things, our perceptions can be narrow-minded and our experiences are carefully selected to repeat a known experience rather than to seek and explore the unknown. This might be a safe way of living your life, but it's also pretty dull—and you can also miss some extraordinary things that are right in front of you!

For instance, when we look at the sunlight, most of us see only the radiance of light. But if we hold a crystal prism inside the light, we see it refracted into many different bands of light frequencies. Well, guess what? Those colors were always present. It just took the right tool to bring them out.

Healing energy is also always present, but many of us lack the knowledge and healing tools needed to access it. We simply need to reawaken the knowledge about giving and receiving healing, and then it's ours just for the asking.

Platonic Solids

The Greek philosopher Plato believed that everything we need to know about the earth and life on it is accessible to us in five basic shapes. *Everything* is composed of these basic shapes—our physical bodies, DNA, plants, cells, minerals, the cosmos—you name it. These shapes are called the *Platonic solids* and consist of the following lattices in solid formation:

- ◆ 3-sided tetrahedron
- ◆ 4-sided cube
- ◆ 8-sided octahedron
- ◆ 12-sided dodecahedron
- ◆ 20-sided icosahedron

def•i•ni•tion

The **Platonic solids** are the five basic shapes that compose the structure of every solid material known to us.

The five Platonic solids.

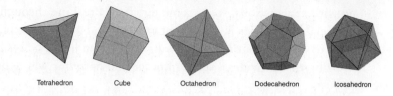

Tetrahedron   Cube   Octahedron   Dodecahedron   Icosahedron

Do these molecular structures have anything to do with the vibration frequency of a crystal? Yes, very much so! The architectural and mathematical perfection of these natural crystal structures is like a cosmic receptacle for divine energy.

The crystal matrix is like a blueprint for the source energy that the Divine Spirit forms into matter. On a larger scale, Gaia (Earth) is a cosmic receptacle of divine energy. It is said that the crystals on Earth hold the matrix of divine energy.

Each type of crystal provides a specialized link for your life force resonance. As a specific train track takes you to your chosen destination, so can a crystal be used as a tool to repattern your life force.

Crystals, then, can be seen as tools that help us access and transform the patterns of stem cells, the basic blocks in the crystalline matrix. Because they hold the ions of elements from the beginning of time, crystals can absorb and radiate different frequencies to the fluids in the body that contain electrolytes. In other words, you can use these crystals to resonate with your own energy and re-create cellular patterns. You could be resonating with the cosmos, with the environment, or with a higher spirit.

Crystal Clear

Experiments in Russia at the Institute of Clinical and Experimental Medicine in Novosibirsk in the 1970s have shown that the DNA in living cells can communicate with the surrounding cells by way of energy transmission. In more than 1,700 trials, the transmission of energy from one group of cells to another through a quartz window allowed the passage of energy in the form of ultraviolet light in the range of DNA radiation (the movement of energy). The results show that energy can move between cells independently of their biochemical and functional organic systems.

Crystal Resonance: Good Vibes

The crystal resonance or vibration of a crystal is very powerful because it can essentially reprogram the patterns of substances nearby, including—but not limited to—human energy patterns.

Take, for example, the work of Masaru Emoto. In the late twentieth century, he experimented with the crystallization of water and found that when the mind was focused on pleasant thoughts, images, or music, the water crystals had a surprising quality and intricate matrix. When water was exposed to negative thoughts, the water crystals were incomplete, lacked structure, and generally looked misshapen.

If we can consciously direct the crystal resonance to perform in specific ways, then unhealthy human cells should be able to regenerate from the influence of nearby healthy cells. Crystals can facilitate the focus and direction of consciousness to work toward healing.

Contagious Energy

Here's a more familiar way of thinking about this kind of energy: Have you ever been in a bad mood and run into a light-hearted friend? Suddenly, your own state of mind improves. You've been affected by your friend's resonance and now you are actually vibrating on a higher level. Another way to say this is that your friend's positive energy has been transferred to you.

Crystals are bioenergetic transducers, working in much the same way as an upbeat friend. They have the ability to transform and transfer energy of living energies and substances that have a crystalline structure. We'll look more closely at this crystal resonance in Part 3, along with how to use crystals for restoring harmony and balance to our own bodies, minds, and spiritual energy structures.

Sacred Healing

When we take the work of men like Plato and Emoto and combine it with what we know about crystal resonance on a personal level, we start to understand how crystals heal the human body, mind, and spirit. It's not just science—it's sacred science! And it's also what we call *sacred healing*, one of those therapeutic processes that can't necessarily be explained by scientists, but one that seems to work well for some people regardless.

def•i•ni•tion

> **Sacred healing** is a term used for the processes that are not governed by the conventional application of medicine or medical procedures. These can include all kinds of alternative therapies, such as working with crystals.

So many of us seem to have an idea that something outside of us, such as medicine, therapy, or even a new life situation, is necessary to precipitate healing. We also have a perception that healing has to take a certain amount of time. Perhaps we think a broken leg takes six weeks to heal, while a broken spirit might take six months.

But lo and behold, one day we wake up and realize we're feeling better. We have arrived at some level of acceptance, or maybe we've detached a little from our problems. But in any event, something has changed inside of us—we've begun to relax our mental effort and need for a specific outcome. When you realize that you have control over how you see your problems, you will see how sacred spiritual healing works.

You Have the Power to Flip the Switch!

There seems to be an invisible switch for turning on sacred healing. Some people will turn it on themselves; others need to be led to it. But the switch can be flipped only when the person is ready. Some people describe this as a change of attitude: There is a sense of renewed energy and wanting to find a way to heal. There's a feeling of being reconnected to life and wanting to get out there and do things again.

Yellow Flag

Sacred healing is not a panacea for everyone. If you have a known medical condition, consult with the best-qualified medical help you can find and use your best judgment.

Spiritual healing is finding a place in many hospital and clinical settings these days. Doctors know they can provide only so much physical and psychological treatment for their patients. When all the medical avenues have been exhausted, a physician sometimes refers a patient to spiritual services to help a patient find inner healing, spirituality, and prayer in the most difficult times. As one doctor said, spiritual services can help a patient make room for a healing to occur.

Sacred healing comes through many channels, such as meditation or visualization exercises, and anyone—and I mean *anyone*—can access these tools. They're already within you! Crystals can play an important role in facilitating the healing by assisting in these exercises and by providing a connection to the crystalline complex, where healing can happen and miracles are possible, too.

The Four Classes of Illness

Spiritual purification practices help to remove the negative imprints on our mind that cause illness to arise. Regardless of your faith or spiritual and religious teachings, everyone can benefit from a positive mental outlook because even if illness does occur, your suffering will be less.

Illness in the Buddhist concept is a display of the mind. Everything we experience is the result of cause and effect. Our past deeds, both positive and negative, influence our experience. Sufficient good deeds or virtuous actions accumulate positive *karma*, so medical procedures will be effective in recovery from illness, even for serious illnesses.

def•i•ni•tion

Karma is the accumulation of positive or negative merit based on past action.

The four classes of illness in the Buddhist tradition are as follows:

- The first class of illnesses is inconsequential. You will recover from them regardless of whether you seek medical care or not. This would include cuts, bruises, and colds.

- The second class of illnesses contains illnesses that are very dangerous but can be cured by medical intervention. Medicines include chemotherapy, surgery, and even acupuncture.

- The third class of illnesses contains illnesses that one cannot recover from simply with medical intervention. Spiritual practices—the healing power that is in the nature of all things—need to be accessed and activated. People are able to cure themselves of illness that medical procedures cannot. These might include things such as addiction, depression, and the like.

- The fourth class of illnesses contains nonrecoverable, nonreversible illness. Death is inevitable, regardless of medical intervention.

So I just told you that Buddhists believe illness is a display of the mind. Take, for example, my friend Jake, who recently hired a construction firm to do some home renovations. He was quite upset that things were not going well. The workers were doing more damage than repair work, and the original week-long project was now taking more than a month. He felt like he was being deliberately targeted by the workers for an expensive bill.

In the middle of the work, Jake had a gallbladder attack, so on top of his suffering an endlessly poor renovation job, he was also in pain. He still made no connection between his condescending attitudes toward the workers and his illness. Finally, in exasperation Jake shouted, "The gall of those workers trying to wreck my place!" Then he realized that his own anger was causing an increase of stress in his body and that this stress is what had triggered the gallbladder attack. Jake calmed down and distanced himself from the workers without further incident of gallbladder pain. The job was eventually completed to his satisfaction.

There are times when demonstrating anger is helpful, especially if it helps prevent harm to others. Unresolved anger, however, is like poison and there are consequences to holding onto negative attitudes and emotions such as illness and bad luck.

How can crystals intervene in these conditions? By accessing and changing the energy of the body. The crystal lattice (see Chapter 2) is constantly changing throughout our bodies, even when we are ill. So one moment a diseased, angry, or scared cell is there and the next, it may not be, perhaps thanks to the energy emitted through crystal therapy. And when all the errant tissues are no longer there, we consider the tissue matter to be healed.

The Meditative Mind

Meditation is an important and integral part of sacred healing, but the very idea of meditation is still quite new to Westerners who have not yet experienced a true form of it. Often they have been told by ecclesiasts to think of meditation as a time for spiritual reflection or deep introspection. You meditate *upon* something, they say. Well, that's not true meditation because contemplation is still "thinking." There are usually words going on inside your head, with some expected outcome from all that thinking.

Meditation is about *not* thinking. At all. Period. A clear mind is the place where true healing energies can take hold and grow. We'll talk more about meditation in the following section and in Part 3, but for now know that when you use a crystal (such as amethyst, clear quartz, rose quartz, sodalite, or smoky quartz) during meditation, the results are clearer due to the crystal resonance keeping all your energies strong and aligned. (For the best results, hold a crystal in your left hand to receive its mind-stabilizing energies.)

Beginners' Meditation Exercise

Now that you know what true meditation is—and what it isn't—and how it can help flip that sacred healing switch, let's try a simple exercise to introduce you to the process:

1. Sit upright in a chair or cross-legged on the ground. Let your hands fall naturally into your lap or rest them on your thighs. If you have time, go through an inventory of body parts to check for tension. Check your feet, legs, and hips; your stomach, lower back, upper chest, and shoulders; your arms, hands, and fingers; your neck, mouth, jaw, temples, eyes, and finally your scalp. Relax everything. With every breath, draw in feelings of relaxation and expel any tension you feel in your body parts.

> **Crystal Clear**
>
> Guided meditation is different from traditional meditation because it uses visualization and other methods to enhance healing.

2. Focus on your breathing for a minute, being aware of your chest moving in and out with each breath. Bring your focus to your nostrils, feeling the air slipping in over the nostrils. Close your eyes if it will help you focus.

3. Follow the breath in as you inhale. Try not to force any awareness. Let your focus be gentle and natural and go as far into the esophagus as possible. The next breath may take your awareness deeper into the lungs.

4. As you exhale, follow the breath out, feeling the air sweep up the esophagus and over the nostrils. Do you have any awareness of the breath from your lungs? Does it feel warm or cold?

You might become more aware during the meditation that your mind is full of "noise," or mental distractions. There may be bits and pieces of thoughts floating by. Maybe you have some mental yellow sticky notes floating around in there. Perhaps you hear a part of yourself trying to reject your meditation experience. This is all expected and is only the first stage of many that we must go through to achieve an empty mind. It's all right for those thoughts to be there; simply allow them to float up and out to the outer edges of your mind so that your focus is not on them.

An empty mind is a good thing, and an essential thing for healing. In time, the mind relaxes during meditation and becomes like clear water.

Crystal Clear _____

Studies in neuroscience using brain-imaging technology have shown that when the left frontal cortex is activated through meditation, stress and pain are reduced. The medical community is particularly interested in the results of these experiments as a means to decrease healing time and to promote a healthier life style.

Set some time aside every day for a meditation practice. Start with 10 minutes, once a day at the same time and place if you can. Your body and mind will grow used to sitting quietly. When you feel ready, try two sittings a day for 10 minutes each. The first sitting is to tame your mind. The second sitting will really count, as you will have emptied most of the mind traps from the first sitting. Increase the sitting time each day until you are able to sit quietly for 20 minutes at least once a day, preferably in the morning when there are fewer distractions. And do not be discouraged. It takes practice.

Group Meditation

When you meditate with others, you belong to a group harmony that seems to promote a better meditation. The reason is that when you are with people who are basically all doing the same thing, you are all putting out the same vibration. The meditative experience is much more powerful for everyone. You may experience a deep sense of peace and broader awareness.

An experienced meditation leader will usually initiate the group session and may give some guidance on how to conduct yourself during the session so you do not disturb others. You may be asked to sit in a certain way, chant special words, or focus on something to relax your mind. Group sessions may seem long for beginners, but they will help your meditation with their shared energy. Check first with the organizers so you know what to expect.

Meditation groups are often found with martial arts organizations, as part of training in yoga, and other spiritual and religious groups.

Into the Alpha State

If you want to know if there is a scientific explanation for why meditation works to heal the mind and body—why, yes, there is!

There are four types of brainwaves that can be determined using an electroencephalogram (EEG) instrument used to measure brainwaves:

- **Alpha waves** are associated with an awake, relaxed, and effortless alertness.

- **Delta waves** are present only in the deepest part of sleep.

- **Theta waves** are present during light sleep and deep meditative absorption.

- **Beta waves** are present during times of stress or when it is difficult to focus and concentrate.

Meditation is known to activate the left frontal cortex of the brain and to induce an alpha state of consciousness. When you reach the alpha state, your consciousness has switched from an awake state to a meditative state.

When we do not spend enough time in the alpha state, the experience of stress breaks down various mental and body functions. Over the long term, health declines and mental stability is compromised. When we stay in the alpha state for a longer period of time, we become more resourceful and more creative. We have less anxiety and more ability to apply concentration to problems. Our immune system strengthens. Even sports performance is enhanced!

 **Yellow Flag**

We seem to spend a lot of time in beta states from the time we wake up to the time we rest for the night. We rarely slow down long enough to induce an alpha state, let alone a theta state. So it's not uncommon for people to feel as though they can't relax—they're just not used to the feeling!

Prayer and meditation are ways to connect to that alpha state, where we become peaceful yet attentive. You'll experience a calmness and a clarity of thought, yet your mind is still and is not chattering on a mile a minute. You can experience the theta state when you rouse yourself from sleeping and just lie there with the awareness that you are awake, yet calm and alert. For some, this is the time when there can be a deeper connection within oneself to the transcendent self or to the divine. It is a time to explore!

Altered states of consciousness from meditation have been found to be highly beneficial to health and well-being. Some of the reported benefits are lower blood pressure, a happier disposition, and fewer stress-related disorders. Research has also shown that when people meditate while physically sitting or lying inside a pyramid structure, alpha brainwave activity increases. These deeper states of consciousness can also be achieved by using the crystals mentioned earlier (amethyst, clear quartz, rose quartz, sodalite, or smoky quartz) to enhance the alpha and theta states.

You don't have to have a physical pyramid to gain the benefits of relaxation, however, as long as your imagination is ready and willing to do some work. You can simply visualize yourself sitting inside a pyramid structure. Feel your mind starting to slow down and relax. See how long you can stay aware of the pyramid around you. See if you notice your breathing slowing down or becoming more regular. After a few minutes, allow the image of the pyramid to dissolve like a fading rainbow and slowly bring your awareness back into the room.

By the way, did you know that the 51.43° angle of the Great Pyramids of Egypt is the same as the angle of a quartz crystal? Marcel Vogel, a noted IBM research scientist and leader of crystal healing, cut crystals to exactly 51° to focus the "universal life force." Try this visualization exercise with the pyramid. The results may surprise you.

The Power of Intent

There is a new way of looking at healing, called *intent medicine* or *intent healing*. When the power of conscious mental intention is focused on healing, it has been shown to change the pattern of energy. William A. Tiller, a distinguished scientist featured in the movie *What the Bleep Do We Know*, leads investigations in the related field of *psychoenergetics* and has shown that both thought and visualization together can affect the human energy system. His experiments have shown that the energy released by healers using thought, intention, and healing hands were capable of releasing electrons and affecting change at a cellular level.

def•i•ni•tion

Intent medicine is the power of conscious mental intention (this can include prayer, meditation, or other like practices). Intent medicine has been shown to change the pattern of one's energy. **Intent healing** is the application of mental intent to cause a healing response. **Psychoenergetics** is a relatively new field of science that investigates the meeting of consciousness, energy, and matter and the nature of reality.

Experiments by Dr. Leonard Lascow, author of *Healing with Love* (see Appendix C), have also shown that both imagery and intent together are shown to influence health.

Dr. Larry Dossey is another leader in the field of intent medicine. He reported that in a double-blind experiment in 1998, a group of 40 advanced AIDS patients were randomly divided into two groups. One group received standard medical treatment but were not told that they were also receiving *distance healing* from healers scattered throughout the United States. The control group received standard medical treatment only. After six months, the results showed that the group receiving distance healing had fewer new AIDS-related illnesses, lower severity of illness, and fewer visits to the doctor or to the hospital with fewer days of hospitalization. This group was also significantly happier.

def•i•ni•tion

Distance healing is the ability to influence the restoration of another person's health from a distance.

Other similar studies have also shown that subjects receiving distance healing were able to block the effect if the healing was unwanted. For those who had a positive mental outlook and wanted distance healing, healing was more beneficial.

If you remember the earlier section on group meditation, people who share in meditation are combining their strength of intent. This is one reason why healing circles that gather several people to focus healing on select people maximize their healing intent, even from a distance. We seem to spend a lot of time looking for healing. How many of us really spend the time to look at what we want to happen? We need some new skills for healing, not just new medicine. If we put together the amazing properties of crystals with the power of intent and imagery, we can focus the mind on healing in a very powerful way. Intent medicine is more than a placebo, it's a reality!

The Least You Need to Know

♦ Sacred healing is a form of healing that cannot necessarily be explained by traditional science or medicine.

♦ The five Platonic solids relate to everything we know in the world—humans, plants, DNA—and help us to connect to the healing resonance of crystals.

♦ Crystal resonance can affect the internal energy of all things.

♦ Meditation calms the mind and can assist in healing. Certain crystals can enhance this process.

♦ The intent to heal is a significant factor in healing.

Chapter 4

The Crux of Crystal Healing

In This Chapter

- Crystal healers show you the way
- How and why crystal healing works
- Understanding crystal energy therapy
- Combine gemstones with Reiki healing
- Using crystal power to boost traditional symbolism
- Correct your astrological shortcomings with crystals

Now that you have a good base of knowledge about where crystals come from, what they're all about scientifically, and the metaphysical ways we can think about them, let's get into some therapeutic talk.

What is it that a crystal can heal that traditional methods overlook? It's the spirit, that idea of who we are and where we're headed in life. A crystal healer can come in many forms—a friend with a passion for crystals, a Reiki practitioner who uses crystals as part of his or her healing session, a trained crystal healer, or you can look in the mirror and let the healing begin! This chapter will let you in on how and why crystal therapy works and how you can ensure that it will work for *you*. (Hint: there's a little thing you must have called *faith!*)

Crystal Healers

The purpose for seeking healing is generally that we want to feel better about ourselves. Health is a matter of balance between the physical, emotional, and mental states—at least that's what the doctors can treat if you are ill. Yet our sense of self and well-being comes from our spiritual state and frames how we experience the health of our bodies, our emotional responses, and our thoughts. Sometimes we need some outside help to initiate our connection between the body, mind, and spirit. That's when a *metaphysician* can be useful.

A healer, on the other hand, is a person who has skill or training to use tools to apply healing techniques. A *crystal healer* facilitates the healing process through the selection and placement of crystals on the client's body. (Although even crystals placed in a room will emit energies or vibrational frequencies that can create a shift in energy dynamics and consciousness.) A crystal healer may use a variety of techniques and will have a number of different types of crystals that will be used for different purposes.

def•i•ni•tion

A **metaphysician** is a philosopher who examines the nature of reality—the mind-body connection—and sometimes will enter the border of the supernatural to seek explanation for what is beyond established laws. **Crystal healers** understand the crystalline complex and how to use crystal energy to create a curative transformation at the physical, emotional, and psycho-spiritual levels of being.

Within Tibetan Buddhism, crystals represent the highest level of purity and clarity of mind. Why is this? Well, the crystal teaches us that our minds should be clear and free from afflicting emotions and illness. And like a mother who cannot help but love her child unconditionally, a crystal refracts light unconditionally. If you put a clear crystal ball on a colored cloth, you will see the colored cloth underneath. Put a clear quartz crystal in water and the crystal disappears. Put simply, nothing material seems to stick to it.

Crystal healers know that if we strive to have the qualities of a crystal, we will hold a higher energy within ourselves and will radiate this light unconditionally throughout our being. Illness will not stick to our bodies and our minds will be clear. This is ultimately what we hope to find in crystal healing.

What Is Crystal Healing?

We've been using the term *crystal healing* a lot in this chapter, but what does it really entail? In crystal healing, crystals are applied selectively to the human body to affect a change in the subtle body energies and promote healing and relaxation. We'll talk more about the subtle energy bodies in Chapter 6; for now, think of it this way: Energy can get stuck in the body. When this happens, it affects every part of the body, mind, or spirit. Crystal healing helps to clear those blockages and get everything back in balance.

Crystal Clear

The use of crystals for healing has been around for thousands of years. Ancient civilizations in China and Meso America used jade as a preservative for the human body in its journey after death. The Egyptians used copious amounts of gold, lapis lazuli, carnelian, and other precious stones to decorate the tombs and possessions of their sacred pharaohs.

The use of crystal healing is relatively new to Western culture, although we do use crystals and minerals in many products such as fluoride in toothpaste, calcium in stomach tablets, and limestone in cement making. Many other crystals are used in the pharmaceutical industries. Even our computer chips are made from a crystal known as silicon dioxide. Other areas of the world use pure forms of gemstones for healing. For example, Indian Ayurvedic medicine uses crushed gemstones such as sapphires and pearls, and Tibetan medicine uses crushed calcite and turquoise among other crystals.

How Does It Work?

In the time before chemistry became a science in Europe, there was alchemy, which was devoted to finding the right composition of raw materials that could be used to manufacture gold. This gold would provide incredible wealth and longevity. However, metaphysicians and philosophers said that the most precious jewel was that of the human spirit. They called this gem the Philosopher's Stone—another name for the spirit that lies within us. The quest to find the Philosopher's Stone would lead us to enlightenment, bliss, and immortality.

When we have the right composition of materials near us, we can create what we need for personal transformation, ascension, or connection to our Higher Self. You've already learned that crystals resonate on particular levels. Their healing properties depend on their resonance.

So for a broken heart, we would want to hold or use a crystal known for its properties of healing the heart chakra. Rose quartz would be the perfect choice. For a diseased heart, we would use malachite (which is high in copper, helping in electrical recharging) or kunzite (high in lithium content to help dysfunctional behavior such as alcoholism) for psycho-spiritual healing. For throat complaints such as timid speech or sore throats, you might wear turquoise (known for its ability to open and protect the throat chakra). For back or leg pain, we would place hematite, which has magnetic properties, along the spine or leg, and so on.

Knowing which crystals to use for which issue is only part of the healing work. There is also the person's individuality to consider. A crystal healer will have a greater understanding of the crystals and their uses and will be able to activate the crystal resonance for healing purposes.

Why Does It Work?

We tend to attribute certain value to crystals, as we do with gold. The more rare an item is, the more interesting it is and the more value we place on it. But there really is a transcendent nature to crystals. They depend on the user having an open mind—something we also call a *consciousness opening* or a *spiritual initiation*.

There actually is some real energy in the crystals, too, of course. You can even measure their properties scientifically for electromagnetic energy, piezoelectric energy, and known chemical substances. But when you learn how to use these physical attributes on an esoteric level, crystal energy can be used even more effectively.

There is also a line between the physical and the metaphysical. With crystals, your mind set—your intention—is a carrier for energy.

I owned a crystal store for two years before moving into full-time crystal healing. A number of people would come into the store looking for healing. On some occasions, people received spontaneous healings, such as with personal issues. I recall a few:

◆ A young man had swollen hands and asked if there was a crystal to use for his complaint. I suggested halite, which is also known as rock salt. I asked him to put a small piece in his hand. During the next few minutes, his hands started shaking and when he opened them there was a puddle of water in the palm of his hand that ran off onto the counter. The swelling in his hands had shrunk, and he claimed he could bend his fingers more easily.

◆ One man came into the store to tell me about how a crystal had helped his family. He said that his son had cut off the tip of his finger. He had quickly wrapped his son's finger with a bandage. In the bandage he'd put his clear quartz crystal, which he'd bought only a few days previously after we'd been talking about crystals used for healing. He said that it seemed like a good idea to wrap the crystal in his son's bandage. He said his son felt no pain and that the surgeons were amazed to find the damaged area was in good condition for this type of injury. The doctors were also a little startled to see the crystal drop out of the bandage. They sewed the tip back on, and the son healed more quickly than expected.

◆ An elderly woman came into the shop asking me if I recognized her. I didn't. She reminded me that the last time I'd seen her was about two months ago and that she'd walked in using two canes. Clearly, she had no canes with her this time. She said she used the copper and garnet for her arthritis I had suggested and that it had worked so well that she no longer needed the use of her canes.

◆ Others have told me that their thyroid medication had been reduced after using crystals, usually amethyst. Amethyst is known to work on the subtle energies related to both the pineal and thyroid glands.

Crystal healing is satisfying for many people because they can participate either actively or in a passive manner—whichever is appropriate to their healing. Sometimes, the crystals do all the work. Sometimes, the person does all the work. And sometimes, a higher force does all the work.

Yellow Flag

Many skeptics question the use of crystals for healing. One author has even suggested that crystals are the ultimate placebo, having no inherent value or healing quality at all. Here's the bottom line: Crystal healing works if you believe crystals work. Just a small opening of consciousness is enough to make a positive connection with a crystal or anything else in life. Remember that there is no room for healing with a closed mind.

Crystal Energy Therapy

Some crystals are used to help access deeper levels of the human psyche and release emotional and karmic energy trapped in layers or bands around the person's body. Crystals have a unique connection with these bands because the energy of a crystal is compatible with the subtle and psychic energies of a person.

def•i•ni•tion

A **crystal energy therapist** is a person trained both as a crystal healer and as a psychotherapist or life counselor.

This is where a *crystal energy therapist* comes in. Using psychotherapy methods with crystal healing techniques, a crystal energy therapist can identify where the trapped energies are and select the appropriate crystal for transformation.

This type of deeper healing session with a trained crystal energy therapist should not be compared to any other type of healing. It is a modality on its own, involving a dynamic interchange of energies passing to and from different layers of the body and of consciousness by using crystals as the transformation tool as facilitated by the therapist. These sessions are not for everyone because they involve deep transformational forces that can be perceived as uncomfortable (but necessary) due to the force of rapid change.

Self-Therapy

The good news is that you don't need to seek out a healer to get the benefits of crystals. Many books (including this one) compile the meaning of each crystal and will guide you on your way to self-therapy. (See Appendix C for a good selection.)

Let your intuition guide you as to which crystals you need. Experiment with your feelings by selecting a crystal and wearing it throughout the day. Make a note of any changes you feel in a journal and add any specific events that might have been unusual for you and any reactions from other people. (Were they friendlier toward you? Less friendly?)

Is there a vibration to crystals like an earthquake or a truck rumbling by? No. The vibrations of a healing are subtle, very gentle. Many people need to be led to open up to another level of consciousness to actually feel and use the energy of a crystal. Without this knowledge and sensitivity, the crystal is just a rock.

It is easiest to wear crystals in jewelry, hold them in your hand, or just have them near you. Give each crystal about three days to settle into your energy matrix and begin to resonate with your own vibes; then try a different crystal. Explore each crystal one at a time and be aware of the specific message they bring to you. Remember, sometimes the healing is on more subtle levels, so check how you feel physically, emotionally, psychologically, and spiritually.

When you get used to their energetic output, you might want to wear one type of crystal to get a special effect over a longer time, maybe a few weeks. It's okay if you want to wear more than one crystal of the same kind. The effects will be stronger. Try wearing two different crystals at a time and later add one more for optimum healing effects. You can wear up to seven crystals at one time. More than that and you might feel overwhelmed!

As a starter kit, you might like to wear a rose quartz pendant at the heart or throat level for a week to open your subtle energies. Then add clear quartz to purify and amplify your subtle energy. After wearing both the rose quartz and clear quartz for a week, add amethyst to provide transformation and stability to your energy. Wear all three crystals during the third week to complete a 21-day energy change cycle.

 **Yellow Flag**

If you feel light-headed or dizzy, take the crystals off for a while to integrate the changes. You may also need to work with fewer crystals until you build up your stamina for crystal energy.

Reiki and Crystals

Many Westerners are already familiar with the practice of "hands-on healing" or "laying on of hands" within a spiritual context. The Bible refers to this ability, and this type of healing through touch has been practiced throughout time. Even the Shaolin monks in China perform a type of energy healing.

More recently, hands-on healing has found its way into complementary health care fields with various forms that include therapeutic touch, Jin Shin Do, Tibetan Pulsing, and *Reiki* (a gentle healing therapy). The name Reiki is a Japanese word symbolizing the universal life force and our personal life force. Reiki evolved out of the experience and dedication of Mikao Usui, a healer who started Reiki healing schools in the 1920s in Japan. Reiki was introduced to the West during the 1980s.

Many people receive benefits from Reiki energy therapy—adults, seniors, children, even pets. Reiki has been used to treat stress, burn-out, hyperactivity, depression, and related psychological imbalances and various diseases (including HIV, cancers, and various addictions). Reiki can also assist in recovery from injury from sports, car accidents, and so on, where gentle healing would be beneficial to promote well-being and health.

Reiki is an ideal treatment for seniors and disabled persons who may respond well to healing touch therapies. A person receiving Reiki can expect to feel deeply relaxed and balanced with a general feeling of well-being. Reiki can be a profound experience of deep relaxation and inner quiet. It can allow you to shift gears into a deeper sense of self and personal priorities. Reiki is a way of being that assists in creating more peace, harmony, balance, and a state of grace in your life.

The use of crystals in Reiki is not part of the traditional Usui teachings; however, crystals certainly provide a benefit and are used to augment a Reiki healing session. The Reiki practitioner might place Reiki energy into the crystal by holding it in her hands for a while before placing the crystal on the client. Advanced practitioners put universal energy symbols into the crystal (something I talk about in the following section). When the crystal is placed on the client's body, the energy is released and transferred.

Combining Crystals and Symbols

If a crystal can hold an energy pattern constant, then if we put another energy pattern—such as a symbol of peace—into the crystal, it will also retain that energetic structure. This means the energy of the symbol is available to be energized by the crystal. When the crystal discharges its energy, that energy will include the pattern and force of the symbol. It is a transference of the resonance of both the crystal and the symbol. Some samples of symbols are a dove representing peace or a rose representing love.

If you would like to experiment using crystals and symbols, here is an exercise to try. First, select a clear quartz crystal (see Chapter 10 for selecting a meditation crystal) that has been cleansed and is fully charged (more on these processes in Chapter 7). Then follow these steps:

1. Place the symbol in front of you and gaze at it for a few minutes while holding the crystal in your right hand. If you close your eyes briefly, you should see an image of the symbol in your mind.

2. Hold the crystal in front of you and see this image over the crystal. Hold the image steady in your mind and when ready, draw in a deep breath and blow sharply over the crystal. This will transfer the image into the crystal. This is a form of crystal programming that is discussed in Chapter 7. The breath is a carrier for the image. The crystal will resonate with the symbol in its structure.

3. Take the crystal and hold it to your heart chakra or third eye; see what you feel from the symbol.

You might find that you feel tingly—that's okay because it means your energy is being activated with the vibration from the crystal. Try sleeping with the crystal under your pillow and record any dreams in your journal stimulated by the symbol.

Ayurvedic Crystal Healing

Since ancient times in India and other countries, astrology has been a guidance and governance of people's lives. When people are born, the planets may be aligned in both auspicious and nonauspicious ways. According to *Ayurvedic* beliefs, when we need some help to balance the energies that are out of balance due to the planetary weaknesses that were present at the time of our birth, we can wear crystals or gemstones. The gemstones will also increase the strengths we were born with.

def•i•ni•tion

> The term **Ayurvedic** refers to the Hindu method of healing, which has been practiced for thousands of years. Ayurvedic gemstones are believed to balance any cosmic energies that were out of balance when you were born.

The natural electromagnetic radiation of gemstones helps with the alignment of glands, organs, and chakras. As subtle energy interacts with the body and mind, subtle corrections are made. A person wearing gemstones to balance energy will benefit from a longer life and be more free from the effects of illness and other discomforts than someone who does not have access to gemstones selected for his or her health.

Ayurvedic Gemstones by Astrological Sign

Astrological Sign	Ruling Planet	Birthstone
Aquarius	Saturn	Blue sapphire
Pisces	Jupiter	Yellow sapphire
Aries	Mars	Coral
Taurus	Venus	Diamond
Gemini	Mercury	Emerald
Cancer	Moon	Pearl
Leo	Sun	Ruby
Virgo	Mercury	Emerald
Libra	Venus	Diamond
Scorpio	Mars	Coral
Sagittarius	Jupiter	Yellow sapphire
Capricorn	Saturn	Blue sapphire

In Ayurveda, gemstones are selected for each person based on planetary alignments at birth and his karmic predispositions. Here, size matters, and it is not uncommon to see gemstones of several carats set into a pendant or ring to correct the imbalance of a planet! Usually a ceremony is performed by a priest to provide purification and blessings to the gemstone and to activate its properties. Jewelry such as a pendant or ring must be worn over the proper body part for healing and balance. Each finger, for instance, represents a different planet. In the case of a ring, it must be open at the back to expose the gemstone so that it touches the skin. Thus, the gemstone will provide subtle energy and vibrations to correct the imbalance within a person's life or body caused by planetary imbalances at the time of his or her birth.

When deeper karmic healing is needed, the gemstones are crushed and ingested as medicine. In Tibetan medicine, it is not uncommon to see turquoise, red coral, and other precious and semiprecious substances ground up with medicinal herbs. I personally have taken many of these precious pills, some containing substances such as ground pearl and gold, silver, copper, iron, sapphire, emerald, diamond, turquoise, and ruby in the detoxified ash form or oxides. These special compounds are made by Tibetan doctors called *Emchi*, who have trained for 12 years.

Yellow Flag _____

Do not ingest powdered crystals, minerals, or gemstones unless under the strict supervision of an accredited practitioner of a traditional healing art such as Traditional Chinese Medicine (TCM). Special processes are used to extract and prepare gemstone medicine. Many untreated crystals and minerals can be extremely dangerous to your health if taken internally.

Among some Amerindian groups, quartz crystals are retained in lodges to provide healing throughout the community. Sometimes large crystals are placed back in the land at strategic points to balance spirit energies. The ancient Druids of northern France and England also placed stones strategically, although their purpose is still a mystery. All these cultures have different methods, but they know one thing: crystals and their healing powers are a natural part of the environment.

The Least You Need to Know

◆ Crystal healers strive to help their clients mimic the characteristics of crystals: lightness of being and freedom from material and worldly concerns.

◆ Crystal healing works on two levels—the way the body or mind interacts with the actual energy of the crystal and the way we perceive the healing or expect it to take place.

◆ Hands-on healing methods like Reiki can be enhanced with crystal energy.

◆ Crystal energy can combine with the energy of an iconic symbol—a peace sign, for example—and amplify the resonance of both.

◆ In some cultures, crystals are used to compensate for astrological weaknesses that might have been present at the time of one's birth.

The Beginner's Guide to Buying

In This Chapter

◆ Narrowing down your choices

◆ Where to buy crystals (and where *not* to buy them)

◆ Getting to know your crystal

◆ Different shapes and sizes

◆ Crystal-inspired changes

◆ Keeping a journal

By now you are probably pretty excited about the potential of crystals and want to get started using them. This chapter is geared toward the beginner, guiding you to the best places to find crystals—and what to do when you get there and find that there are hundreds to choose from!

Of course, after you make a decision about which crystal to buy, your work is really just beginning. Bonding with your crystal is just the first step in the amazing journey you are embarking on with your crystal.

So Many Choices!

If there were a type of crystal for every illness, the list of crystals and their meanings would be endless. (Actually, the list *could* be endless, as far as anyone knows because not all crystals have been discovered yet!) Fortunately for those of us who love and admire these gemstones, there are plenty of crystals to choose from. But how do we narrow them down to manageable choices? A few tips that might help you pick and choose are discussed in this section.

Crystal Clear

Crystals sometimes discharge the energy stored inside them. Some people feel this harmless discharge of energy as a small electrical wave and might be more surprised than shocked! For most people, just holding a crystal causes them to feel more calm and relaxed. Sometimes physical pain lessens, such as headaches go away. Sometimes people feel less sad and more energized.

Hold Me Tight

When you are purchasing a crystal for the first time, selecting a suitable stone—one that you will do great work with—is critical to your experience. Keep these points in mind:

- Before you head out to buy a crystal, ask for spiritual guidance to direct you to the crystals you need and for the crystals needed to be there for you at a price you can afford.

- Set a budget for yourself. In most gem and mineral shops, *tumbled stones* are inexpensive, usually around a dollar for a small piece. A rule of thumb is that the better the quality, the more expensive the crystal. Because crystals are like eye candy, it's easy to want a lot and you can easily end up overspending your budget. So concentrate and choose only what really speaks to you!

def•i•ni•tion

Tumbled stones have been smoothed to a glossy finish using a rotary tumbler as part of a physical process. It takes several days of continuous rotation to transform a jagged rock into a highly polished stone.

♦ It is best if you can make your crystal selection when you are not in a negative mood. If you are upset or feeling resentment, the crystals you purchase will only absorb your bad mood.

♦ If you are buying specialized crystals, be prepared to pay more for quality. Look for any imperfections such as irregular coloring, which might give away that the stone has been dyed. Some crystals should also have specific markings that are desirable in certain types of crystals, such as dark concentric rings in malachite or light wavy lines in blue lace agate. Ask the staff for help in selecting a crystal. They are usually knowledgeable about good examples and they might even pre-select some crystals for you to look at.

When you've narrowed down your choices, you can see whether you and a particular crystal are a good fit. Hold the crystal in your dominant hand at about arm's length. If it has a point or tip, point it toward yourself. Slowly bring the crystal in line with your heart chakra (in the general area of the heart in your upper chest—more information on this in Chapter 6), drawing it slowly closer to your body. You're trying to feel the power of the crystal and whether it is connecting and interacting with all your energy fields. You might feel a pulling or a tingling, indicating the energy of this crystal is in tune with you.

You can also hold the crystal directly to your heart or solar plexus chakra to see what effect you are getting. If you are looking for a crystal for your third eye, look for a smaller crystal and hold it to your forehead to sense its energy. (See Chapter 6 for more on chakras.)

Be Decisive!

Here's a good rule of thumb for any wishy-washy shoppers out there: If you see a crystal and are not sure whether you want it, don't leave the store without making a definite decision either way. The reason is that a crystal is a totally unique energy on the planet. There really is only one like it. The signature of the crystal you touched will still be with you when you go home. You might even have dreams about the crystal. If you

Yellow Flag

Be sure your purchases are packaged properly and wrapped up very well for the trip home. You do not want to get home and find that the tips on your crystals are chipped, as chipped tips don't hold or direct energy well enough for healing purposes.

make a connection like that, then that crystal should be with you. And if you go back to buy it and it's gone, you'll be out of luck and missing out on some potentially great healing sessions!

Sometimes crystals feel sticky on the surface. This is usually from many people handling the crystal in the store and leaving negative energies behind. It is best to flick your hands at the finger tips or shake out any energies that might have been picked up along the way. If a crystal feels sticky, it is best to leave it there in the store. Its energy will be depleted and the crystal will need to be both cleansed and recharged before it can be used.

Shopping for Crystals

The Internet is a great source for finding and learning about lots of crystals, but the downside is that you don't get to hold them, see what they are like, or connect with them until you've purchased them. For these reasons, I'm a big fan of supporting local business when you're actually making a purchase. You have to know exactly what you're getting.

If you travel, find out where the crystal shops are and drop in. You might see something different or unusual to bring back with you. Check out the rock hound clubs and gem and mineral shows. Many hobbyists and prospectors bring their rock and mineral finds from the field in to sell or trade at shows.

Registered gemologists often have great connections with others in their field and can help you find someone reputable to purchase from. Some may be able to conduct testing on a gemstone if you are uncertain about the authenticity of a gemstone.

If you are new to buying crystals and don't know if you are getting a genuine gemstone, please be aware that fraudulent merchandise and disreputable dealers have been in this business for centuries. Fortunately, many crystals used for healing are not that expensive. If you were misled into purchasing jade that was merely colored glass or resin, you will have lost only a few dollars. However, I'll leave you with a few stories to consider before you make any larger investments. Remember "caveat emptor"—buyer beware!

I know of one reprehensible dealer who puts a zero at the end of a wholesale price as the retail price. If he buys a polished fluorite crystal for $40, he adds a zero, making it $400 retail, and sells it to people as a gimmick to remove bad family karma. One of my own clients told me she bought two crystals from this dealer. I made her return one that she paid $300 for, because I knew it was only worth $30. She was able to return that particular crystal, but not the other one, for which she paid $700! One gemologist sold me a high-quality, AAA-grade, clear quartz crystal necklace. When I looked at the necklace more carefully at home, I noticed a small bubble in one of the beads. I was curious and when I looked at some of the other beads, I noticed there were other bubbles. These bubbles were caused by gas and do not naturally occur in quartz. There was no question that these crystal beads were actually glass and were not the high-quality, premium-priced quartz I thought I was getting. I called the gemologist to bring this to his attention. He was quite surprised and had been unaware he was sold something being passed off as quartz from a person he thought was reputable. After checking his stock, he immediately discontinued the beads from his inventory.

Initial Introductions

Once you're home and you've unwrapped your new crystal, you'll need to cleanse and recharge it. (Read Chapter 7 for complete instructions on both processes.)

Now you can spend some quality time with your new crystal. And remember that even the smallest crystal can be effective in opening your consciousness to a whole new level because it is a portal to the expansion of awareness. After you've chosen a crystal, it's time to really get inside it (and I mean that literally) and see how the two of you affect each other.

For your first *crystal initiation*, select a clear quartz crystal with a natural tip, one that hasn't been polished. This is an all-purpose crystal, perfect for people who have never been through this ritual.

Again, be sure that your crystal is cleansed and fully charged before you begin. Sit quietly in a room that has natural light, which is best for seeing inside a crystal. Spend a few minutes looking outside the crystal, all over the surface of it. Observe its lines,

def•i•ni•tion

> A **crystal initiation** is a session during which one meditates and enters into the crystal matrix.

faces, and sides. Be aware of its dimensions. Feel the bumps with your fingertips. As you handle the crystal, be aware of your breathing. Maybe your breath becomes quicker; maybe it slows down and is barely audible.

Get the Inside Information

Now look inside the crystal. Look through the sides of the crystal. Look at any veils (discussed in Chapter 10) and other inclusions. Look through to the other side, and observe any distortions. Tilt the crystal and look through the tip. Look down inside to the bottom, to the floor of the crystal.

After you have truly explored the crystal inside and out, select a spot inside the crystal. Focusing on that spot, breathe in and out until your breath slows and becomes regulated by the crystal. When you are ready, close your eyes and feel yourself enter into the crystal. Explore what you see inside the crystal now, using your inner eye and your deeper connection. Be prepared to see something special. Maybe there is a rainbow of colors. Maybe you hear music. Maybe you see someone there and have a chat! The power of crystals is limitless, so anything is possible here.

When you are ready to return, take a deep breath in and mentally say the word *release* to bring your consciousness back into this reality. As your breath begins to speed up again and you are taking deeper breaths, open your eyes. If you are feeling a bit light-headed and need to get more grounded, drink some water with a little lemon juice in it to gently wake your senses back up. Walking around in some fresh air will help as well.

Now that you and the crystal have been introduced to each other, keep the crystal constantly near you for at least three days so your energies become well integrated.

Crystal Coldness

If you find that getting to know your crystal is leaving you cold, you could be blocking incoming messages. There's a simple fix for this. Hold your crystal and repeat this affirmation aloud and slowly three times to open subconscious blockages:

"I, [your name], am open to all there is in life."

Your subconscious takes in direction without judgment so it doesn't worry about whether the statement is true. The crystal will also help you by amplifying the affirmation. Now try the whole introductory process again. I'm willing to bet it's going to go a whole lot more smoothly this time around.

Type A and Type B Crystal Personalities

In the 1950s, two California-based doctors, Meyer Friedman and R. H. Rosenman, theorized that people could be loosely grouped under one of two categories. According to this study, Type A people are impatient, stressed, and very goal driven. Type Bs are relaxed, easy going, and will tell you it's the journey that counts. These are the people who wear the "Don't Worry, Be Happy" T-shirts.

The energy charge held within some crystals can be similar to these human traits. In Type A crystals, the matrix seems to store more charge and a higher level of activity. The energy they store is used to do a deep healing job, and the work is done quickly.

Type A crystals *look* intense—they're usually precise or chiseled, almost like a super-fit body. Their color can also look more intense than Type B crystals. When you hold them in your hand, they feel heavy with energy. These crystals have a job to do and are very assertive. If you need to clear a blockage in the subtle energy system or address an urgent physical or emotional issue, Type As are ready to get the job done.

Type A crystals include the following:

◆ Rutilated quartz

◆ Obsidian

◆ Smoky quartz

◆ Chrysocolla

◆ Malachite

◆ Purple fluorite

◆ Certain configurations of clear quartz crystal, such as a laser wand

Type B crystals, meanwhile, have a slower, gentler energy release that is more like a shift in consciousness or a relaxation into another level of awareness. These crystals seem to be lighter in weight and might have some less distinct lines than the Type As. When Type Bs are placed on the body, there might be a slow gathering of energy, like water backing up behind a dam, followed by a slow gentle release of the energy.

Type B crystals include the following:

◆ Amethyst

◆ Rose quartz

- Citrine

- Sugilite

- Sodalite

- Certain configurations of clear quartz crystal, such as a rainbow

Keep your Type A and Type B crystals fully charged to experience the quality and depth of their healing. (See Chapter 7 for more information on charging crystals.)

Crystal Clear

Should you store Type A and Type B crystals together? There are pros and cons to this because their very different vibrations can cross and absorb into each other. If you do store them together, the crystals learn from each other and can ultimately provide a balance of energy, neither too brazen nor too reserved, but just right for the person receiving the healing.

Unusual Shapes, Uncommon Power

Crystals come in all sorts of shapes and sizes—some of these shapes, especially, are intended to magnify the effect of the crystal's power and can produce amazing effects in your home or in your outlook!

Obelisks

The Egyptian obelisk is a magnificent piece of stone, often quarried from several kilometers away and carved with the local history of famed rulers. Obelisks are wider at the base, pulling up yin energies from the earth (see Chapter 6 for more on yin and yang). At the top of the tall, four-sided, tapered spire, the tip is in the shape of a pyramid.

The symbolism is that the obelisk is life-giving. The healing aspects of obelisks draw negativity from the environment, shooting the energy up the shaft to be replaced on its journey with positive energy. The four sides of the pyramid tip are like a lighthouse, beaming the positive energies out from its tip over the community or relaying energy to other obelisks, like antennae.

If you have kept even one obelisk crystal in the middle of your room or home, energies will be kept in circulation, releasing pent-up energies that have accumulated. When used for healing purposes, you would place the base of the obelisk over an area of the body or chakra to be healed; the crystal pulls up energies for transformation.

Geodes and Clusters

Geodes are formed when volcanic activity spews out lava and forms balls that cool on the outside. The balls contain various gases that promote the growth of various crystals inside, such as amethyst. Some geodes are like caves, as big as a person. When they're broken open, you'll see pristine sparkling crystals inside, like a whole colony of crystals. Sometimes small pieces are broken off of the geodes and sold as clusters.

Clusters are groupings of crystals of the same or different type. They are used in *feng shui* for balancing energy in a room, a garden, and buildings. (See Chapter 9 for more information on crystals and feng shui.)

Like an acoustical microphone, geodes are cupped to pick up negative energies. They can be positioned within a room to absorb and transmit energy. Place one on each side of a doorway, or facing a door, to catch and cleanse negative energies on their way in.

def•i•ni•tion _____

Feng shui (pronounced *fung shway*) is an ancient art of placement based on the principle of an eight-spoke wheel where each spoke represents a part of one's life and environment. Using "cures" for bad influences, objects and colors are placed in the areas of the home or building elements to restore balance and to achieve harmony.

Other Shapes

A crystal carved into the shape of an animal represents the spirit or energy of that animal. In ancient traditions, an animal's spirit might help guide you or protect you. For example, a lion represents courage. When we see or wear the image, we feel empowered by the animal's spirit as a reminder to be courageous. Ask yourself in a meditation to be shown in your mind's eye which animals walk with you to guide and protect you. Next time you are looking for crystals, see if you can find your spirit friends as crystals. Keep them with you to be worn as jewelry, or place them in your sacred place or altar.

Changes in Thought and Presence

As you begin to work more and more with your crystals, you'll become more comfortable and start to feel enlightened. What's happening here? Is it real? Is there a name for it? There sure is—it's your intuition popping up to say hello. Get used to it because it's going to stick around now for a long, long time!

Let Intuition Be Your Guide

What is intuition? How do you know if you have it? Intuition is the knowingness that is already inside you. Sometimes people refer to intuition as their "gut feeling," the ability to know what's right, or a warning that something is wrong. Our own intuition is something we trust because it comes from within ourselves.

When you hold a crystal, you may get an energy rush as your intuition awakens and guides you through a new learning experience. Intuition is activated from the energy of the crystal, releasing its energy into your subtle energy fields. It's your own energy that the crystal energy is supporting and enhancing.

If you can sense this awareness or feel other sensations while using a crystal, your consciousness is opening to another level of perception. The more you work with crystals, the more your awareness and intuition open. As your intuition opens, you will have the ability to know how connected you are to the infinite universe and to the possibilities of love, peace, and healing.

Quick Change

A *quickening* is an amazing experience that often happens when you work with crystals. Your awareness expands and you find that you are living life on a whole new level. Your energy is revitalized and you become more stimulated about living your personal truth. Spiritual understanding happens subconsciously and progression is rapid. You seem to gain a lot of information very quickly. Most of us can't really explain it; it's just a broadening of the mind and spirit. Sometimes you just don't have the vocabulary to explain it even to yourself. Such is the illuminating path of working with crystals. Sometimes you feel dumbfounded about what you know.

def•i•ni•tion

Quickening is a transformational process that speeds up spiritual awareness and development.

Quickening is an amazing personal experience, but it can frighten or confuse the people around you. They might say things like, "Oh, she's into her crystals now. I just don't understand her anymore." Try not to be hurt. Just remember that regardless of your own enthusiasm, others are not ready to take on this type of change themselves. Give thanks for your newfound wisdom and go ahead and revel in it!

And here's a wonderful side effect of crystals and quickening: The positive energies amplified by the crystals can be seen in the way you look, the way you act, and the way you interact with other people. Don't be surprised if others are drawn to you. They feel good in your environment and are feeling uplifted and happy around you!

The Flip Side

For every action, there's an opposite and equal reaction. You've just learned about the ultimate in positive crystal power, intuition, and quickening. However, due to the indiscriminate nature of crystals, negative energies can also be amplified and the negative emotional energy will be stored in the crystal until the crystal itself is cleared (more on this in Chapter 7). Negative energies are usually associated with a strong negative emotion; a physical trauma; or unwanted disturbances at the psycho-spiritual level, such as grief, trauma, or mental disease. Calmness is the name of the game when handling crystals. You don't want to take an already bad mood and crank it up to an unbearable level.

Yellow Flag

Never destroy a crystal in an angry fit, and do not use crystals with the intent to harm others. Your negative intent is absorbed by the crystal and will come back to you in the form of bad karma!

Keep a Crystal Journal

One of the best ways to keep track of your crystals and your experiences with them is to keep a journal. You can write down details such as where you purchased the crystal, its cost, the country and area from which it was mined, and special characteristics such as inclusions or other crystals growing with it. You might also want to write down your first impressions or images that resonate with each crystal.

Later you might want to review your notes to fill in your collection or to determine a constitutional crystal for long-term use.

The Least You Need to Know

♦ Before you purchase a crystal, you should take the time to hold it and determine whether you have a connection with it.

♦ A crystal initiation is a method used to bond with and really get to know the intricacies of a crystal.

♦ Like people, crystals have different personalities. Some are quite aggressive, while others are more mellow.

♦ Buying stones on the Internet does not allow you to feel their energy and their potential for working with you.

♦ Working with crystal energy can bring about amazing transformations in your intuition and general outlook in life—harness that power and work with it!

♦ Consider keeping a crystal journal to record your crystal purchases and your experiences with them.

Part 2

Starting Your Crystal Collection

Selecting crystals for different uses is always challenging. A large toolkit of colorful crystals is not unusual because different types and forms of crystals are needed as healing tools. Each crystal has a job to do and is selected based on the issue being addressed.

Preparing crystals for healing involves several processes from general cleansing and activation to self-attunement and programming. Developing sensitivity to crystals is a process of awareness that takes some self-training and practice. Feeling comfortable with crystals activates and supports the energy of healing. Research and experimentation shows that using visualizations and affirmations increases the effectiveness of healing.

Some specialized areas where crystals perform well to change subtle energy is in the environment. Using crystals in feng shui practices is beneficial to harmonize your home or office. Crystals and gemstones are also effective when worn as jewelry. Stone and setting selection are important, as is the location on the body where they are worn. Part 2 gives you the skinny on getting your crystal collection rolling.

Chapter 6

Shifting Energy with Crystal Power

In This Chapter

- What is subtle energy?
- Understanding chi, meridians, and grounding
- The seven chakras in the body
- Discovering your aura
- The power behind crystal balls, wands, and pyramids
- What healing feels like

Crystal healing has been around for many centuries and has brought about dramatic improvements in the physical health of countless people. But there's more to healing than meets the eye. That is, crystals can be used to address imbalances in the unseen energetic forces that are whirling inside each and every one of us. When these systems are out of whack, we don't feel well—and we may not know why. The good news is that with the right gemstone, the energy can be shifted right back to where it should be.

In this chapter, I talk about some very familiar-sounding forms of crystals and give you the real story on how to use them to harness positive energy!

Experiencing Subtle Energy

Some people can read subtle signs around them and tune into their environments. Have you ever smelled the ozone in the air before a good rainstorm or seen the leaves turn over when the wind shifts before a storm? Have you tried to predict the future by reading tarot cards or tea leaves?

Subtle energy is all around us, even in our own bodies. By learning about subtle energy, we can become skilled at sensing and feeling it, recognizing it visually, and even reaching a higher level of knowingness about the subtle energy in others. When we're really in tune with this form of energy, crystals can be useful in helping to heal at the subtle body level.

Crystal Clear

If you were lucky to have had someone close to you explain subtle experiences such as knowing about events before they happen or reading tarot cards or tea leaves, your mind will be more open and relaxed to experience a wider range of extrasensory experiences!

Middle Eastern Traditions

In India where there are major teachings of yoga and *Ayurveda,* the traditional medicine of India, the word *prana* means "breath." Prana is light and airy and is considered to be the vital energy in the human organism that flows along a subtle energy network called *nadis.*

In Tibetan medicine, the subtle body energies are called *tsa, lung,* and *tigle.* Tsa are the channels or pathways; lung is the pranic energies; and tigle are the seeds of subtle energy that are like pollen in the wind, moving with the subtle winds of the body and leaving you feeling happy and content. Within the subtle body are different levels of subtlety. The channels are larger, with the lung or pranic energies being more delicate; the seeds of energy are the most subtle of all. The mind will experience well-being and happiness when there is balance in the channels.

Restoring Balance to the Subtle Body

Subtle energy is an entire network designed to keep you in balance. When the subtle body is balanced, energies float freely without restriction along the channels. Feelings of joy, happiness, love, compassion, and well-being will flow freely, too. The mind rides along with the tigle in the energy channels, like a horse and its rider.

When the subtle body is disturbed through fear and other negative mental states, the tigle seeds of energy become restricted. Because they can't spread around, they start to recede and cause depression, anxiety, and unhappiness.

To revive these energies and well-being, the subtle body needs to be restored and balanced. By working with the subtle balancing energies of crystals, the tigle are influenced and our minds and any blockages become more relaxed and clearer. We're returned to peace and happiness! Constant exposure to crystals and other forms of healing that balance subtle energies helps to maintain the subtle body through which we can experience all kinds of love.

Chi and Meridians

In traditional Chinese medicine, *chi*, like prana, is the life force that sustains a person's vitality. Among Chinese chi masters, experts in understanding the subtle energies of chi, it is well understood that thoughts can direct and affect the flow of chi. There is no question that the mind and consciousness are all intimately related. Chi is a natural component of your health.

Our awareness of chi is something we can all become more aware of and more sensitized to. We can take classes in Tai Chi, Qi Qong, and other Asian methodologies that focus on the movement of chi through the body. We can also be more aware of when we feel chi increase—such as with laughter, which is the increase in the flow of chi; and sadness, which is the decrease in chi. You can even get positive chi just talking to another person. You'll know because you'll feel good. Strong emotions can generate or reduce the flow of chi.

Since chi, as a vital force, is all around us, just breathing while walking or any kind of motion causes chi to flow freely. When chi flows, health is affected in a positive way. Meditation also helps to stimulate the flow of chi. As chi masters already know, our thoughts and our consciousness can also control chi.

def•i•ni•tion

Chi, a Chinese word for "air," is used to describe a person's vital life force. **Meridians** are the pathways in the body on which subtle energy moves about.

Chi is generally associated with *meridians*, pathways on which the subtle body energy travels. The body contains 12 meridians. Each meridian is a channel for subtle energy to travel along that correspond to a specific organ and a set of physical and psychological functions as shown in the following illustration.

Chakras/Meridians.

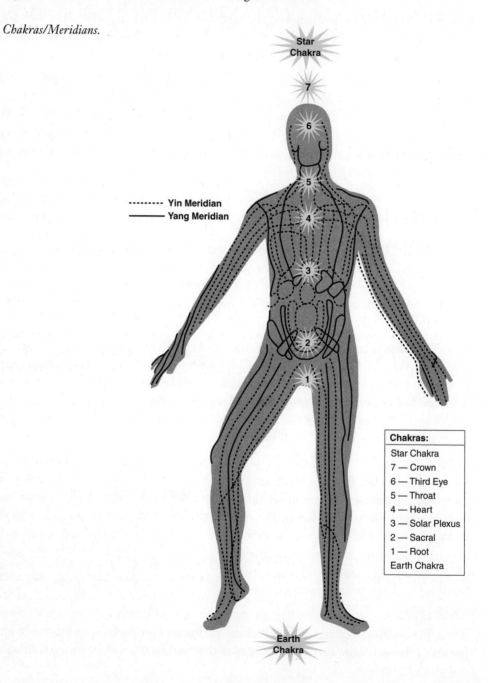

Star
Chakra

7

6

5

4

3

2

1

- - - - - - - - Yin Meridian
———— Yang Meridian

Earth
Chakra

Chakras:
Star Chakra
7 — Crown
6 — Third Eye
5 — Throat
4 — Heart
3 — Solar Plexus
2 — Sacral
1 — Root
Earth Chakra

Subtle energy usually stays within the body. Like the trunk and branches of a tree, there are major arteries for the energy to travel along. Some of these pathways lead to the health of major organs. When in balance, with neither too much energy nor too little energy, the organs remain healthy. When imbalanced, health is affected and immunity to disease is compromised.

When crystals are placed along an imbalanced meridian line, especially at the beginning and end of a meridian line and over the area of imbalance, a rebalancing of that meridian line occurs. We'll talk more about healing the meridian line in Chapter 11.

Yin and Yang Energies

To understand how chi energy is balanced, you need to understand yin and yang, opposing energies that are contained in all things. Yin and yang represent the balance between positive and negative attributes, and also the balance between feminine (yin) and masculine (yang) energies. Both are part of the whole. Together they must always be equal in a dynamic equilibrium. If one disappears, the other must also disappear.

When an imbalance occurs, there is more yin or more yang. If there is more yin, there is less yang somewhere; conversely, if there is more yang, there will be less yin somewhere. For example, where there is a flood on the planet, there will also be a drought somewhere else. If there is too much energy in the subtle body system, there will be too little in the physical body, which can manifest as illness. When the yin and yang are restored to balance, health and well-being continue. Hopefully we can do the same for our planet.

Balancing Yin and Yang

When it comes to crystals, some types and forms of crystals will be more yin- or more yang-balancing. The shapes and qualities of crystals put them into gender-based categories. The important part is that crystals can be very powerful in increasing or decreasing energy, and the right crystal must be selected to balance yin and yang energy.

For instance, if you're feeling stressed at work and a bit hot-headed, maybe yelling at people and feeling upset a lot, this would indicate an overabundance of yang energy. To balance this level of yang energy, you would need to select a crystal that would either decrease the yang (anger) or increase the yin (calm). So you have two choices: either find something to calm yourself down by removing or absorbing the excess yang energy or find a powerful yin crystal that will match and balance the level of excess yang energy.

You also have a third choice: you select both yin and yang crystals to bring yourself more rapidly into your center of balance—one to dispel negative emotions and the other to create positive emotions resulting in emotional harmony.

In this case of being an overstressed worker, you would select a yang crystal such as the dynamic smoky quartz, best known for absorbing negative energies. You would also select a yin crystal such as moonstone, which is best known for its icy coolness and calming abilities. Together they each do their job to achieve a yin/yang balance and a harmonic wholeness.

Crystal Clear

Yin crystals include agates, amber, amethyst, aquamarine, calcite, clear quartz, fluorite, jade, moonstone, and rose quartz. Yang crystals include carnelian, diamond, fire opal, garnet, lapis lazuli, malachite, obsidian, rutilated quartz, smoky quartz, and sapphire.

Yin and yang are also associated with the sides of the body, so to balance this person's energy, I would recommend holding the smoky quartz in the right male-yang-dominate hand and the moonstone in the left-yin-dominate hand. Balance will be restored as the extreme polarities of yin and yang reach harmony.

There are a few ways to enhance the balancing effect:

- Take a long breath of coolness, directing your breath to draw in from the moonstone. (In other words, you would take a breath from the hand that is holding the moonstone.)

- Slowly breathe out any heat and negative thought from your body into the smoky quartz, letting the crystal absorb the excess energy. This hot/cold tune-up usually doesn't take more than a few minutes and calms and centers your yin and yang energy.

After such a session, it's normal to feel a little light-headed from breathing so much, but overall, your body will feel more relaxed and your mind will be clearer.

Even though a crystal might be considered more yin than yang, there are many degrees of yin. Conversely, there are different degrees of yang crystals. In Chapter 5, I mentioned that there were Type A and Type B crystals. Type A are more yang and Type B are more yin. So next time you are selecting crystals, be aware of what degree of yin or yang a crystal is and select the crystal according to how active or passive your needs are.

Get Grounded

Change is difficult for many people because we like the familiar ways of doing things. We like to get up in the morning and have toast and coffee for breakfast. We like to take the dog for a walk at night. We like the same laundry detergent, the same brand of milk, and the same burger from the same drive-through, time after time after time. And that's all right—these are things we can count on as being the same in this vast, sometimes confusing world.

This is not to say we're inflexible. We might grumble a bit if there's no coffee in the morning, but most of us will get on with the day despite the discomfort. The real inflexibility comes when we are asked to change the inner parts of ourselves. This is different from changes in the subtle energy body, because these are changes we're consciously bringing upon ourselves. Fortunately, crystals can help soothe these transitions through a process called *grounding*. Grounding helps us keep centered when everything else is changing around us.

def•i•ni•tion

Grounding is a method that opens channels in the body and allows for unwanted energy to travel into the ground.

When personal change occurs, it can feel unsettling and uncomfortable on many levels. For instance, changing a bad habit, such as interrupting people while they are speaking, can be incredibly frustrating. After all, you have things you want to share, too. But you're waiting and learning about the give-and-take of conversation … and it feels like all you're doing is waiting while your friend blabs on and on and on!

Aggravating, right? Well, all that unspoken and unspent energy builds up inside and waits to be released at a later moment when it's finally your turn to speak. That energy is like water behind a dam and needs to go somewhere or you'll burst and spit out all the words at once. This is where grounding comes in. Grounding takes that excess energy and diverts it someplace else so that it causes no harm to yourself or others.

Move That Energy Safely

Like a lightning bolt hitting a tree and traveling through the roots into the ground, your surges of energy need a place to go where they aren't going to cause harm to you, your psyche, or your loved ones. During an electrical storm, you would be advised to be in or on a safe surface, one that would not conduct electricity.

Grounding your personal energy is similar, except we're going to use a material to draw that energy out and into the earth.

When you are grounded, the energy travels though the energy pathways in and around your body. When these pathways are open, energies can travel along them without getting stuck along the way. This means that the energies you need for health and healing will be readily available, while negative energies can be removed altogether.

Here's an example. Imagine experiencing the emotional shock in learning that a co-worker has been stealing company money. The energy hits you in your solar plexus, the gut of your emotions. Your head is spinning just thinking about the news. You feel sick, you can't think, you just need to get out of the situation, or you think you might blow up.

When you are grounded, all of this unwanted energy passes right through you so that it doesn't harm your physical, emotional, and spiritual body. Sure, you may still be concerned about the situation (naturally!), but the effects on your body will be lessened when the energy has a place to go.

Grounded for Life!

So how do you do a grounding? It's a fairly simple process that requires focus and a dark crystal. Take a deep breath, and follow these steps:

1. Sit down with feet flat on the floor. Do not cross your legs, because energy will be unable to travel with restriction. Feel your weight on the seat of the chair, focusing on your tailbone.

2. Center yourself. Look inside and feel that part of you called the core, the center of your being. This is the part of you that nothing can shake. Using your breath, inhale into the core and exhale, sending light-filled energy throughout your body into every cell until you are filled with light.

3. Place a dark-colored crystal such as garnet or obsidian, or a rock such as black granite, between your feet. The crystal will provide the anchor for your energy and will keep you tied to the earth plane instead of allowing your energy to fly off and get lost on some other dimension.

4. Visualize tree roots coming from under your feet. See them growing deep into the earth, traveling faster until they reach a big boulder, as big as you can imagine, below the surface of Earth. Anchor the roots by winding them several times around the boulder. This is one of the simplest methods of grounding.

5. If you feel you need to go deeper into grounding, draw in a big breath from the boulder, inhaling the heaviness and stability of that boulder's energy up through the tree roots. You may feel a tugging as your body sinks deeper into the earth. Bring the root energies up through your physical body, following the energy pathways and expanding the energies around you into the subtle body. Breathe in from the boulder, drawing the energies through and around your body. Do this a total of three times. Take your time. You will feel very heavy and really grounded.

6. Visualize that the roots are released from the boulder. Bring your focus to your heart center. Visualize a white ball of light from the center of your chest radiating throughout your physical and subtle body. The light will create an energy balance for the grounding exercise.

7. End the grounding session by smudging yourself. Light up a little sage in the room. The smoke will clear energies away from the body that are not necessarily for your highest good.

Crystal Clear

Drink plenty of water. Water is a carrier in your system for energy and provides a flow for energy to follow. If you are dehydrated, you may feel like your energy flow is a bit like a finger running over sandpaper—everything sticks and catches along the way.

Clearing Blockages

When you have repeated stresses such as emotional shock, worry, physical traumas, and feelings of being spiritually shortchanged, the ability to pass unwanted energy through energy pathways becomes weaker. Sometimes obstacles to clearing unwanted energy will build and blockages will form, like the formation of plaque in arteries when the pulmonary system is overloaded with cholesterol. Some of these obstacles are not recognizing or ignoring signs of physical and emotional distress, hiding emotions, ignoring needs of the self, or staying in a mind space that is harmful to your self.

Grounding is a way to keep the pathways open so energy doesn't get stuck along the way, or get built up and fester until it causes a problem finally noticed by yourself or others.

The really harmful thing about these types of blockages—and really, what I'm talking about are long-term hurts and stressors—is that they are a big cause of major imbalances in the body, something I'll talk more about in the following section.

The Chakra System

The word *chakra* in Sanskrit means "wheel" and describes the spinning centers of energy at various points in the body. There are seven major chakra centers, each associated with the glandular system and the general physical health of the area of the body to which it is closest. The chakras are part of the subtle energy of the body and provide for movement of prana.

def•i•ni•tion

> **Chakra** refers to the spinning wheels of energy that provide circulation of prana to the nadis and contain vital energies as well as spiritual energies.

Color Therapy and Chakras

Color therapy, which is used to balance the chakras, has been around for a long time. Avicenna, the eleventh-century physician, observed that certain colors were connected to disease and healing. For instance, red was associated with movement of disease through the system, blue was cooling (as in calming a fever), and yellow took heat away (as in dispersing inflammation). In the chakra system, red is seen as vitality, blue is associated with healing, and yellow with intellectual pursuits. There are many systems and interpretations of what color means. What we can agree on is that each color has a special meaning.

In the chakra system, the higher the vibrational frequency of the color, the more it relates to the higher chakras—the seat of consciousness. When positive and negative ions merge as white light in the highest chakra center, the crown chakra, there is such an illumination of energy that ignorance of the mind is dispelled and enlightenment occurs.

The chakra system also disperses energy to lower chakras where the endocrine system is affected. Fluids are secreted along the delicate nervous system, which in turn provides mastery and regulation of a unified mind and body. Fluctuations can cause subtle changes in mood, initiative, and other responses to external stimuli. The internal energy system can be modulated using various therapies, including crystals.

Crystal Clear _____

Imbalances in the chakras are indicated by the opposites of the attributes listed—in other words, an imbalance in the root chakra would manifest as physical weakness, melancholy, or infertility.

On the following pages, you'll find all the information you need to work with and heal the chakras with various crystals. One important note: you will get a bigger self-healing effect if you also place one of the chakra crystals directly on top of each chakra and then sing the chakra sound for a few seconds to activate and awaken the chakra energy. Do this one by one for each chakra, starting at the root chakra. Let the crystals rest on top of your body for at least 7 to 15 minutes to soak in all the energies.

The First Chakra: The Root or Base Chakra

The first chakra is between the legs at the perineum, the space (ahem!) before your anal opening.

The root chakra provides physical strength, the will to live, sexual and reproductive energy, grounding, and the fight-or-flight response.

Red, black, or brown crystals work well to balance the root chakra. Red crystals can include garnets or rubies. Obsidian and black tourmaline work well in the black range, and brown crystals include mahogany obsidian and brown jasper.

Colors: Red, black, brown

Sound: LAM Note: C

The Second Chakra: The Sacral, Spleen, or Sexual Chakra

The second chakra is easy to find. Simply place your hand with closed fingers flat against your stomach below the navel with your thumb just at the navel. In the center of your torso four finger widths down from the navel and just below the little finger on your hand, press and find a soft spot of about 3 to 4 inches wide. That is the location of your second chakra—the sacral chakra.

The sacral chakra provides self-esteem, self-awareness of emotions, openness to new ideas, connecting to others, assimilating experiences, and our definition and identity of sexuality.

Crystals that are in the orange color range heal this chakra and include carnelian, orange calcite, jasper, and coral.

Colors: Orange, orange-red, orange-yellow

Sound: BAM Note: D

The Third Chakra: The Solar Plexus Chakra

The third chakra is the soft spot below the sternum in the center of the upper torso. This is the area of the "gut feeling" many people have. In the martial arts, you can disable your opponent by hitting this area. Sometimes this chakra moves around, either higher or lower depending on your interaction with life—trying to get more out of it or trying to hide from it.

The solar plexus chakra provides personal power, self-confidence, logical thinking, decision-making, and intellectual pursuits.

Yellow is associated with healing in this chakra. Crystals that are in the yellow color range include citrine, golden topaz, golden or yellow calcite, smoky quartz, apatite, yellow jasper, and amber.

Colors: Yellow, golden yellow

Sound: RAM Note: E

Yellow Flag

I once wore a large green emerald for more than three months at my solar plexus chakra. I was affected with more green to the area than I needed. I had a stomachache and an overproduction of bile. When an aura photo was taken, a large green ball was shown to be at the solar plexus. After I took off the emerald and wore citrine for two weeks, I could feel the area cool down. The moral of this story? It's possible to oversaturate an area with color with detrimental health effects! As with anything, check on your progress when working with crystals and know when you've had enough.

The Fourth Chakra: The Heart

The fourth chakra is in the center of the chest, about halfway between the bottom and top of the sternum. This center is usually found in times of great joy or great sadness because it either feels wide open with love or closed down in pain and grief.

This chakra can move around as well, either higher or lower depending on what you've encountered in life. If the chakra is higher on the chest, it signals some level of spiritual ascension.

The heart chakra provides compassion for self and others; love; and balance between mind, body, and spirit.

This chakra needs both pink and green colors: pink for divine love and green for healing and nurturing. The heart chakra is the seat of compassion and the source of love and radiant light.

Crystals that are in the pink color range include rose quartz, kunzite, rhodonite, rhodochrosite, and pink tourmaline. Crystals that are in the green color range include emerald, malachite, dioptase, peridot, and aventurine.

Colors: Pink, golden pink, green

Sound: YUM Note: F#

The Fifth Chakra: The Throat Chakra

The fifth chakra is located at the soft spot at the base of the throat, above the well that forms where the clavicles meet. People who use their voices for speaking and singing have a well-developed fifth chakra that is usually a bit higher over the vocal cords.

The throat chakra provides creativity, communications, speaking truth, and the will to take action.

Turquoise is the color associated with healing the fifth chakra, as it is focused on open expression and communication.

Crystals that are in the turquoise color range include turquoise, blue lace agate, celestite, aquamarine, blue tourmaline, natural blue topaz, and sodalite.

Colors: Turquoise, light blue

Sound: HAM Note: G#

The Sixth Chakra: The Third Eye

The sixth chakra is the hardest to locate. It varies on each person. Generally, it is a disc about the size of a walnut located in the center of the forehead. For some, this chakra is lower—slightly above the top line of the eyebrows. When activated, this center tingles. To test where you think the sixth chakra is, wet your finger and place it on your forehead. You will feel a cooling tingly sensation not unlike what it feels like when your third eye is open. (Chakra activation is covered in further detail in Chapter 8.)

The third eye chakra provides the seat of your intuitive seeing and knowing, extra-sensory perception (ESP), clairvoyance, and a higher understanding of others.

Iolite crystals are used to balance the third eye chakra. Iolite is an unusual color in that both a sapphire blue color and gray seem to combine with a drop of red from iron to form it. These blues are attuned to bringing truth, harmony, and protection because blue is calming for the emotions.

Crystals that are in the indigo color range include iolite (also known as cordierite), sodalite, lapis lazuli, blue fluorite, sapphire, and azurite.

Colors: Indigo, deep blue

Sound: AH Note: A

The Seventh Chakra: The Crown Chakra

The seventh chakra is at the top center of the head. You might have noticed some tingling in the scalp sometimes for no reason. Maybe they were incoming messages from Beyond!

The crown chakra provides the merger with the higher self, basic identify with god, spiritual growth, self-realization, and spiritual peace.

Violet crystals are used to heal the crown chakra because this color has the highest vibration and provides a transformational flame, turning negative energies into positive ones. Crystals that are in the violet color range include amethyst, sugilite, purple fluorite, and charoite.

White or transparent crystals are also sometimes used on the crown chakra. These may include selenite, apophyllite, clear quartz, and diamond.

Colors: White, purple

Sound: OM Note: B

The Chakra Tune-Up Kit

One of the most important tasks when starting on crystal healing is to assemble a chakra tune-up kit. Keep these specially selected crystals for each chakra handy for when you need them. If you already have a collection of crystals, get them all out and group them together by chakra color to see if you are missing any.

Begin by looking at what color crystals you have been collecting the most of. That is a clear signal that you are trying to get your healing in that chakra and should probably be wearing the crystal as a pendant to increase your vibration in that particular chakra. Now look at your crystals again. Which color(s) are you lacking? Let's say you have a lack of yellow crystals. This signals that you are trying to avoid issues related to the solar plexus chakra (whose color is yellow), including self-confidence, logical thoughts, and decision-making.

The following table gives a minimum list of crystals for your chakra kit. Crystals should be at least 1 inch in diameter if you can find them, either tumbled smooth or in raw form.

Chakra Tune-Up Kit

Chakra	Chakra Crystal
1—Root	Garnet or other red crystal such as red calcite.
2—Sacral	Carnelian or other orange crystal.
3—Solar plexus	Tiger eye, jasper, or any yellow crystal such as honey calcite.
4—Heart	Rose quartz or any pink crystal such as rhodochrosite, and/or green crystal such as jade, malachite, or dioptase.
5—Throat	Turquoise or light blue crystal such as blue lace agate or sodalite. White coral can also be included.
6—Third eye	Lapis lazuli or other deep blue crystal such as iolite or blue topaz, or golden topaz or apophyllite.
7—Crown	Amethyst or other purple crystal such as purple fluorite, or clear crystal such as selenite.

Spinel for Your Chakras

The mineral kingdom provides a number of different types of crystals in a full color palette for the chakras, such as calcite, fluorite, and spinel. Spinel is often used for jewelry because it is a clean crystal, meaning that it is easy to find without inclusions and flaws, and comes in a number of different colors, corresponding to the color of each chakra. Spinel can be used to replace more expensive gemstones.

Crystal Clear

Spinel is also known to be a blood purifier and restorer of energy. As such, spinel is known to provide powers of immortality.

There is often confusion between a spinel and a ruby. Both gemstones are deep red and vibrant, and both were identified as rubies until the eighteenth century, when science clarified that ruby was from a material called corundum.

When used for spiritual growth, spinel provides a vitality to the chakras that enhances the energy of the chakra. The colors match the chakras perfectly! Wearing a pendant containing a spinel of each color would be very therapeutic:

◆ **Red**—Increases strength and regeneration of physical energy through the first or root chakra.

◆ **Orange**—Enhances creativity and stimulates sexuality in the second or sacral chakra.

◆ **Yellow**—Stimulates personal power and self-confidence through the third or solar plexus chakra.

◆ **Green**—Helps to develop compassion, love, and altruistic feelings through the fourth or heart chakra.

◆ **Blue**—Improves self-expression and communication through the fifth or throat chakra.

◆ **Dark blue**—Enhances intuition, clairvoyance, and channeling through the sixth or third eye chakra.

◆ **Clear**—Aligns the chakra system through the seventh or crown chakra.

What's Your Aura?

When mood rings were first introduced in the 1970s, they were offered as a means to determine the color of a person's *aura*. A thermochromic (heat-sensitive) material under a plastic shell containing liquid crystals would change color with the heat from a person's finger. In response to different body temperatures, the crystals would twist in their matrix, altering light wavelengths that could produce as many as 12 shades of color. The ring would show the color blue if you were calm and relaxed, yellow if you were stressed and unapproachable, and red if you were feeling sexy. While clever as a commercial application of liquid crystals, mood rings are not really reliable as an indicator of the human aura.

def•i•ni•tion

An **aura** is a reflection of the colors of the chakra system. Different colors can indicate which chakra and its associated systems are strongest in your body.

So what *is* an aura, anyway? When chakras spin, color projects around the body into different layers of the auric system. Each layer is a little bit different in how it handles energy perception, but the crux of the issue is that depending on the color of the aura, you might be way out of balance! Unfortunately, most people can't see auras, so they have no idea that they're walking around with energy all blocked up somewhere inside their bodies.

One way to train yourself to see other people's auras is to see your own. For this exercise, you will need a clear quartz crystal (1 to 3 inches long). Hold it in your right hand in front of your chest with the tip pointing in toward the center of your heart chakra. This amplifies the energy field and makes it easier for you to visualize various colors.

Sit or stand quietly in front of a clean, streak-free mirror. Gaze just to the side of your hairline. Try to not focus on anything; just look past your own image. Breathe softly but do not blink, even if your eyes water. You might see various distortions in the mirror, but after about 5 minutes, lights and small colored streamers may start to float around. You might see the aura as transparent color, like a rainbow.

What do these colors mean? Well, in a nutshell:

- Purple indicates that you are a spiritual person.
- Blue means that you are at peace with yourself and the world.
- Turquoise indicates that you are a high-energy person.
- Green means that you are a natural healer.
- Yellow means you are a joyous person.
- Orange means you are a power-hungry, controlling person.

◆ Red indicates you have materialism on the brain.

◆ Pink is the aura of someone in love.

Now try the same technique by gazing past a friend's head (and try not to giggle as though it's a staring contest). You might even like to draw what you saw as an aura portrait!

Harnessing Power with Familiar Forms

In the last chapter, we talked about crystals that have been formed into other geometric shapes and how their crystalline alignment is more powerful (for example, a pyramid can amplify the power of a crystal). Now let's talk about some familiar forms of crystals—so familiar, in fact, that many of us don't think of them as crystals at all! And yet, their power to shift and move energy is every bit as genuine as any other gemstone.

Crystal Balls

Most people associate crystal balls with looking into the future. Crystal ball gazing, also known as *scrying*, is an ancient form of divination. A seer or clairvoyant will look into a crystal ball for images that tell the reader about events of the future.

However, crystal balls are not just for gazing. They can be used for massaging the body, for clearing and saturating chakras with energy, and for dream work. You can even perform energy massage therapy by rolling the crystal ball over areas of pain and discomfort. Be sure to cleanse and charge your crystal ball after each use to keep it in tip-top shape.

def•i•ni•tion

Scrying is an ancient form of divination using a reflective surface such as water or a crystal ball to see images that can relate hidden or future events.

Crystal balls come in different types of crystal, such as amethyst, rose quartz, sodalite, and obsidian. Many of them are cloudy with inclusions (flecks or specks in the crystal) or are opaque. These are good choices for energy massage therapy but take the time to hold the ball in your hand and listen to and feel what its energy is telling you. Make your purchasing decision based on this personal interaction.

For scrying (which is just a form of harnessing energy with a crystal ball), you'll need a very clear crystal or glass ball. Perfectly clear quartz are hard to come by but are worth the money because they provide a clear surface for the mind to project upon.

Scrying takes practice. You'll need several sessions of sitting with the ball and just gazing softly into it. There is a relaxation within the physical eye after a while, and a connection opens to the inner third eye. You might start to see images. At first these will be subjective, like seeing your own dreams. For those with natural talent, reliable images will be seen along with impressions about them. The interpretation of these images is up to you and your intuition, which of course is strengthened by the crystal itself.

Crystal Wands

Wands are really an extension of your arm and your own energies, which are amplified through an interesting charging effect that happens inside the chamber of the wand. As your hand heats the wand instrument on the outside shaft, ions get excited and begin to align. When a critical mass has accumulated, it starts to fire in a straight line up toward the crystal. The energy passes through the crystal and can be directed for whatever purpose the wand master deems. Making your own crystal wand is considered to be more powerful for activating energy because you make a special connection with it as a healing tool by intent.

How do you make a wand, you ask? You will need:

◆ 7-inch-long copper tubing, wide enough to secure your crystal

◆ A copper cap to fit one end of the tube

◆ A clear quartz generator crystal or an amethyst 2 to 3 inches long

◆ Epoxy glue

◆ Leather or silk for wrapping the crystal to the top of the tube

Now you're ready to assemble! Place the crystal slightly inside the top of the tube with the point facing out. Add some cotton or other natural filler to keep the crystal steady and centered at the head of the tube. Add glue to fill in any gaps. Apply glue to the banding material, and wrap the top of the wand to cover the base of the crystal. Let it dry completely. Add the bottom cap and leave the metal exposed so the cap can slip off. Decorate the wand with feathers, leather, paint, and additional crystals glued anywhere on it.

Using a Crystal Wand

To harmonize the wand to your energy, keep it with you and warm it up from time to time in your hand—without using it—over a few days. It's like starting a car on a cold morning. A wand needs a little time to warm up and to align its energies.

Now it's time to purify and activate the wand:

- ◆ **Crystal wand purification.** Light a white candle and hold the crystal wand in both hands. Pass it back and forth over the heat of the flame, being careful not to burn the wand. After several passes, the heat of the candle will have purified the crystal.

- ◆ **Activation prayer.** While rolling the wand back and forth on your knee or between your hands, visualize a white light surrounding you and recite the following prayer to activate your wand:

  "I now invoke the love and wisdom of my higher self to be present and guide the energies for this wand activation.

  "I now dedicate the healing energy of this wand to benefit all others in the highest service of all mankind.

  "I now encapsulate this wand in the triple healing light—pure white light, green healing light, and the purple transmuting flame to seal and protect this wand from any misuse.

  "I now call on my master, teachers, and guides to help me serve in the highest intention for use of this healing wand.

  "I now activate this crystal wand for the highest good of all who may receive healing from this tool."

A wand is for focusing and moving energy for healing purposes. You can hold the wand by either one or both hands and point it a few inches above the surface of your body to send healing energy. Try visualizing white light or colored chakra light coming from the wand's crystal tip into the body.

If you would like to send energy out farther for distance healing, hold the thought of the person in your mind, or gaze at a photo of the person. Hold the wand straight up in front of you with both hands on the shaft to charge the wand. Imagine the person in front of you. Aim the wand toward the visualization and at any special areas that need healing. Hold the wand steady for several minutes. You can either say an affirmation for the person or ask for a healing or a blessing.

Crystal Pyramids

If you are drawn to pyramids, you might be looking for structure in your life. The pyramid gathers and shapes sense from the chaotic mental and psychic energies into a logical creative life force.

Interesting, right? But how do you put this to use in your life? Well, a pyramid structure used during meditation harnesses and focuses your energy. If you have a small crystal pyramid, you can use it as a guide for visualization and hold it over your head. If you're lying down, simply place it above your head.

A crystal pyramid makes it possible to move into other dimensions where information can be accessed and you can create manifestations on a material plane. Pyramids are the teachers for students learning to use the dynamics of energy!

> **Gem of an Idea**
>
> Some people claim that pyramids act like room air fresheners, removing bad smells or bad energy. A small crystal pyramid with the base held against a sore tooth will help reduce pain. You can place a crystal pyramid over a person's photo to send her distant healing. To increase psychic abilities, you can tap a small crystal pyramid made of labradorite or amethyst over your third eye.

There are several healing properties of meditating with a pyramid:

♦ **Physical**—Increases regulation of all body systems, speeds healing, reduces aging, and smoothes wrinkles

♦ **Emotional**—Reduces stress and worry, decreases feeling of alienation, and assists in emotional releasing

♦ **Mental**—Increases mental clarity and dreaming; improves memory, communications, and logic; develops a deeper sense of one's self; and improves creativity

♦ **Spiritual**—Improves psychic abilities (clairvoyance), enhances spiritual connections with other beings, assists in astral travel, helps access deeper levels of esoteric knowledge, and strengthens all energy fields

What Does Healing Feel Like?

Now that you've been introduced to how crystals can be used to balance or heal systems in the body, the obvious next question is, "How do I know it's working?"

Sometimes the effect of crystals on the human energy field is very subtle and difficult to describe because there is no real physical feeling such as "hot" or "cold." Each person has a different level of perception, different levels of receptivity, and different levels of sensitivity.

Crystals can definitely warm up in your hand if you hold them even for a short period of time. A transference of body heat and other subtle energies into the crystal occurs. If you hold a crystal for a while, put it down, and return to pick it up even after a minute, you will find the heat is still inside. Tibetans living in the higher altitudes will sometimes place crystals in their armpits to heat up and then hold the warmed crystals in their hands to protect them from frostbite.

When you have a pile of crystals on you for a healing session, you can feel very relaxed, often entering a different state of consciousness. After a healing session, many people seem to have a healthy healing glow on their face. Muscles and wrinkles seem to relax and pain subsides. Emotional issues seem less important or resolved. Over the next one to three days, the subtle energy in your body is recharged and you might feel more energetic and your head will be clearer.

The healing effects of crystals are often experienced as very refined changes to the four levels of being: physical, emotional, psychological, and spiritual. Each will be discussed in Part 3.

The Least You Need to Know

◆ Crystal power is used to harness and shift energy.

◆ The body is comprised of a subtle energy system, which, although unseen, affects your sense of well-being.

◆ Yin and yang are part of the subtle energy system; they are always working together.

◆ Chakras are part of the subtle body, and each is associated with distinct colors and sounds.

◆ Crystal balls, wands, and pyramids are also used to shift energy.

◆ Because everyone has a unique energetic field, the healing and/or shifting of that energy feels different for everyone.

Chapter 7

Preparing Your Crystals for Work

In This Chapter

- ◆ Cleansing your crystal externally and internally
- ◆ Energetic recharge!
- ◆ Activating your crystal and programming your intention
- ◆ Protecting yourself from negative energy
- ◆ Six essential crystals every healer should have
- ◆ Caring for your crystals

To prepare your crystal before using it for healing or meditation purposes, it should be first cleaned physically of any mud, oils, sand, or other debris. Then using a cleansing technique, any negative energies should be removed from the crystal so that you do not transfer residual energies onto yourself or others.

For maximum healing effects, charging crystals will ensure the crystal is ready electromagnetically and is saturated with ultraviolet light, which energizes each crystal. To "wake up" your crystal, you might need to activate it into its role and mission. And finally, program your crystal to direct the energy for a specific outcome or for support during a healing session.

External Cleaning

If you purchased a crystal with mud on it, chances are it still has part of the growth *matrix* on it. The matrix is the part of the earth that the crystal grows in. It's full of mineral nutrients and fortifies the crystal with its unique energy.

def•i•ni•tion

A crystal **matrix** is the earthen structure that the crystal actually grew in.

The matrix provides a great place for the crystal to grow and absorb its specific energy from the earth. But now that you have it in your hands, you want to see the beauty of the gemstone, so let's get rid of the muck.

When removing the dirt from your crystal, be careful because the crystal might be softer than the matrix it grows in! A warm water bath in a high-foaming dishwashing detergent and a stiff scrub brush work well for coarse crystals; a bath and a flexible, soft toothbrush is best for more fragile crystals.

For really tough situations, a soaking might be necessary. For example, the matrix on quartz crystals is usually yellow and somewhat cakey-hard, like mud. It sometimes requires a bath of oxalic acid for 2 to 5 days to get it completely clean. (A chemist/pharmacist may be able to get the oxalic acid for you, or try searching for it on the Internet.) Use one part oxalic acid to two parts water.

When the crystal is clean, let it dry in the sun so that it soaks up the ultraviolet (UV) rays. (More on why this is important a little later in this chapter.)

Internal Cleansing

After you have physically cleaned the crystal, the next step is to cleanse the crystal of unwanted vibrations and energies that come from other people handling the crystal during its mining or from people packing, transporting, unpacking, and touching it before it has actually reached you. Crystals tend to take on energy indiscriminately and, like wearing someone else's clothing, you can feel that something's just not quite right.

To cleanse the crystal of this type of energy, I recommend a salt water bath. Salt is really good for removing negative energies from most crystals; however, some crystals like angelite, barite, and howlite, and some marbles and pearls are sensitive to salt and their surfaces can be damaged very quickly in a salt bath. For those, you can use the smudging technique I talk about at the end of this section.

To cleanse a crystal you wear regularly, a 7-hour salt bath every 2 weeks or so is fine. Get a plastic bowl large enough to hold your crystal(s). (Glass is fine, but it is a hard surface and you could chip your crystal easily.) Fill the bowl with enough water to cover the crystal. Room-temperature water is fine, and it would be best to have spring water, which is "alive" with nutrients that crystals like.

Add 1 teaspoon of salt for every 8 ounces of water. The "perfect" cleansing solution is a 30 percent solution of sea salt and spring water. (If you have genuine sea water, use that!) You do not need to actually mix the salt into the water. I usually just throw a handful of salt over the crystals in a bucket and leave the entire thing in the sun for the crystals to soak up the rays and recharge.

When you pour off the salt water, do not touch the water because you will be transferring the negative energies back onto yourself. Pour it into the earth and then rinse any salt residue from your crystals. Let the crystals dry on newspapers or tea towels. If you leave them in the sun, you can also charge them! (Some crystals don't need cleansing; we'll talk about these a little later in the chapter.)

Different Salts

You might wonder if there is a difference between using sea salt and table salt (rock salt). There is. I find that sea salt leaves the crystals with a different feeling than table salt.

Sea salt has a more refined energy signature with a lot of small rainbow-colored vibrations. Table salt is like a workhorse—it is less subtle, is more coarse, and has clunky yellow and gray-blue vibrations. If you plan to use a crystal at the upper chakras (third eye or crown), cleanse it in sea salt because these centers are very refined on the body and prefer the more subtle vibration. (Wouldn't you?)

To feel the energy signatures from different salts, get them from health or food stores or pick them up while traveling. I have tried ordinary table salt, Celtic sea salt, sea salt from the Dead Sea, sea salt from California .... Each provides its own type of energy and vibration.

Gem of an Idea _____

> Try soaking two crystals separately overnight—one in sea salt and one in table salt—using about 1½ teaspoons salt in about 1 cup of water for each type of salt. Rinse the crystals off thoroughly the next day and then see whether you can tell the difference energetically by holding one and then the other.

Smudging Technique

As I've mentioned, some crystals should not be soaked in salt water. These are generally porous or water-soluble crystals such as halite, marble, angelite, and barite. Salt can also pit the shiny exterior of a polished crystal.

def•i•ni•tion _____

To **smudge** something is to use smoke to clear it of negative energy. Sage, sweet grass, and incense are commonly used for smudging.

As an alternative, *smudge* these crystals with sage, sweet grass, or incense such as frankincense to cleanse them. This is a particularly good method to use if you have a cabinet full of crystals or some that are very large and awkward to bathe.

Spend about 3 to 7 minutes doing a smudge, fanning the smoke over the crystal with a feather fan. As the smudging smoke rises, it pulls the negative energies away from the crystal, so it's very important not to fan the smoke with your hand. Passing your hand in this smoke will track these negative energies onto yourself.

When you've finished cleansing the crystal, give yourself a good smudge to clear your own negative energies—especially your hands, which have been handling the crystal directly.

Recharging the Batteries

Sunlight recharges crystals with UV light, sometimes called light radiation. When the crystal comes from the earth, it is has been nurtured in yin or feminine energy from the earth (see Chapter 6). The crystal has been taking nutrients from the ground—gases, water, various minerals, and other nutrients—to develop into a crystal. When it is "harvested" from the earth, it is removed from the yin energies and needs now to receive yang or masculine energies as its source of energy renewal. So the UV light from sunlight, the full spectrum of light, restores the crystal's depleted energies.

Recharging time depends on the crystal's capacity to absorb the light (its individual crystalline energy structure has a lot to do with it), the stage of energy depletion within the crystal, and (I think) the will of the person who has been handling the crystal. (A stubborn, strong-willed person is going to wear out a crystal more quickly than someone who's pretty laidback.) Typically, I find 4 hours in the sun once a week keeps a small crystal energetic and alert.

Keep your crystals by a window for constant recharging in the strong UV rays. Some people say that glass refracts the UV rays so it is best that your crystals get direct sunlight. But if that were so, then the plants raised under glass greenhouses probably wouldn't survive.

> **Gem of an Idea**
>
> Tape your crystals to your windowsill to prevent them from being blown away by a strong gust of wind, or put them all in a basket for easy transportation in and out of the sunlight.

Wakeup Call: Activating Your Crystal

Sometimes, a crystal can be a "sleeper" and needs a little nudge to be made aware that it is going to be used for healing or meditative purposes. You can activate your crystal through an initiation ritual (discussed in Chapter 5) or by simply holding it, rolling it quickly back and forth in your hands, sleeping with it, gazing at it, washing it, and generally handling it.

To awaken its consciousness through ritual, offer some sage, sweet grass, or tobacco and indicate your intent for use of the crystal (for example, for healing). You can speak out loud, or you can simply meditate with your intent. This can be something as simple as, "I intend to use the power of this crystal to heal me of this illness."

Touching a tuning fork to the crystal or using bells will also initiate its energy.

Remember to fully recharge your crystal as described in the previous section after you've been handling it for activation purposes.

Programming for Intent

Each crystal has its own mission, or its own programming for healing. Crystal people sometimes say that a crystal resonates with a particular chakra, for instance, or that it has a mission to clear a past life. We don't want to harm or change that type of programming. Even if it's not what you need right now, you might want that energetic help sometime in the future.

Blank Slates

All right, so we know that every crystal has a task and we don't want to mess with that preprogrammed energy. But here's the interesting thing: Each crystal also comes with its own blank database, a subtle or spiritual energy center that has the ability to store new instructions, just like humans have an infinite capacity for instruction and spirituality. The crystal can translate and absorb an energy signature from outside itself and store it into a crystalline energy structure within itself. Now this is the real esoteric work of a crystal!

Yellow Flag _____

Folklore says that crystals may have been programmed by alien beings. It is up to your own belief system to decide whether there were extraterrestrials or others who have loaded instructions into crystals, but you'll want to be sure you have removed any programming that is not to your highest and greatest good.

This blank database sometimes gets filled up with unconscious instructions from people handling the crystal. So we want to be sure that the database is cleared of that kind of programming before using it. Once it's cleared, we can add our own set of instructions. The crystal will then resonate with those instructions, amplifying, broadcasting, and projecting the new set, of energy patterns in its work.

A Breath of Positive Air

When we're talking about programming crystals, we're really talking about infusing them with positive, helpful energy. There are several ways to do this. Here are some different programming techniques used with crystals:

♦ Write a thought on a piece of paper, and then place a crystal on top of it to absorb the thought energy. The crystal magnifies the thought and acts as the transmitter, sending the thought in its amplified state to the universe.

♦ Program your crystal by holding it in your hand, breathing in through your nose, holding the thought in your mind of what you want, and forcefully breathing out (snort!) through your nose into the crystal. Do this on each side of the crystal. There are six sides to a clear quartz crystal; for tumbled or round crystals or gemstones, hold them in your hand and snort directly over them six times.

◆ Hold the crystal in your hand and focus on your intent. Use a circular breath by breathing slowly and naturally through your nose into the crystal and then breath energy back in from the crystal. Repeat this circular breath for 3 to 5 minutes. This is an effective meditative technique and is quite powerful to directing your mind for positive results. This is a good technique to use on crystals that will be given to others for their healing purpose.

Crystal Clear

The reason you pass air through your nose is that the mouth is considered vibrationally inferior—you cough, say bad words, and eat using your mouth so the vibration is not as pure as passing air through the nose.

You can put as many thoughts, affirmations, or items such as holographic images into your crystal as you like. Whenever you want to clear them out, just hold the word "CLEAR!" in your mind and then forcefully breathe (snort through your nose) into the crystal six times to clear the crystal of unwanted programming.

Oh, and by the way, if you are holding a crystal and thinking bad thoughts, *stop*. Put the crystal down and clear your mind. Revisit your intent; then you can return to the session—unless you need to cleanse the crystal of any negativity it has picked up or to clear it of any unintentional programming.

Learn to Attune

After selecting a crystal and cleansing the crystal in salt water, you are ready for the process of *attunement* to your crystal.

To get you more attuned to crystal energy, hold a clear quartz crystal with a good point (the tip of the crystal) in your right hand (if right handed), pointing it down into the palm of your left hand, and run it slowly over and over the palm of your hand about

def•i•ni•tion

Attunement is the process of aligning your energy with that of a particular crystal.

1 inch above the surface without touching the skin. You will feel the electrical energy of the crystal. Now do this with the other hand. Then run clockwise circles very slowly around your heart chakra, feeling the sensation of crystal energy in your heart chakra to get a strong connection to the crystal. Hold the crystal in front of you and say the following Dedication Prayer or one of your own choosing.

I dedicate this crystal to the Universal Purpose. From this moment on, I undertake to utilize its energies to benefit all life. For I am one with the creative mind and therefore one with all life forms. In that which I am, I now activate the life energy within this crystal, in order that its power will be utilized to serve the Universal Purpose.

(Reprinted with permission from Sharon Ellis, www.essence-of-wisdom.com)

Then simply place the crystal on your chest, over the heart chakra with the tip pointing up. Just lay quietly with the crystal on your chest for 15 to 20 minutes to get a full attunement. Make note of any images or thoughts you receive during this time in your journal.

Protection Techniques

As you work with crystals and open up energy centers and feel vulnerable, you also want to feel protected from any harm or misdeeds (such as negative energy). This is where special protection techniques can be used.

def•i•ni•tion

In most major faiths there is a concept of three sacred elements, also known as the **sacred trinity**. For instance, in the Catholic faith, the Holy Trinity is the Father, Son, and Holy Spirit; in Buddhism, there is the Buddha, Dharma, and Sangha.

Recite a protection prayer, preferably three times, to express your higher will and to initiate the *sacred trinity* of your faith or belief system. You can make up your own prayer or modify the crystal wand activation prayer found in Chapter 6. Simply ask for spirit guides or angels to stand guard for you. You can envision a golden net with white light over the room, sealing out any unwanted energies. Maybe you'll envision a ring of fire for protection. Use your imagination. Whatever works for you will have more meaning and power behind it.

Alice Bailey, a twentieth-century mystic, said The Great Invocation Prayer was a world prayer for use by everyone. This very potent prayer distributes powerful spiritual energies and is used to bring light and love to the planet:

From the point of Light within the Mind of God
Let Light stream forth into human minds
Let Light descend on Earth.

From the point of Love within the Heart of God
Let Love stream forth into human hearts
May the Coming One return to Earth.

From the center where the Will of God is known
Let purpose guide all little human wills
The purpose which the Masters know and serve.

From the center which we call the human race
Let the Plan of Love and Light work out
And may it seal the door where evil dwells.

Let Light and Love and Power restore the Plan on Earth.

(Adapted version; reprinted with permission from Lucis Trust)

Six Essential Crystals

Now that you know how to get started with your crystals, I want to tell you about six crystals that many crystal healers would not be without. I'm not saying you have to add them to your kit right now, but somewhere along the way, you'll want to make sure to pick these up for their healing benefits.

Kyanite

Kyanite is known to energetically align chakras, both vertically and horizontally. Point the tip into the chakra and hold it steady for a count of 7 or 21 seconds, or up to 3 minutes for particularly stubborn chakras. For a full alignment treatment, hold the crystal at each chakra. Your hand might wobble a bit with the energy at first, but it will steady as the chakra becomes aligned. Kyanite is one of several crystals that do not seem to need cleansing, due to its unique internal structure, which is constantly providing its own alignment.

Selenite

It is said that at the time of the legendary King Arthur of England, the wizard-druid Merlin died in a crystal cave filled with selenite. Merlin projected all his knowledge into the crystals. There is no doubt that selenite opens the crown chakra and offers esoteric information telepathically to those wishing to know. You might even be able to access Merlin's knowledge!

This crystal can be used at the highest levels for healing—to align chakras, to cleanse the aura, to remove obstructions such as tumors, to open to higher states of consciousness, and to increase creativity.

def•i•ni•tion _____

The word **ethereal** indicates a subtle energy field that exists between the physical energy field and the emotional energy field.

Selenite is another crystal that does not need cleansing because its lustrous light and internal structure eliminates energy from being absorbed in the first place. This is an *ethereal* crystal, meaning it provides a connection between the physical body and the rest of our subtle energy layers.

Fluorite

Fluorite is a very interesting crystal because some of it comes in an octahedran shape, looking like two pyramids end-to-end at the base. It also comes in varied colors. Green fluorite often comes from China, and is used for physical healing. Yellow fluorite is considered to be a crystal of high mental stimulation and creativity. Also look for rainbow fluorite, which is banded with many colors, for a full spectrum of healing.

One of the features of fluorite is its ability to glow when under UV light. This crystal certainly holds a tremendous amount of white light! When there are stubborn blockages in the chakras, drop a purple fluorite into the chakra for several minutes to loosen up those emotional and mental strong-holds.

You might also find that joints stiffened by extra cartilage will benefit from fluorite crystals around and on the joint for several minutes over a few applications. Use fluorite at the crown chakra to clear energy passages from the third eye to the crown and to provide an increase in intuition and clairvoyance.

Calcite

Like fluorite, calcite comes in many colors. Calcite isn't a very hard material, so you'll need to be careful not to drop it or bang it up too much.

Calcite has many forms, but it is found where water flows. Calcite, like water, is cooling and calming of emotions, dousing the intensity of stress. The nature of this element is to fill things (think stalagmites, stalagtites, and limestone deposits, which are all calcite), so it's commonly used to fill energy gaps in the chakras.

Hematite

The natural magnetic quality of hematite makes it a perfect crystal to use instead of commercial magnets to ease nausea and pain at specific points on the body. Obtain several flat pieces of hematite for your tool kit and tape them onto joints and the spine if you need more energy. As blood pumps by the crystal, it will pick up needed magnetic energy and increase the circulation in the area of the crystal.

Hematite is also a blood purifier and relates well to reducing anger and eliminating toxins stored in the liver.

Infinite

This opaque green crystal is also called "The Healer's Stone" and seems to contain loving energy that pulls out pain. It provides relaxation and rest to the worried and wearied. Hold the crystal to the area where there is pain for as long as necessary to sense pain reduction. Some people wear the crystal for chronic issues. The stone can be held in the hand at night for a more restful sleep or placed on the belly to induce relaxation.

Treat Your Crystals with Care

As you begin to build your collection of crystals, you will want to have a number of different crystals available for various physical, emotional, and spiritual issues.

You might be wondering if you have to separate crystals according to their uses or vibrations. The answer is no! Keeping your crystals together is actually helpful because they tend to resonate to the highest crystal frequency. As they are all together, they will also share healing memories, so they will learn from one another. Finally, if there are any crystals that have not been cleared of negativity, the vibration of the other crystals will clear the crystal.

To transport them in and out of the sun for recharging, use a basket or fishing tackle box, with a good handle that's strong enough to hold the weight of the crystals. You don't want all your crystals to tip out or drop as they could become damaged.

> **Yellow Flag**
>
> Some crystals are photosensitive and the color can fade over time if left in the sun. Sometimes dyed crystals will fade quickly as the dyes are not fixed. If you are not sure about your crystal's sensitivity, consult a mineral website or a minerals guidebook.

A note of caution: Even though it's fine for your crystals to "live" together, it's very important that they do not bang against each other. You can wrap individual crystals in cotton batting or silk and larger crystals can be slipped into old, clean socks. For third eye or crown chakra crystals, a container kept separate from heavier crystals will keep the softer or more refined crystals better protected.

The Least You Need to Know

◆ To clear crystals of negative energy, cleanse them in salt water. The energy of the crystal will be more powerful and flow more freely without obstruction.

◆ The sun's ultraviolet rays are a perfect natural recharger for crystals.

◆ Crystals can be programmed with positive energy using breath and intent.

◆ To keep negative energy at bay during a crystal healing session, simply say a prayer for protection, or call upon your spirit guides to stand watch over you.

◆ The six essential crystals that every healer should have in their kit are kyanite, selenite, fluorite, calcite, hematite, and infinite.

◆ It's fine to store crystals together—in fact, it can even be helpful, because all of the crystals will begin to vibrate with the resonance of the highest-energy crystals in the group.

Chapter 8

Crystal Sensitivity Training

In This Chapter

- ◆ Confronting your fears about crystal healing
- ◆ How to initiate and feel crystal energy
- ◆ Activating your chakras
- ◆ Using crystals for meditation
- ◆ Relaxation techniques

When trying crystals for the first time, there is a way to tell if you are making a good connection. You can actually feel the crystal energy in your hands. For some it is a tingling sensation, for others it feels like a cool breeze. This might seem a bit strange at first, but it signals the beginning of conscious awareness of crystal energy!

Of course, you might have some fear that you are doing something wrong as your consciousness opens, your chakras become activated, and you bond with your crystal. Trusting your inner process is really what matters. Without that, crystals are simply pretty gemstones. They need to connect with your energy to get their work done!

Awakening Your Intention

You might have opened this book to learn about crystals for personal reasons or because you want to help someone else in her healing process. Maybe it's drug or alcohol abuse, sexual or psychological abuse, disease or illness, trauma to the body from accidents, bad luck, unemployment … the list of possibilities goes on and on. The problem doesn't really matter. What matters most is whether you're truly ready to heal. Without that intention, healing can be difficult.

> **Crystal Clear**
>
> To heal, we need to get to a place of wholeness in body and spirit, and that can only happen if the person who needs healing is open to experiencing that healing. So if you are trying to help a friend or loved one, you must wait until that person is ready to heal.

When you start working with crystals, an awakening begins. You become more aware of your surroundings; you might feel energy moving more freely through your body; your mind will be more alert; and your breath will be deeper as you breathe in new life, sending oxygen into your body. You may find your surroundings more pleasant. Your emotions will be more balanced and it will be easier to express them. Your eyes will be brighter, and you might have a spring in your step. In short, you'll have a feeling of hope—one that you perhaps haven't felt in years!

Controlling Fear

Fear is a huge factor in life. It's what slows us down and holds us back. To overcome fear, we have to challenge the deeper parts of ourselves to take on change and new information. We have to be willing to step out of our comfort zones and into the unknown, but that takes time.

Some people don't believe in crystal energy; others fear it. If you fall into the latter category, keep in mind that crystals have been sitting in the ground for hundreds of thousands of years, without causing any problems there whatsoever. Crystals provide a means for connecting to a vast energy network to promote healing and meditation.

Unfortunately, there are some "crystal readers" out there who will scare you into thinking the only way to improve your life is to drop several hundred dollars on a "karma cleansing." Walk away from these dubious deals, and contact your local police to report such fraudulent dealings.

Nothing to Fear, Everything to Gain

I have heard people say that they can't work with crystals because the practice goes against their religious beliefs. And while I respect that, there is no need to feel you are harming yourself or that you have crossed some religious or cultural line when you work with crystals. Crystal healing isn't an introduction to black magic or the world of cults or new age. Crystals work on scientific principles and have been successfully used by countless people for centuries!

If you are looking for a place to put feelings of skepticism, put them into a spot called "wonderment." You already know this place—it's where you were as a child, enjoying unrestricted access to new information and investigating the world around you. Only later do we face the disapproval of parents and teachers when they want us to "mature." As long as you enter a learning process—indeed, as long as you are alive!— wonderment should be there. Whether it is learning about computers for the first time or designing a new injection mold for plastics, let your life be one long learning process.

Yellow Flag

You can't enter wonderment if you have already been programmed to reject anything you are not already familiar with. So above all else, please come into crystal therapy with an open mind, and then just see what happens!

Developing Sensitivity to Crystals

Bonding with your crystal is a way to align your biochemical energy structure with the crystalline structure in the crystal. Having a crystal close to you for a while will also open the subtle energy bodies and your consciousness which will help you become more sensitive to crystals.

To train yourself to feel the energy of crystals, take a cleansed and charged clear quartz crystal, 2 to 3 inches long with a point at one end. Hold the point about $1/2$ inch away from the surface of the palm of your hand. Make small circles over the surface of your palm. You might immediately feel some pressure or tingling at the surface or under the skin. (If you don't feel it right away, keep trying. Your consciousness will eventually open up to the sensations.)

Now run the point of the crystal up and down your fingers. Play around at the tips of the fingers. The crystal will help to activate your internal electrical energy system, clearing meridian lines that carry chi energy, and it will also help to open up subtle energy channels called *nadis* (refer to Chapter 6).

Your feet are also very sensitive to energy, so you can also run the point of the crystal over your toes and ankles. You can also run your crystal over your arms and legs, lingering over sore spots. What does it feel like on your face? Run the tip of the crystal around your eyes where there is so much tension.

If, after 4 or 5 minutes, you still aren't getting a feeling of energy, heat, or tingling, put the crystal down. Open and close your hands several times. Rub the palms of your hands together and shake them lightly. Pick up the crystal and try running the crystal over your hands again, keeping the tip ½ inch away from the surface of your skin. Experiment by moving the crystal 2 inches away and going back and forth to your skin surface. You can also try closing your eyes and rotating the crystal 2 to 4 inches away from your face. You are looking for subtle energy, like a breeze. You may not even notice it at first. Give yourself time to feel it.

Chakra Activation

A way to stimulate deeper healing is by using visualization techniques with crystals for chakra activation. When a chakra is active, its structure is in motion, distributing energy to other parts of the subtle body system. Why would anyone need to exercise their chakras? Well, sometimes a chakra will be sluggish in its rotation or be blocked with excess emotional congestion. The following chakra activation alleviates these symptoms and promotes health in the chakras.

First, find a quiet spot free of distractions and get grounded. (Information on grounding is included in Chapter 6.) Use the visualization technique of seeing roots growing from under your feet down into the earth, anchoring your energy.

To begin your chakra activation, follow these steps:

1. Using your chakra tune-up kit that contains a crystal for each chakra (as discussed in Chapter 6), place each crystal on the respective chakra. For the root chakra, place your crystal just on your pubic bone. And don't worry if you don't get them exactly aligned.

2. Allow the crystals to rest for a few minutes, to connect in with the crystal resonance of each chakra.

3. Using the chakra sound (see Chapter 6) for activation, sing the vowel associated with each chakra while mentally focusing on that chakra. Try long tones at first; then sing the chakra sound in short repetitive tones. For example, for the third eye, sing *aaaaaahhhhhh* first. Then sing the vowel *ah-ah-ah-ah*. You can also visualize the color of the chakra while singing for more effect.

Gem of an Idea

If you are having trouble with your singing, you can easily find guided chakra meditations on CD or DVD. You will be able to hear the tones and sing along through each chakra. They are great for a tune-up. There are a number of music distribution companies that have chakra music and guided meditations; search for those keywords on the Internet.

4. As you sing, visualize the color in the center of the chakra as a ball of brilliant transparent light, about 4 to 5 inches in diameter, sitting just above the chakra.

5. If you feel light-headed, don't worry. Just stop and catch your breath; then continue. Build up your stamina by working each chakra for 30 to 60 seconds until you can do 3 minutes at each chakra.

At the end of the activation cycle, rest quietly with the crystals still on the chakras. Let your breathing become regular. When you want to get up, remove the crystals or let them fall gently off as you roll to one side. Get up slowly and gently. You have had an energy workout, and getting up too quickly might be a bit of a shock to your system. Drink some cool water and walk around a bit to restart your not-so-subtle energies.

After a chakra activation, keep a record in your crystal journal of what happens over the next day or two. When chakras are open, you might feel more vulnerable about certain issues. It is worth noting what those issues are because they indicate which chakra might need more work.

If you want to try another chakra activation, instead of working bottom-up from the root chakra to the crown chakra, start with the heart chakra, the center of love. Then open the third eye, throat, solar plexus, sacral, root, and then crown chakras.

Visualization Techniques

You just used a visualization with a colored ball for your chakra activation. Now let's try something a little more complex to create something you'd like to happen, such as winning a sports competition.

First, select one of the crystal forms from the set of Platonic solids from Chapter 3. Start with a cube or tetrahedron at first; then move to the more complex shapes. If you don't have one, use a clear quartz crystal. Assume your position for meditation or visualization. You know the drill by now—find a quiet spot with no distractions.

Hold the crystal in front and gaze softly at the crystal. Think of something you would like to have happen in the next few days. Alternatively, you can think about an upcoming activity you'd like to successfully navigate.

Now visualize the image of yourself inside the crystal going through each and every motion very clearly, right down to the words spoken, what people are wearing—as many details as you can come up with. See the complete scenario in the most positive way. Move through it slowly, deliberately, and whole-heartedly. The crystal will store the energy. Keep the crystal with you; it will hold the energy. Then see what happens.

Chakra Oils

One of the nicest ways to treat yourself is to use essential oils with crystals. The resonance of the crystals amplifies the energy of the essential oil. Use the following table to find a complementary scent to help activate the chakras with the crystals. You can combine several scents. An aromatherapy diffuser works best to bring the scent into the room. If you don't have one, you can improvise and add a drop to a candle or place a drop on a tissue and place in front of a fan to scent the room.

Gem of an Idea

Add a drop of an essential oil such as lavender to be absorbed by a porous crystal, and leave the crystal beside your pillow at night for a restful and refreshing sleep.

In the following table, you can select an oil and one of the complementary chakra crystals from the list to help amplify the healing effects of the oil. Place the oil on the crystal, rub it in, and set the crystal on the chakra for 10 minutes. A drop of rose oil on rose quartz will create a soothing, loving vibration that will help open the heart chakra. However, if rose oil is dropped on lepidolite, the effects will be physically relaxing and relieve stress. Try different combinations for different effects.

Chakra Oils Chart

Chakra	Essential Oils	Gemstones
1—Root	Vetiver Sandalwood Cinnamon	Smoky quartz Obsidian Garnet
2—Sacral	Ylang-ylang Tangerine	Carnelian Citrine
3—Solar plexus	Peppermint Rosemary Clary sage Lemon	Malachite Yellow calcite Hematite Citrine
4—Heart	Rose Neroli Melissa Jasmine	Rose quartz Pink tourmaline Lepidolite Fluorite
5—Throat	Geranium Frankincense	Turquoise Blue calcite
6—Third eye	Cedarwood Patchouli Amber	Lapis lazuli Blue topaz Celestite
7—Crown	Myrrh Lavender Wild rose Sandalwood	Amethyst Clear quartz Diamond Sugilite

Gem of an Idea

Incense or essential oils are used to help focus the mind during meditation. Do not use perfume because most of them contain chemicals and alcohol that disturb subtle energies. Some natural scents that are commonly used include sandalwood (for quieting the mind), patchouli (for focusing the mind), jasmine (for calming the mind and emotions), and amber (for alerting all the senses).

Crystal Clarity of the Mind

The benefits of meditation have been recognized by the scientific and medical community for years. Some people associate meditation with Eastern religion and steer away from it because they're afraid it conflicts with their own beliefs. Although meditation originated in the Far East, it's so commonly used these days that it isn't tied into any particular religion. In fact, you've probably meditated without realizing it. Do you remember cloud watching as a child, the way you could shut off your mind and not think about anything? That was "sky meditation." Now as an adult, you can do "mindful meditation." And although you can certainly meditate without crystals, using a crystal can help you calm the erratic energy of a busy mind.

> **Crystal Clear**
>
> The crystals that are most frequently used for sitting meditation are clear quartz and amethyst. Dark crystals such as smoky quartz and obsidian ground energy very well and help center a wandering mind.

Start by holding a clear quartz crystal in your left hand, pointing upward or toward the body. Alternatively, you can place the crystal 6 to 8 inches in front of you so it's in your energy field. In this instance, it should point up or toward you. Then follow these steps:

1. Sit either cross-legged on a cushion or in a chair with your feet flat on the floor. Let your hands relax into a natural position, in your lap or on your thighs.

2. Bring awareness to your breath as a way to quiet your mind of thoughts. Inhale through your nose for a slow count of eight, pulling in your diaphragm on the inhalation. Hold your breath for a count of four. Exhale through your nose for a slow count of eight, relaxing your diaphragm completely.

You'll know you're in a state of meditation when your body is relaxed, your mind is not in thought, and you are not falling asleep. You will feel awake and aware, yet totally at ease in your body. If your mind starts to wander off, bring it back gently by focusing on your breath for a while; then relax again into mindfulness. Rest in meditation for as long as you can. It's not unusual for beginners to be able to meditate for only a few minutes. Each time, hold your meditative state a bit longer, eventually extending it to 20 minutes.

To enhance your meditative experience, try the following tips:

◆ Try to find a place where you will not be disturbed. This means no distractions. No kids, no pets, no loud or jarring sounds that will knock you back to reality before you're ready.

◆ Be aware that music can help or hinder the meditation process. If you find that music distracts you, try white noise instead, such as running a fan. The constant sound numbs background noise.

◆ Light a candle. Preferably, use one made from ecologically clean beeswax. It will help purify the air by pumping fully balanced negative ions into the air and either sending dust, toxins, and odors to the floor or eliminating them all together.

◆ Plan a regular time when you will meditate. As your meditation becomes habitual, your mind and body will go into meditation more easily. Try not to mediate when you are already sleepy because you risk falling into an actual deep sleep.

If you're having trouble getting yourself into a state of meditation, try a guided meditation CD or DVD. These tools provide helpful visualizations and mental stimulation that slide you into a state of relaxation and then into meditation.

Physical Relaxation

We hear it all the time: "Relax! Take it easy!" Why should we slow down the physical body? Won't we have time to rest when we're old and weary?

It's important even for healthy, younger folks to take a physical break once in a while. When your body is relaxed, your subtle energies flow more easily and your mind becomes quiet and still. And when both mind and body are relaxed, a deeper healing (physical and/or emotional) can happen on many levels.

Here are some guidelines to achieve a deeper state of physical relaxation using a relaxation technique for 10 to 20 minutes:

1. Put on some light and airy nonvocal music or turn on a fan to block out any background noise. Lie down, comfortably supporting your neck and shoulders with pillows and cushions. Prop your knees with a pillow underneath to support the sacral area and to flatten the stomach.

2. Place a clear quartz crystal at the solar plexus chakra to help alleviate emotional stress. Draw a light blanket over your body to prevent your body from losing heat during this process. Perform a grounding exercise (outlined in Chapter 6), visualizing yourself anchored to the earth by roots.

3. Bring your focus to your toes and feet. Wiggle them gently to release any tension. Focus next on your ankles, calves, and knees. If there is any tension, draw it in with the breath and release it on the exhale release. Check in with your thighs, buttocks, lower back, and lower torso (groin). Search out tension in your middle torso, upper chest, and back and shoulders. Be aware of any tension in your fingers, hands, lower arms, and upper arms. Do you feel tension in your neck, jaw, cheeks, mouth, eyebrows, or temples? Finally, feel your hair line, your scalp, and the back of your head where it meets the pillow. Breathe in and out to release any tension.

4. Allow your back to sink into the mattress or ground. Let your body feel heavy. Feel each joint drop into the floor, fully supported by the earth.

5. Bring your awareness to the crystal sitting in your solar plexus chakra. Now visualize a bright golden radiant light, like the sun. See this golden light spreading throughout your body. First, send the light through your bones. Then send it through every organ. Finally, send the golden light to your skin.

If there is a particular area of healing your body needs, focus the golden light intently on that area for a while. When you are ready, bring your focus back to the golden light above the crystal at your solar plexus and let your mind relax there. This relaxation exercise unifies mind and body energy and provides a healing awareness. When you are ready, take the crystal off and get up gently, trying not to disturb your energy. You may feel quite refreshed and your vital energy restored.

The Least You Need to Know

- An open mind is one of the most important aspects of working with crystals.
- You can test your sensitivity to crystals by running them over your hands.
- Chakra activation gets the body's energy centers whirring and helps with healing.
- Crystals can be used to help with meditation and relaxation.

What *Can't* You Do with Crystals?

In This Chapter

- ◆ Crystals around the house and office
- ◆ Balancing the subtle body with jewelry
- ◆ Improve your luck with crystals
- ◆ Enhance feng shui with crystals
- ◆ Dream a little crystal-infused dream

Believe it or not, you can use crystals in almost every aspect of your life to provide a little boost here and there—and their use can be so subtle that you'll be the only person who knows what's really going on!

The use of crystals in everyday living provides a continuous field of energy that can help keep you aligned to your highest vibration. Whether you want to balance your body, your unconscious mind, your appliances, or your home, there's a crystal that can get the job done.

Daily Crystal Use

Just as there is a crystal for every illness, there is a crystal for every situation—and I mean *every* situation, from studying to soothing sore feet to enhancing the crop in your garden!

All crystals will provide some level of healing, and most of the enhancements I'm talking about are just specific forms of healing. You will get the best results from particular placements of crystals, and that's what you'll learn in this section.

Gem of an Idea

Place tumbled crystals of different colors in a bowl and leave them by your front door. As you leave the house for the day, randomly select two or three crystals, and slip them into your pockets for a little boost!

Crystals for Learning

Many types of crystals are useful for students. A clear quartz cluster or amethyst cluster on your desk will help with your focus and concentration. Or bring a double-terminated quartz crystal to an exam and gaze into it when you need your mind to be clear.

Got a big test coming up and need to memorize lists, names, and dates? A lapis lazuli or a clear quartz window crystal (window crystals will be discussed in Chapter 10) can help get your mind in gear. Tape a piece of either crystal onto your third eye to reduce fogginess while you study, or wear a crystal headband (something you'll learn to make shortly).

Crystals for Sore Feet

Hot, burning, painful soles? Tape crystals to the bottom of your feet or tuck them into your socks before settling into bed for the night. You can also drop crystals into a foot soak. Try hematite for pain or use rose quartz, jade, or aventurine to soothe tired feet. Garnets provide more energy and are an especially good choice for anyone who has been on his feet all day.

Just be careful when you wake up. Remove the crystals before putting your feet on the ground; otherwise, you'll just hurt those tootsies all over again!

Crystal Bath

Add a crystal to your bath water to soak up the benefits of crystal energy. To wash your troubles away, try the following:

- Rose quartz for love and relaxation
- Sodalite to ease the mind
- Lepidolite for stress relief
- Chrysocolla to quell emotional mood swings
- Smoky quartz to dissolve anger
- Tiger eye for mental clarity

If you have lots of tiny crystals, put them in a cloth bag or tie them up in a washcloth or cheesecloth and then place the bag under the tap while the water is running to infuse the water with energy.

Crystals on the Brain

A soothing bath is great, but sometimes we need to recharge on a deeper level. To increase your intuition and open higher chakra centers, glue or tape a crystal such as clear quartz, lapis, celestite, or Herkimer diamond onto a stretchy headband. Wear it at your third eye at the center of your forehead, slightly above the eyebrows. You can also sleep with your headband at night to increase dream clarity. The crystal energy goes right through tape and cloth without altering its signal.

Crystals for PCs, Appliances, and Cars

Placing a crystal on or near electromagnetic equipment such as your computer, large appliances, and even car engines will help regulate subtle energy fields. (This is actually one of the scientific qualities of crystals; see Chapter 2.) Ongoing use of crystals for appliances should promote a longer life span with fewer breakdowns.

A Crystal Garden

Not exactly the green thumb type? You can boost the way your garden grows without fertilizers and without breaking your back. Just try the following little crystal tricks.

♦ To help an ailing plant, place crystals (try clear quartz, amethyst, rose quartz, aventurine, or sodalite) in a circle around the plant. To give the roots and the rest of the plant a helping hand, stick part of the crystal into the soil, about 2 inches away from the main stalk. If a specific tree limb or branch needs more healing, place the crystal directly on the branch and wrap it with soft copper wire. Leave the crystals in place until health is restored (this could take a couple of weeks, so be patient).

♦ Use broken pieces of quartz crystal and dark stones such as onyx or obsidian underneath tomato plants. The quartz energy is very grounding for the plants, and the darker crystals keep garden pests away. Eating crystal-energized fruits and vegetables is especially nice, because you know you are getting a good vibration from a happy plant! The crystals help with the internal alignment of the plant's energy. You may find more production from the plant and that the fruit or vegetable tastes better.

♦ Try wrapping a crystal inside a flower and leave it until wilted. The beautiful, soothing energy of the flower will be transferred into the crystal. Use the crystal in the heart or crown chakra for one of the meditations from Chapter 19.

Just seeing crystals combined with your plants can give you a little pick-me-up. Place crystals in glass water containers with bamboo sprouts or tulips for a pretty display. Or make your special flowering plants, like orchids, even more attractive by placing gem-quality crystals in their containers.

Gem of an Idea

Place your crystals in the moonlight, preferably outside, for two days before a full moon, during the evening of the full moon, and 1 day after the full moon. The crystal will absorb the feminine or yin lunar energies. Use the crystals on your belly to draw the healing energies into your body.

Adorn Yourself with Crystals

The extraordinary actress Elizabeth Taylor is well-known for her collection of exquisite jewelry. In her book *Elizabeth Taylor: My Love Affair with Jewelry* (Simon & Schuster, 2003), she says, "I'm fortunate to have some very important pieces of jewelry. I don't believe I own any of the pieces. I believe that I am their custodian, here to enjoy them, to give them the best treatment in the world, to watch after their safety, and to love them."

I love her thinking on this! She has some of the biggest, purest gemstones and she not only knows that they truly belong to the earth, but also knows of their power to heal, to soothe, and to boost energy. Of course, Dame Taylor is a lover of diamonds, but you can benefit from much more reasonably priced crystal jewelry.

Wear Them

The easiest way to benefit from crystals on an ongoing basis is to wear them. Activate the lower three chakras (base, sacral, and solar plexus) by wearing rings, bracelets, and belt buckles or by slipping them into your pockets or a purse. When it comes to jewelry, the bigger the crystal, the more powerful the effect because a larger crystal stores more energy than a smaller one does.

Here are a few guidelines to follow:

♦ To soothe or activate the solar plexus chakra, use a crystal in a pouch or necklace that extends to reach your abdomen.

♦ To reach the heart chakra, wear a necklace that is 18 to 22 inches long.

♦ For the throat chakra, wear a choker, a necklace that is 12 to 16 inches long, or a gemstone pin to provide more direct healing.

♦ The third eye and crown chakras respond well to crystals in earrings, tiaras, headbands, or hats with gemstone pins.

There are some cautions to follow when choosing crystal jewelry, such as the hardness or softness of the stones and how much wear they'll receive. Because we use our hands a lot, any stones set into rings should have a minimum hardness of 4 on the Mohs hardness scale (see Chapter 2); otherwise, they will chip, flake, or scratch easily with wear. If softer crystals are set as a pendant for the upper chest area or for earrings, they are less likely to show obvious signs of wear.

Conductive Crystal Energy

Metals provide electrical conductivity for the energy of the crystal, but each metal transmits power differently. This means that some will feel right for you, while others might be unbearable. For example, I went through a stage where I could not wear yellow gold because it produced too much fire for my subtle body. I would feel electrical sparks around my ring finger, and I had to remove the ring and keep it off for several days.

Here are some general rules of thumb when it comes to choosing metals:

- **Gold**—It is the master of all metals. Gold emits solar, fire, yang, and the masculine and enhances intelligence and the higher mind. Gold gives a sense of power and connection to great strength, along with a sense of absolute purity. Gold has the ability to link with the matrix of other crystals and is an activator of their electrical circuitry.

- **Silver**—The qualities of silver are the feminine, yin energy, and the moon. When silver is worn, energy is retained and circulates throughout the subtle body. Silver also provides a balance when used with other crystals. It is the metal of choice for many jewelers and artisans for gemstone wrapping because silver wound around the crystal does not block the energy of the crystal.

Gem of an Idea

When choosing a metal in which to set your crystals, place the metal against your skin and close your eyes. Does it feel right, or is there something about it that's making you feel uncomfortable or "off"?

- **Copper**—It is a conductive material and can pass electrical pulses along its matrix without interference. It is a servant to other energies, both human and crystal, by stabilizing energy transfers.

Be aware that, as you continue to work with crystals, your sensitivities to crystals *and* metals will change. This is progress (and gives you something to look forward to!).

Rings on Her Fingers, Rings on Her Toes

When looking for a ring, find the right balance between the quality of a gemstone, a size that fits your body type and personality, and your budget. Consider that some jewelry needs to be highly functional for everyday wear (a ring that would suit an office worker might not be the best choice for a landscaper, for example).

After you've chosen the metal and a gemstone, think about the shape of the stone. Each figure has a story:

- ◆ **Circle**—A circular stone is a symbol of wholeness, completeness, and unity. Energy circulates and is renewed.

- ◆ **Oval**—An oval stone holds the energy of both the sky (spirit) and the earth (groundedness) flowing throughout the subtle bodies.

- ◆ **Triangle**—A triangular stone represents the sacred trinity, a pyramid to focus energy for visions, dreams, and goals in life.

- ◆ **Square**—A square stone aligns and structures energy to provide stability and security.

- ◆ **Emerald**—An emerald-cut has a series of steps to the facets that produce a mirrorlike quality to the light caught by the gemstone.

Deciding on which finger to wear your crystal ring is significant and can influence your energy and luck. Rings will open the energy in your fingers and hand chakras. Use the following illustration to figure out which crystals suit you best.

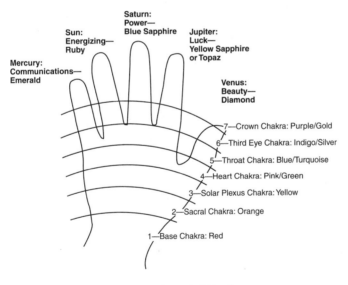

Chakras, planets, colors, and gems related to hands.

Lunar gemstones activate benevolence, gentleness, and creativity and should be worn on the left hand, which is the receptive side. If you are a person who angers quickly or might be a bit arrogant and rash, consider wearing lunar crystals on your left side to tone it down a little bit. (Really, just a little. It's for your own good.)

Wear traditional lunar gemstone rings on the mercury (emerald), jupiter (yellow sapphire or topaz), and venus (diamond) fingers.

Solar gemstones are those that are activating for wealth, fame, friendship, and health, and they should be worn on the right hand. Wear traditional solar gemstone rings on the sun (ruby) and saturn (blue sapphire) fingers.

Bracelets

The ever-popular chip stone bracelets are easy to wear, are inexpensive, and do provide some crystal benefits, as your body picks up particles of crystal energy and distributes them throughout the body and aura by following the meridians and other channels of energy. However, this is not a very focused energy. Think about it: Your hands are waving around all day and are never stationary long enough to get a good saturation in any chakra. It's worth noting, though, that they're closest to the solar plexus and sacral chakras (so if any chakra has a shot at absorbing this energy, it's those two). If you want to get more concentrated crystal energy, you can remove the bracelet and place it on top of a chakra.

You can also find ceremonial bracelets that combine powerful crystals and metals made by artisan-healers. These specialized bracelets provide a shot of energy—just think of Wonder Woman and her magic bracelets she used to deflect flying bullets!

Bracelets provide significant energy coming into the body if worn on both wrists. Generally, if there is a crystal with a tip, it should point up on the left side to bring energy into the body. On the right side, a crystal with a tip should point away to release energy outwardly as directed by the wearer.

Pendants and Earrings

Earrings can be worn close enough to activate the throat and third eye and will also influence the crown and heart chakras. Pendants are usually worn at the throat, heart, or solar plexus chakras.

When wearing a crystal pendant to activate or reenergize the solar plexus or heart chakra, choose a crystal that's at least a half-inch large. Anything smaller is not going to be very effective. If the chakra is burned out, overworked, and lacking energy, a larger restorative crystal such as rose quartz can be very soothing.

Should the tip of the crystal point up or down on a pendant? Pointing down, the crystal discharges energy downward and provides for much needed grounding. Wearing the tip pointed up tends to rush energy upward into the higher chakras and can make a person feel light-headed. A crystal with a point at each end worn vertically provides for a two-way energy exchange and energizes and balances the flow of subtle energy. However, I would pass on a crystal that is set horizontally unless you are trying to restore balance to, say, the left and right brain hemispheres or the left and right inner ears.

 Yellow Flag

You might be more sensitive to crystals worn closer to your head. If you feel dizzy and disoriented, remove your crystal jewelry, sit down, and drink water to ground your energies. Breathe deeply, relax, and allow the energy to dissipate.

Pouches of Power

Crystals are sometimes placed in pouches to be worn at the heart or solar plexus chakras. Other sacred items might also be placed inside the pouch, such as buffalo wool, shells, bone, and other natural objects that have ritualistic significance. In Tibet, special decorative metal containers called *gao* are made for carrying sacred medicine and blessed crystals.

Yellow Flag

Never touch someone else's sacred pouch without permission! Getting into someone else's space and energy uninvited might cause an energetic mishap for you *and* the pouch-wearer.

Leather and silk are the best materials for making a pouch because they allow the energies to circulate unimpeded. Use a leather string to maintain the energy transference. If you are vegan or an environmentalist, hemp or bamboo are suitable alternative materials.

Increasing Prosperity and Luck

Using the programming technique we talked about in Chapter 7, you can program your crystals to increase wealth and prosperity. Ruby and citrine are good crystals to use for attracting wealth. Put a small piece of either crystal in your purse or wallet, next to your money, to magnify your money. If you have a cash register, drop a citrine in there, too.

If you would like to program several small crystals or gemstones, slip them into both hands and hold them in front of your nose. During programming, ensure that all the crystals make contact with your breath. Point the crystals toward your targets of success, if possible. You can also point them toward a symbol of your goal, such as a map of Europe if you want to travel overseas or a pile of money if you want a more successful career.

Try to make a deep connection with the energy available to you. It's not enough to program an affirmation by saying you want a home theater. Try something more general that will send the energy on its way, such as "I, [your name], am open and willing to receive all of life." If it happens to include a home theater, then so be it!

Gem of an Idea _____

Some wealth affirmation suggestions:

- ◆ "I, [your name], fully accept prosperity and abundance in my life."
- ◆ "I, [your name], attract money and abundance to flow freely to me."
- ◆ "I, [your name], choose to attract wealth and prosperity to me."
- ◆ "I, [your name], can choose to create whatever I want in life."

Feng Shui

Feng shui is the ancient Chinese art of placement. It is related to the I Ching, the Book of Changes, and the principles of yin and yang—the feminine and masculine in balance.

Feng shui is a complex field of study, but the results are so powerful that a business using feng shui principles can augment its sales rapidly. Consequently, some of the more famous feng shui masters in Asia are booked years in advance and command a significant fee. In the West, feng shui has become more popular but is used mostly in residential settings. Crystals are used in feng shui to provide balance to the environment.

What's a Bagua?

A *bagua* is a tool used to determine areas in your home or work environment where there might be an energetic imbalance. Crystals can be used to adjust these imbalances when you understand the bagua and a few other concepts.

def•i•ni•tion

A **bagua** is a diagram of eight symbols used to represent different directions, yin/yang principles, seasons, elements, and family members. Each section of a home or garden or other surface maps to one of the eight segments in the bagua. By using different cures or remedies in the segments, imbalances in the environment and home can be influenced and balance can be restored.

A bagua is used in a room or house by overlaying the pattern over the floor plan. The bottom segment, the Career segment, is aligned with the entrance to the front door of the house or the entrance to a room. To the immediate left of the door is Knowledge. To the immediate right is Helpful People, such as friends and others who help us. Travel is also included.

Opposite the door is Fame/Rank. Fame is what you are best known for, what you are good at, or are certified to do. To the left of Fame is Wealth. Wealth can include possessions or things such as an heirloom stuffed duck worth $10,000 (really, there is such a thing called a Labrador Duck). To the right of Fame is Marriage, which includes partnerships and anything that takes two or more for wholeness to be accomplished.

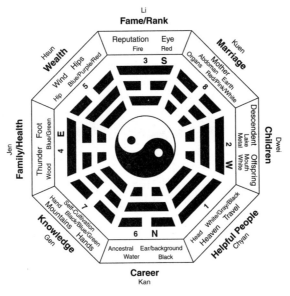

The bagua and its corresponding elements, body parts, colors, and life situations.

Align the front door along this plane

The left middle side of the room is Family/Health and our ancestors who provide continuity of wisdom. (Even if we do not have known family, we can still use the wisdom of our ancestors, real or imagined.) To the middle right is Children, who provide inspiration and creativity. (And even if we do not have children, we can energize the energy of being a child with great imagination and the freshness that unimpeded joy brings.) The center of the room, called Tai Chi, represents you in total harmony with All That Is. The symbol of tai chi, the balance of yin and yang energies, is shown in the illustration by a circle with a black and white motif in the shape of the number 69. There is a drop of yin in the yang and a drop of yang in the yin. When chi is balanced, there is health and harmony.

Too Much, Too Little

To harmonize a segment, take a look at your life and where it is now. In the following table, place a check mark in the column that you think best represents what you'd like to improve and make more active or perhaps tone down by making it less active so harmony and balance is restored. If you feel a segment is just right, you can check that column, too. Life can change and you'll want to keep track of what you did and didn't change so you can continue to make effective adjustments.

You will then purchase crystals and place them in the segment of the home where you can see them. In a few days, the subtle energies will ripen and blend with your surroundings and you will see the results. Take your time setting up the feng shui in your home. It can be a powerful shift as you are altering the subtle energies of your environment and your own body. Make minor adjustments as needed and keep track of the results in your crystal journal.

Segments to Harmonize

Segment	More Active	Less Active	Just Right
Career	❑	❑	❑
Knowledge	❑	❑	❑
Family/Health	❑	❑	❑
Wealth	❑	❑	❑
Fame/Rank	❑	❑	❑
Marriage	❑	❑	❑
Children	❑	❑	❑
Helpful People	❑	❑	❑
Tai Chi (your self)	❑	❑	❑

Making It More Active

If you want to be more active in a segment, select the crystal and color for that section from the following crystal bagua chart and look for a shape from the following list of yang crystal characteristics:

♦ Tall, pointy shapes, narrow, angular

♦ Shiny, smooth finish

♦ Transparent

♦ Spires

♦ Pyramids

♦ Obelisks

♦ Faceted crystals

♦ Single-pointed crystals

♦ Dark-colored crystals

♦ Clusters with a high profile, more than 4 inches in height

For example, if you want to increase the energy in your career segment, you might select one or more black crystals. If you can find a black obelisk to place for decoration in this segment or even tack a photo or postcard of opals on the wall, you might find your career gets launched or that you have become more noticeable at work. (See Chapter 6 for more on yin and yang crystals.)

Toning It Down

If you want to have more time to spend in other areas of your bagua, tone down the overactive segment by selecting the crystal and color for that section from the following crystal bagua chart. Look for crystal shapes from the following list of yin crystal characteristics:

♦ Short, rounder shapes, plump, soft edges

♦ Dull surface, might be pitted or smooth

♦ Opaque, not transparent

♦ Lighter pale colors

♦ Geodes

- Crystal balls

- Tumbled stones

- Clusters with a low profile, under 4 inches in height

Crystal Bagua Chart

Wealth/Purple/Red Amethyst Purple fluorite Ruby Sugilite Geodes	Fame/Rank/Fire/Red Garnet Carnelian Fire agate Peridot Your "personal" crystal	Marriage/Pink Rose quartz Moonstone Pink tourmaline Kunzite Twin crystals
Family/Health/ Wood/Blue Green Malachite Petrified wood Amber Crystal wands	Tai Chi/Earth/Yellow Sulpher Citrine Yellow fluorite Clear quartz Yellow calcite	Children/Metal/White Pyrite White calcite Selenite Hematite Agate Silver, gold, copper Crystal clusters
Knowledge/Blue/Green Chrysocolla Azurite Lapis lazuli Sapphire Crystal balls	Career/Water/Black Black tourmaline Opals Pearl Coral Black onyx	Helpful People/Black/ White Agate Marble Granite Snow quartz Channeling crystals

The Art of Bagua Maintenance

Monitor the energy generated from the crystals in each segment to ensure you haven't overactivated the sector. You can place a colored silk cloth (the color of the sector) over the crystal(s) to tone down its overactive effects.

All this energy will need to be balanced and cleared from time to time. Remember to cleanse, program, and care for your crystals (see Chapter 7). Let them get recharged in the sunlight from time to time. To cleanse and refresh the energy of the bagua, replace them with new or different crystals.

Program a smooth polished clear quartz crystal to balance and clear environmental energies. Hold the crystal in an upright position in the middle of the tai chi (center) of the bagua. Holding the crystal at the base, slowly turn the crystal to the right, visualizing white light filling the room and being conscious of clearing out all negativity in all sectors. You can use this technique to clear energy from the bagua or to clean out individual sectors by rotating the crystal from the middle of the segment.

Dream Enhancement

Sleeping with crystals can encourage both dreaming and recalling those dreams by providing increased clarity of mind, mental recognition of the dream state, and awareness of your own consciousness. Crystals do not need to be used only at night to achieve this awareness. Wearing and using crystals throughout the day will also increase awareness of the dream state.

Programming Dreams

There are three aspects of dreaming to program into your crystal. First, you need to direct yourself to actually dream. Next, your program should help direct you to remember the dream. You have to store the information in your brain as a function of memory. Part of this memory will be patterned with the crystalline energy of the crystal and your bioenergetic systems. The third part is to recall the dream. Your mind has to retrieve the information from the memory store.

If you want to reenter a dream, program your crystal to pick up where you left off. If you want to receive a message to help resolve an issue or address a problem, program the crystal to give you an answer.

How do you do this? It's really very simple. When you wake up in the morning, try not to move. See if you can recall the dream you just came out of. If you need a little help, hold your crystal near your third eye and remain still for about 5 minutes. If you still can't remember your dream, that's all right. Get up and get on with your day, but remain receptive to recall. Sometimes, the energy will take a while to filter through your system. You might be sitting eating breakfast or driving to work (or maybe even driving home from work) when the dream suddenly comes to you.

Crystals for Dream Enhancement

Just about any crystal will help you connect within your dream state. Some crystals have a particular mission. The Australian dream stone—mookaite, a form of jasper—is great for accessing dreams and protecting us as we enter another state of consciousness.

Try these crystals for a different experience:

- Amber, jade, and aventurine all soothe emotions and quiet very active dreams.

- Blue tiger eye is a real eye-opener—of the third eye, that is. Use this crystal to go deeper and deeper into your dreams.

- Celestite keeps your crown chakra active for receiving messages from friends and family and from subtle spirit energies who use the dream state to teach us.

- Herkimer diamonds produce memorable dreams, sharpen your memory of them, and provide a nice healing at the mental and spiritual planes.

- Labradorite and moldavite produce spacey, prophetic, visionary dreams.

- Lodalite inclusions in quartz are known as the shamanic dream crystals. Lodalite enhances your ability to enter into the dreamtime and to access other dimensions.

- Moldavite provides a powerful connection for communication to the stars and our extraterrestrial friends.

- Moonstone is protective for astral traveling. It softens difficult dreams and nightmares.

Your dream crystals can be tucked into your pillowcase overnight to prevent them from rolling around. You can also just hold them in your hand or tape a small piece of crystal onto your forehead between your eyebrows with white surgical tape to intensify your dream state. If you find you are awake all night, remove the crystals or switch to a less active crystal.

The Least You Need to Know

◆ Crystals can be used to enhance learning, alleviate stress, energize a vegetable garden, and balance the energetic fields of your appliances.

◆ Different metals and the different cuts of stones will affect how crystal jewelry feels and the way it works for you.

◆ Wearing crystal jewelry is a terrific way to keep your energetic centers whirling all day long! Be sure to wear crystals over the chakras to enhance their balance.

◆ Crystals used in bagua sectors activate energy and create a yin/yang balance.

◆ You can program your crystals for dream enhancement by holding a crystal above your third eye chakra upon waking in the morning. Sit quietly for several minutes and allow the crystal to absorb the memory of your dream.

Part 3

Healing Properties of Crystals for Body, Mind, and Spirit

Crystals can be used for long-term treatment when worn as a constitutional for persistent issues of the body, mind, and spirit. The use of a pendulum in selecting a crystal can provide a good second opinion when you have many crystals from which to choose. The Five Master Healers are crystals that can provide a simple approach and general healing for many ailments.

It is not enough to select a crystal that is identified to help a particular issue. Knowing what to do with it as a specific treatment and what to expect provides for deeper healing of the physical body, for alleviating emotional stress, and for enlivening the spirit.

Crystals can address specific issues that men, women, teens, and children have in common. If you have pets or other animals, crystals can help them as well. Animals require a slightly different approach because they tend to be more sensitive to crystal energy. So open your mind and prepare to learn in Part 3 uses for your crystals that you probably hadn't thought of before!

Chapter 10

More (Crystal) Power to You!

In This Chapter

- ◆ Assessing your concerns and issues
- ◆ The three-step program for long-term healing benefits
- ◆ The Five Master Healers: clear quartz, amethyst, rose quartz, turquoise, and smoky quartz
- ◆ Choosing a crystal for your disposition
- ◆ Using a pendulum to select crystals

When you start putting together all your different healing needs, you could end up using a lot of different crystals. In fact, you could end up draped in gemstones! While there's certainly nothing wrong with that, some techniques are helpful in analyzing which crystal you need.

So far in this book, I've been talking about all kinds of crystals and their corresponding powers. In this chapter, you learn how to combine some of your concerns and issues and how to choose powerful stones to assist in healing them.

Your Personal Agenda

When choosing crystals for healing, you need to first assess the problem areas in your physical, emotional, or spiritual life. If you have been collecting crystals for a while, take a look at your personal crystal collection.

If you have a dominant color choice, that color and the chakra to which it relates is often where your healing attention needs to be focused. Some public speakers, for instance, might have a huge number of crystals and clothes in the color red. Although totally energizing for a speaker, there may be some neglect of other colors to balance the intensity of energy coming solely from the lower root and sacral chakras.

To identify areas that are ripe for healing and identify a constitutional gemstone (I talk about this later in this chapter), jot down your answers to the following questions in your journal:

> **Gem of an Idea**
>
> You can put up to seven crystals into a leather or silk pouch and wear it at the heart chakra. The heart chakra redistributes the energy all over the body, so you do not need to wear a crystal on a specific area of your body.

- What is your dominant color(s)?
- Which chakra(s) does this color tie into?
- Would you like to address physical issues, emotional (feelings) problems, or spiritual questions?
- What are three things you are good at?
- What three things would you like to improve on (underdeveloped areas)?

Excellent! In the next sections, you'll select crystals to work with your strengths and weaknesses.

Three-Step Program

When you wear a crystal, you are initiating a powerful esoteric healing process that requires time to adjust to your energy vibration. This is accomplished in a simple three-step process.

Step 1: Cleansing

In the first week or so, the crystal is making tremendous adjustments within your energy field, matching the matrix of your energy to a larger outer universal energy field that will be used in your healing. We call this the cleansing process.

It is important to keep the crystal on you all the time (24 hours a day) for at least the first 21 days for this cleansing process to be initiated and completed. This is also a period of time where the blockages of energy that are causing the imbalance are removed.

Sometimes a *healing crisis* occurs during these early days. This might occur as a sudden release of energy—an emotional release, a sudden increase of pain, visions, intense dreaming, and other physical and psychological phenomena. Remember, crystals accelerate the change process, so this is normal. Allow these processes to occur without interruption by continuously wearing the stone or crystal until you complete the next two steps. And as always, seek competent medical attention for urgent health issues and use your common sense.

def•i•ni•tion

A **healing crisis** is the physical, emotional, and/or mental symptoms and afflictions caused by repelling illness from the body.

Cleanse your crystal every week and recharge it in the sunlight for at least four hours weekly throughout the healing process (see Chapter 7 for details).

Step 2: Harmonizing and Integrating

During the second stage, beginning in about the fourth week of wearing the stone or crystal, you might notice that your face looks more relaxed. This is because a harmonizing connection is being made within yourself. Your mental outlook, thoughts, feelings, and even opinions can change significantly. All aspects of your energy will be activated, and the result will be a very positive feeling. However, you're not quite finished yet!

You might notice physical and emotional changes in either of the first or second steps as your physical, mental, emotional, and spiritual bodies come into alignment. Some of these changes are caused by throwing off toxins and negative energies during the cleansing process. This will continue during the entire healing process.

You may not feel much physically. If you have pain, you might find it lessens. If your mind has been dull, you might find it's sharper. If you have been down a bit emotionally, you might find your mood has improved. Mostly you will see your awareness grow, and with that comes spiritual confidence—the acknowledgement that you are transforming into the person you want to be.

Step 3: Stabilizing

The third step can take 3 to 4 months—and possibly even longer for some people, depending on the intensity of your original condition. When you are committed to wearing a crystal for stabilizing purposes, you will wear it for a long time, occasionally changing it for a new one of the same type. With continuous wearing of stones or crystals, you will achieve solid stability in the changes you have achieved, whether they are emotional or physical.

"Will I be dependent on this crystal forever?" you might be wondering. No, you won't. So how do you know when it's safe to remove it? You can test your stability by removing your crystals from time to time—maybe just for a few hours or perhaps for days at a time. If you feel desperate and need to put your crystals back on after only a few minutes, you are not even close to stabilizing the energy changes. If you are able to go for a few days without your stones, but then notice you are slipping back into your old ways, consider wearing them for another week or more or only at bedtime before testing again. As you develop deeper sensitivity for crystal energy, you might decide to keep the crystals on much longer to complete the healing process, which can take 4 to 6 months or longer.

Maximizing Crystal Healing

Crystals should be worn next to the skin for best results. The size of the crystal might be relative to your budget. Many semiprecious crystals such as rose quartz are inexpensive, costing around $1. The crystal should be what you can afford and, as a minimum size, should be no smaller than the fingernail on your ring finger, as symbolic of your spiritual heart's need. Your commitment to the crystal is part of the healing process. Let the crystal do the work for you. Although you can eventually work your way up to wearing multiple stones (seven at the very most), it is best not to wear more than two or three stones at any one time if you are new to crystal healing because many people find the effects too distracting. The length of time it takes to obtain the desired outcome will depend on the quality of the crystal (size, color, and energy charge), where and how long you wear it, and the crystal's appropriateness to your healing. (See Appendix A for more information on the power of specific crystals.)

The Five Master Healers

The Five Master Healers are crystals that work well to repair a lot of troubles that we humans get into. They can be used for many purposes at the physical, emotional, and spiritual levels of healing.

These crystals are easy to find and genuinely work as indicated. And you don't have to worry about getting the perfect crystal within each master class because they are very forgiving crystals. For clear quartz, however, it's helpful to know about the various configurations so you can use the one that's right for you.

Clear Quartz: Universal Healer

The basic building block of all crystals is clear quartz. When you first receive a clear quartz crystal, you will probably look it over, but unless you know about this crystal's interesting formations, you might miss something!

In general, clear quartz crystal has six sides and six faces. Because the sides and faces can have different lengths and widths due to growing conditions, different configurations arise. I've put together the 10 basic configurations in the following sections.

Generator

All six sides of the crystal join together at the tip to form a uniform apex that generates energy. Finding a good generator is rare because each face must be perfectly formed to meet at the tip with all the other faces. Most polished crystals are ground by machine to accomplish this level of perfection. This type of crystal is the most basic formation and as such is a good crystal for a beginner. As a universal healer, generators are useful for stimulating healing through all subtle body levels, although they are best used for:

♦ Wearing anywhere on the body to generate healing energy for a specific area such as a chakra, in an area for physical healing, or to keep your aura purified.

♦ Opening the crown chakra while sleeping or during guided meditation.

♦ Teaching yourself about crystals and their basic energy.

♦ Filling in any gaps in an energy field and stabilizing disorganized energy in the aura.

♦ Bringing energy to yourself or sending energy to someone else.

♦ Translating communication with all other forms of energy.

♦ Balancing polarity, the positive and negative electrical charges.

♦ Setting into a ceremonial wand to generate and direct energy.

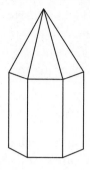

Generator crystal.

Double-Terminated

There are six faces at each end of the crystal. The ends might be like a generator, with all points coming to a common tip, or they might be different. Energy moves bidirectionally, in either direction concurrently. Energy is either drawn or is transmitted depending on the programming. Look for a crystal with a good center so that energy can flow freely and uniformly.

Double-terminated crystals are best used for:

◆ Active wear in the center of the body, for balancing yin/yang energy and balancing dark and light energy.

◆ Chakra alignment. Place vertically at each chakra for 3 minutes. To use for chakra balancing and to harmonize yin/yang, place horizontally at each chakra for up to 3 minutes each.

◆ Telepathic communication. If friends each have a double-terminated crystal and carry them for three days to pick up an imprint of their energies and then exchange their double-terminated crystals, they can be in telepathic communication with each other.

Double-terminated crystal.

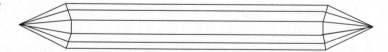

Gem of an Idea

To send a message with a double-terminated crystal, hold it and visualize the message being sent out of one tip of the crystal and being received through the tip of the other crystal. The message will be stored for your friend to pick up later and can be accessed by holding the crystal and inhaling deeply, allowing the images to form in his or her mind.

Channeller

The channeller crystal has a single large face framed by seven sides. This face represents the seeker of wisdom. On the opposite side is a small, three-sided face in the shape of a triangle. The triangle represents the seeker of truth. Hold the crystal in front with the seven-sided face toward you, and tip the crystal back to see the secret pyramid on the other side. This type of crystal should be in everyone's collection to help channel higher energy.

Channellers are best used for:

♦ Seeking answers to gain information. This can be about something specific such as healing information during meditation or for self-development.

♦ Channelling. The seven-sided face represents wisdom as the seven soul qualities: love, knowledge, freedom, manifestation (the ability to project and create), joy, peace, and unity. The three sides of the triangle represent creativity, truth, and expression through speech.

♦ Opening the third eye. For a small channeller, place the crystal at your third eye chakra. For larger channellers, place your thumb on the seven-sided face and your index finger on the three-sided face. Keep your mind clear, focus on your third eye, breathe deeply, and let images and impressions come to you spontaneously.

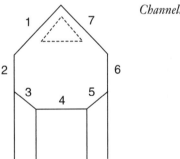

Channeller crystal.

Transmitter

A seven-sided face sits on either side of a three-sided triangle face. These two seven-sided faces should look identical. The edges of the triangle should be uniform and look sharp, clear, and in good proportion. The crystal should be clear and feel slightly heavy because this will show the crystal's ability to hold a greater energy charge.

Transmitters are best used for:

- Providing focus during meditation by holding or placing the crystal in front of you.

- Receiving and transmitting programmed messages and energy.

- Setting into a wand for use in healing the body.

- Focusing thoughts and intentions through the three-sided face.

Transmitter crystal.

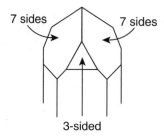

Trans-Channeller

A trans-channeller, also called a dow crystal, combines both a single seven-sided channelling face and a three-sided transmitter face to the left and right of the main channelling face. An even more rare configuration is the alternating of three-sided faces and seven-sided faces to form a special 3:7:3:7:3:7 configuration. Trans-channellers are hard to find but very valuable spiritually.

Trans-channellers are best used for:

- Achieving higher states of consciousness and intense focus for accessing higher energy levels and spiritual dimensions during meditation.

- Providing access to cosmic consciousness and awareness.

- Opening the third eye or crown chakra to direct questions and receive answers.

- Requesting spirit energy to work with. The triangles provide energy portals for the spirit, and the seven-sided faces provide communication portals.

Trans-channeller crystal.

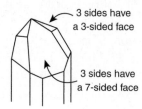

Window

This crystal is a real find! A large diamond shape is created from sloping angles of other faces on the front of a crystal. Like real windows, the best window crystals are ones you can see through. Some crystals have more than one window—one to show you the past (in a smaller face to the left of the major window) and one to show the future (in a smaller face to the right of the major window).

Crystal Clear

Some crystals have more than one major window. These are considered to be "time windows," showing you snapshots of certain events. A window crystal can also be used for unblocking creativity such as writer's block.

Windows are best used for:

◆ Clearing the mind and accessing other realms. Gaze into the crystal for several minutes before meditation or to relax before going to sleep.

◆ Opening awareness to who you really are. Gaze through the window and ask intently to see yourself in your truest form.

◆ Reading auras. Have the crystal window in front of you, pointing toward your third eye. Draw an imaginary line between the crystal and your third eye to enhance imaging.

Window

Window crystal.

Record Keeper

On the surface of the largest face of the crystal are small, slightly raised triangular bumps. These small bumps can sometimes also be found on smaller faces. Keep trying to find these small triangles, moving the crystal face around and looking at the reflected light on the surface to pick up the faint triangles. One of the reasons you might not see them at first is that you are training your consciousness to become more aware. Don't look into the crystal, just look on the surface of the face.

This crystal is sometimes called a "teacher" because the information has much to do with planetary origins, cosmology and planetary evolution, healing information, and higher states of consciousness. If this is so, do not give this crystal away. It has come to you and is meant for you to keep and learn from.

Record keepers are best used for:

♦ Accessing information. Rub the ridges on the fleshy part of your thumb over the little bumps. At the same time, breathe in fully and slowly. Information—whatever you are concentrating on—will be deposited for later retrieval through dreams or when needed.

♦ Catching bad dreams during sleep time. Bad dreams might just become a thing of the past with a record keeper next to your pillow to catch the bad ones.

Record keeper crystal.

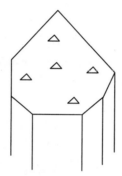

Self-Healed

Due to shifts in the ground and other interventions, the bottom of a crystal will often appear to be broken off. When the crystal regrows, small triangular faces cover the bottom. If a crystal has a large self-healed area, where it has started to regrow itself, it has had a long time to heal, with many lessons learned along the way. An older crystal would be better to learn from than a "younger" one, which is still in the process of rehealing. Newly broken crystals have a glassy, fish-eye look to them at the bottom and the edges might still be quite sharp.

Self-healed crystals are best used for:

♦ Reminding yourself that you can heal. If the crystal can reform through its own internal coding, so can you.

♦ Sending messages of self-healing to the body. For emotional issues, project your disharmonious thoughts into the bottom of the crystal and let the crystal organize them. Turn the crystal around after a few minutes of meditation and receive the organized energy.

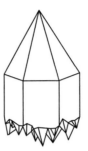

Self-healed crystal.

Rainbow

Rainbows inside crystals are caused by changes in the optical quality of the crystal due to a fracture inside the crystal, probably caused by rough handling such as geodesic shifting, dynamiting, or even the crystal being dropped during extraction from the earth.

Crystal Clear

Another way rainbows are created is when a crack or fissure has opened up due to thermal stress. Cooling and heating expands and contracts at a weak point in the crystal's material and a fracture occurs. There is a space between the walls of the fracture. The various colors of the rainbow are caused by the thickness of the gap picking up a certain light spectrum.

Rainbows are best used for:

♦ Inhaling the colors of love and joy into the heart chakra. Breathe out to dispel negativity and sorrow.

♦ Remembering there is love all around. Rainbows are especially great for children to connect to their inner light during times of trauma or depression.

♦ Wearing. At the heart level, the rainbow light will wink and twinkle and fill in color gaps in the aura.

♦ Filling up the chakras with light.

Veil

A veil is a thin reflective silvery wall or a white wispy cloud inside the crystal. Veils show you the future—not to see the future exactly as how it will unfold, but as a potential of what will come to be, allowing you to prepare in advance. Sometimes inclusions look like veils. The best way to tell them apart is to lay the crystal on its side and roll it back and forth. The veil will not disappear, and your eye can follow it as it looks like a transparent curtain. You might even see what appear to be little bubbles.

Veils are best used for:

♦ Showing how trauma is transformed into wisdom and beauty. We can see behind the veil of ourselves to the beauty masked by our shadows.

♦ Teaching us about our own darkness and about transforming our hidden fears, negativity, and anger. With transformation of our own negative states, we hold a greater capacity to help heal others of their own negativity.

Amethyst: Master Transformer

If you were limited to choosing only one crystal, this would be the one to pick. As a transformer, amethyst is also a purifier of the aura. Its job is to take lower dysfunctional vibrations and clear them by transmuting them to a higher vibrational level. It is very protective of the wearer's energy and acts as a filter for negative energies coming from both the environment and other people. Amethyst heals all things at all levels. Use it for physical problems, for emotional issues and feelings, for changing negative thoughts into higher aspirations, and for accessing higher spiritual planes.

> **Yellow Flag**
>
> Amethyst will need frequent charging and cleansing because it is subject to burnout. Whenever possible, keep it fully charged by the sun's rays. See Chapter 7 for more about cleansing and charging techniques.

If you are using amethyst for meditation, choose a polished single-point generator—the larger, the better.

Wearing an amethyst anywhere on the body will provide some degree of healing. The darker amethyst gemstones facetted and set into gold jewelry settings usually have a higher frequency and should be worn at the heart chakra for greatest benefit.

Rose Quartz: The Love Stone

Rose quartz is the heart chakra opener, oozing compassion into all centers of the body. This is a powerful healing crystal and a bestower of gifts. The wearer becomes aligned with a gracious and gentle energy that can smooth over even the toughest emotional wounds.

When used for physical healing, results are quick. One man had an inflamed scar behind his knee from where a vein had been removed 10 years earlier. After only a few minutes of holding a 3-inch rose quartz to the scarred area, the redness completely disappeared. The man declared that it was the first time since the operation that he finally felt comfortable!

Turquoise: Personal Protector

Turquoise is a protector of the physical body. It aligns all subtle bodies and works with the meridians to unblock and promote the flow of chi.

This crystal is best known as a stone of communications, working enthusiastically with the throat chakra. It provides for the expression of creativity, not only vocally through speech and singing, but also through activity, such as the arts and crafts, music making, and construction.

As a Master Healer, turquoise dispels negativity by providing a detoxifying influence, knocking out self-sabotage and self-harm to those who are near the stone. It is a stone of many virtues and is highly versatile for use with various diseases and ailments.

Smoky Quartz: Spiritual Warrior

Smoky quartz is known for its intensity of going in to do a job by absorbing and dissolving negativity. Some unwanted energies will be transmuted, but much will be absorbed into the quartz structure.

Smoky quartz is highly grounding and yet carries a lot of light in its structure. This crystal is usually used in the mid- to lower chakras because it provides a field of confinement for emotional issues, neutralizing outbursts, uncontrolled anger, and negativity toward others.

Yellow Flag

Larger pieces of smoky quartz tend to amplify negative emotions, so be sure to cleanse it often and wear an appropriate size for your emotional nature.

Selecting a Constitutional Crystal

Finding a crystal that is good for your constitution, or your individual makeup, is a holistic consideration. I would advise selecting a crystal that is beneficial for physical, emotional, and spiritual healing, one that could be worn continuously.

Consider the areas where you seem to have the most trouble—again, this might be physical, emotional, or spiritual in nature—or it could be that it's all tied in together. Perhaps you have trouble speaking your mind, and this is the issue that bothers you the most. However, do you also suffer from frequent sore throats? Feel blocked as a creative writer? A number of crystals could be used individually for these problems, but one in particular would cover most of these symptoms in one compact package. (Have you guessed? I covered this one earlier as a Master Healer. It's turquoise.)

After your constitutional crystal is selected, follow the three-step program outlined earlier in this chapter. Remember to program your crystal with your affirmations and be sure that it is cleansed and fully charged before you begin wearing it. (Chapter 7 contains more information on programming crystals.)

Using a Pendulum

At any point in crystal therapy, you can also use a *pendulum* to help you select an appropriate gemstone for healing. This is common practice as an aid to the selection of crystals and other objects or wherever there is a choice to be made. Pendulums are available from metaphysical and crystal shops. The pendulum works on the basis that your subconscious already knows what you need to know. The pendulum will show you the answer by picking up and amplifying the subtle vibrations from your subconscious, causing the pendulum to swing.

def•i•ni•tion

A **pendulum** is a crystal or metal, charged with positive intent, suspended from a chain or string. It is used to answer your questions about the future or to hone your intuition.

Hold the pendulum between your thumb and index finger with your elbow slightly bent at your side. Use the hand that feels most comfortable for you, and relax. It is important to let the natural vibrations of your own body move through your hand to the pendulum. Your questions should be phrased in such a way that they can be answered with a "yes" or "no."

Interpreting the Pendulum's Response

For many people, when the pendulum swings left and right, this can be interpreted as a "no." If the pendulum swings to and fro, this can be interpreted as a "yes." If your pendulum swings elliptically, clockwise, counterclockwise, or in some other gyration or even stays rigidly still, you must interpret this as best you can.

Here's a hint:

Ask your pendulum something that is true, such as, "Is my name _____?" Note what the response is. This will give you your "yes" motion.

Now ask your pendulum something that you know is *not* true, like, "Is my name Queen Elizabeth?" Note what the response is. This is your "no" motion.

Finally, ask it a maybe question, something you don't know the answer to, such as, "Is it going to rain later?" (providing you have not watched the weather forecast!). This is your "could be" motion.

Suggested Uses for Your Pendulum

Your pendulum will answer any question with either a "yes" or "no," so it is important to structure your question properly. For example, a question like, "Will I find better health with an amethyst?" is great; it can only be answered with a "yes," "no,'" or "maybe." However, if you asked, "Which crystal do I need for best healing results?" you probably won't get any answer at all.

Yellow Flag _____

Consulting your pendulum is not the same as consulting a doctor for informed and reliable information. Seek professional care if you're concerned with a medical issue.

The Least You Need to Know

- Choose a crystal whose color corresponds to the chakra that needs healing. For example, the throat chakra responds to red, so if you have trouble speaking your mind, you might wear a ruby at your throat.

- Wearing a crystal continuously provides deep healing benefits.

- Five Master Healers can be used to heal emotional, physical, or spiritual issues: clear quartz, amethyst, rose quartz, turquoise, and smoky quartz.

◆ Clear quartz crystals come in many configurations.

◆ A pendulum can help you choose which constitutional crystal to wear.

Chapter 11

Crystals for Physical Healing

In This Chapter

◆ How crystals can help with physical healing

◆ Crystals for relieving chronic pain and headaches

◆ Crystals for increasing fertility

◆ What to expect when you first begin healing with crystals

◆ A list of crystals for physical healing

Learning which crystals to use for physical ailments is a journey, although I will let you in on a little secret—although there are literally thousands of crystals and thousands of body parts, choosing a crystal for healing isn't a difficult process! You will need to have a nodding acquaintance with the chakra system, however, so if you skipped Chapter 6, this is a great time to go back and read it.

You might want to write down your experiences of healing with crystals in your journal. Note which crystals you picked intuitively and how they worked for you. Jot down which crystals are most effective for different ailments. You'll be getting some guidance in Chapter 16 on putting your observations, healing techniques, and types of crystals together in a healing session with a partner.

After you have identified the crystal to use for physical healing, the next step is to know how to use the crystal. Do you just wear it, or is there more to know? Of course, there's more to know! Start with an open mind and a positive attitude and then keep on reading ....

How to Use Crystals for Physical Healing

You might be dealing with long-term physical conditions such as asthma or arthritis. It can take some time for crystals to break down these chronic illnesses and clear the way to healing. Acute conditions such as a cold or the flu generally require less healing time, but in either case, the right circumstances have to come together for healing to be activated. Crystals help focus the intent to heal by providing and amplifying a positive energy pattern. Focused intent, breath work, and visualization are all part of the healing "team" and assist in the healing work.

When we are disconnected from the source of wholeness, our energy system is out of balance with our spiritual side. Returning to wholeness requires a multilevel approach of body, mind, and spirit to restore balance and health. Healing is the ability to direct energy to restore that balance. Intuition is very important to help guide us through that process.

Yellow Flag

Crystal healing facilitates the healing process, but it does not replace quality medical care. As always, consult a medical professional for your health issues and use common sense.

If you need some help learning to heal, now is a good time to seek a healer or healing facilitator. The healer provides knowledge and guidance and creates an environment for healing to occur. A healing facilitator is a person who owns and manages the client's process of healing. (In Western medicine, a doctor would be a healing facilitator, for instance.) Chapter 4 has more information on crystal healers.

Healing Takes Four

When a person is looking for a crystal healing, at least four components come together at the time of a crystal healing intervention:

◆ **The client**—That's you. You bring an open mind and the desire to be healed to the table. When you have an open mind, the subtle body energies open and allow healing energy to flow. A closed mind causes disturbances in those subtle energies, making healing all but impossible.

- **The crystal healer**—This person helps unblock the client's stagnant energy using crystals, such as rutilated quartz or purple fluorite, and energy clearing techniques like those described in Chapter 16. Energy that's stuck in the body causes congestion in the flow of subtle body energy. When released, the energy flows and illness is mitigated.

- **The crystals**—Specialized types of crystals are used for specific tasks, connecting the problem area to a larger matrix of life energy for healing purposes.

- **Spirit**—Your subtle spiritual energies connect with activated healing energies at a higher level to effect change and restore health and balance. I talk more about this in Chapter 13.

> **Gem of an Idea** _____
>
> Try healing a small superficial paper cut by holding a long clear quartz crystal 1 to 3 inches long with the tip of the crystal about ¼ inch above the cut. Follow the line very slowly back and forth for about 5 minutes, letting the energy from the crystal align with the internal skin structures. Repeat two or three times during the day. You should find the cut heals quickly; you might also see a black carbonized line where the cut had been signifying the power of the crystal to accelerate healing of the tissues.

With all these components working in harmony, balance and health will be restored. The stronger the connection to the spiritual side, the stronger the energetic connections will be made for physical healing.

Source of Illness

Every system in the body can break down and run into problems. That's just the nature of being human. I don't say this to frighten you; it's important to understand that choosing the right crystal for healing is based on the locale of the illness or problem.

Healing crystals can be loosely categorized into the following six categories. Some crystals within each classification are suggested to help heal illness. If you don't know where to start to select a crystal for an illness from the following section, you can always use one of the Master Healers discussed in Chapter 10 if you are uncertain.

- **Broken bones**—From an accident or a trauma that causes injury. A crystal that helps to repair broken bones is kyanite. Place a piece on top or next to the broken bone or any other tissue such as a tendon that has been severed to ensure the mend is even.

- **Bacteria, virus, fungus**—External organisms create a threat or cause disease and dysfunction in the body. Use pyrite, diamond, turquoise, or Herkimer diamond to protect the body and inhibit the growth of foreign organisms.

- **Negative emotional states/psychological illness**—The way we think causes physical dysfunctions, for example, twitching, stutters, headaches, or cancerous growths. Kyanite corrects mental states that manifest illness on the physical level. Green tourmaline helps nervous dysfunctions to mend by providing an increased electrical signal to cells that will help restore their natural structures.

- *Miasm*—A cloud or fog in the spirit is responsible for chronic diseases (for example, disturbances of the nervous system, psychological disorders, and some physical defects). Green tourmaline is excellent for realigning and balancing energies that hook into the whole body.

def•i•ni•tion

A miasm is a hereditary predisposition making one susceptible to various diseases that appear only if there is a trigger, such as food, the environment, trauma, or the introduction of chemicals.

- **Toxins and chemical reactions**—Illnesses can be caused by toxic proximity environments, such as radiation leaks. Smoky quartz is an excellent grounder of toxic energies. Wearing turquoise can help protect the body from the effects of toxins. Using fluorite in the solar plexus (roughly the middle of the body) speeds detoxing and increases healing.

- **Spiritual beliefs**—Illness can be caused by karma, possession, and curses. Crystals that protect from psychic attack include snowflake obsidian, black tourmaline, and black onyx. Wearing one of these crystals as a pendant or carrying it in your pocket will ground negative intentions.

Crystal Combos

The first step in healing is selecting the crystal to be used, either from the list of crystals for healing chronic pain in the next section or from the list of crystals recommended for various parts of the body at the end of this chapter. If you are unsure which crystal to use, select the crystal by the color of the chakra to which the trouble is closest. For instance, if you had a sour stomach where the nearest chakra is the solar plexus, you could select from the list of solar plexus chakra crystals such as amber or calcite. Place it over the stomach for 5 to 10 minutes to calm excess acid.

A general rule is that red and orange crystals invigorate energy, blues sedate, pinks and greens soothe, yellows neutralize, and purples and whites purify. There are many healing systems, but for crystal healing, these colors work well for these conditions. So for example, using a red crystal for lower back pain would probably increase circulation but would not cool down inflammation. Try using a blue, green, or pink crystal and the following technique to remove excess energy. I've also included information on infusing and increasing energy:

◆ **To remove excess energy**—Place four clear quartz crystals, each ½ inch wide and 1 to 2 inches in length, with the tips pointing north, south, east, and west over the affected area. Place a selected physical healing crystal such as smoky quartz, purple fluorite, or turquoise into the center to cleanse negative energy from the area. These crystals should remain over the area for up to 15 minutes to allow unwanted energies to escape. However, this is just a guideline. If you feel more time is needed, then listen to your intuition and leave them in place as long as necessary.

◆ **To infuse energy**—Place four clear quartz crystals, each ½ inch wide and 1 to 2 inches in length, with the tips pointing inward toward the affected area in the north, south, east, and west directions. Place a selected physical healing crystal in the center to boost healing energy to the area. Malachite or bloodstone is a great choice for energy infusion. The quartz will amplify the healing effects of the malachite or bloodstone and intensify healing energy to the area. Leave it on for up to 15 minutes or longer if you feel the area would benefit from a longer exposure.

◆ **To increase the flow of energy**—To increase the circulation of chi or prana along the internal pathways, use at least four smaller, pointed, clear quartz crystals, each ½ to 2 inches long and ¼ to 1 inch wide. Place two crystals, one above the other, in a line pointing to the area for healing. Then place two crystals below the area in a line with the tips pointing down or outward to carry energy away from the body. You can tape the crystals in place, even on cloth-ing provided you remember to remove them before moving around. If you are unable to place the crystals on the body, place them next to the body, no more than 1 to 2 inches away, pointing the tips away from the body to remove excess energy. Again, leave the crystals on for about 15 minutes or longer, according to how you feel. Sometimes you will feel the flow of energy stop. At that point, the crystals can be removed.

Pain Relief

It is said that everyone deals with pain differently. So first off, try not to resist pain or any emotional feelings that you might have about your pain. Although this can seem to help the pain in the short term, you will be inhibiting subtle healing energy from reaching the part to be healed. And shutting down over the long term might create a lingering and chronic pain. When working with crystals, it's so important to keep that energy flowing!

Crystals for Healing and Chronic Pain

Crystal healing provides a holistic approach to pain; that is, it has the ability to help transform a person's attitude about illness as well as his physical condition. The fol-lowing crystals can help with chronic pain and other conditions—and with your state of mind, too.

Crystal	How It's Used for Healing
Amethyst	A Master Healer. Used for arthritic pain. Use surgical tape to hold the amethyst crystal over the area of pain. For deep pain, use two clusters of amethyst and place them on either side of the joint. For thyroid balancing, wear an amethyst crystal pendant at the heart chakra.
Clear quartz	A Master Healer. Place a clear quartz crystal of any size directly on the affected area. If it's too painful, gather several crystals around the area, with the points facing outward to draw out the pain, infection, or inflammation.
Carnelian	Heals skin, acne, herpes, scars, and wrinkles. Either place it directly over the area or hold one-quarter inch above the area and move slowly in small circles for 5 minutes, twice a day or more.

Crystal	How It's Used for Healing
Copper	Used for arthritic pain. Wear as a bracelet. Natural oxidation causes the copper to leave green marks on the skin.
Garnet	For correcting gynecological issues, PMS, or infertility, wear it as a necklace or pendant, or hold or tape garnets over each ovary. Directions on use for fertility are featured later in this chapter.
Hematite	Use for pain in the legs, arms, or back or to increase circulation. Tape smaller one-quarter to one-half inch pieces down the leg or spine and wear overnight.
Herkimer diamond	Used for alleviating vertigo and dizziness. Keep a crystal in each pocket, or place one at the neck and one at the forehead for 5 to 10 minutes once a day.
Gold	Fortifies the energy fields to be more resilient to pain and increases pain thresholds. Wear as jewelry.
Kunzite	Used for the prevention of heart disorders, for pain in the heart, and post-operative recovery after heart surgery. Wear this crystal unpolished as a pendant at the heart chakra.
Turquoise	A Master Healer, it boosts the immune system and helps alleviate pain from digestive issues and sore throats. Wear as a pendant or chip necklace mid-chest or at the heart or throat chakra.
Malachite	For the prevention of heart disease, wear it anywhere on the body.
Rose quartz	A Master Healer. Cools inflammations as well as emotional issues related to pain (for example, burns or trauma). Wear it as a chip necklace or tape a piece over the area overnight for longer-lasting effects.
Smoky quartz	A Master Healer. Draws out pain and releases negative emotions that might be causing physical pain. Place it over the affected area.

Be sure to cleanse your crystals regularly when they are used for healing purposes. For complete instructions on crystal cleansing, see Chapter 7.

Holographic Healing

In Dr. Leonard Laskow's book *Healing with Love* (see Appendix C), *holoenergetic healing* is produced by envisioning what you wish to release. Like intent medicine, an energy matrix is created with the image of your illness using thought. And in the same way the breath was used to program crystals in Chapter 7, the breath and mind are used together to expel the holographic pattern from the body. A new holographic image of health is solidified in the mind and implanted into the area of illness.

How does this work? It sounds like you're working only in your mind, so how will that help a sore foot, for example? Crystals resonate energy throughout the body, so putting a crystal near the area of physical illness while holding the *hologram*-like image of health in your mind helps to repattern the physical energy fields. It also repatterns the illness into health on multiple dimensions.

def•i•ni•tion

Holoenergetic healing is a holistic healing technique envisioned by Dr. Leonard Laskow that uses energy, intention, imagery, and insight to influence and transform subtle energies. A **hologram** is an object whose image is recorded as light and later reconstructed and will appear as three-dimensional even though the object might no longer exist.

Try the following exercise using a holographic image to practice this technique. Start small, with a cut, a bruise, a wart, a scar, or some other small external physical problem on your body:

1. Select a clear quartz crystal 1 to 3 inches long or a tumbled piece of carnelian 1 inch long. Be sure the crystal you use is cleansed and well-charged.

2. Using your breath, program the crystal using an intention such as, "I am fully empowered to cleanse and heal myself of this [cut, bruise, wart, etc.]."

3. Sit in a comfortable chair. Relax and regulate your breathing. Use a grounding technique such as picturing tree roots coming from beneath your feet and anchoring you into the ground below.

4. Place the crystal on the affected area or hold it in front of you, and imagine the bruise or scar as a holographic image inside the crystal. See the color, the texture, bumps, and even any distortions at the cellular level as a full-dimensional image. If you can, try to imagine the DNA within each cell. Spend a few minutes holding the image in your mind and building the image in the crystal, remembering that the crystal is storing the image. Continue to breathe evenly.

5. When you feel the image is developed enough, bring the crystal just under your nose. Take a deep breath in. While holding your breath, think that with uttering the word, "Release," all the illness from the crystal will be released. Holding the thought of releasing the image of illness will program the air in your lungs with the intent.

6. With a sudden force of breath from your lungs and through your nose (not the mouth) over the crystal in a strong snort, see the image of illness being cleared through the crystal. You will have removed the negative programming of illness at many levels and dimensions. This programming to release illness is now stored in the crystal.

7. Now hold the crystal and start building a new holographic image of a healed area. See bumps even out, broken cells heal, discolorations clearing, DNA twisting and turning properly on its helix.

8. When you have built up the new image, take a deep breath in; while holding the breath, think that with uttering the word, "Heal," the positive image will be transferred into the crystal. Expel the breath through your nose over the crystal, and the image will be transferred into the crystal. The crystal is now programmed for healing.

9. Hold or place the crystal on the area and leave it there as long as possible (a minimum of 20 minutes), or tape it securely to the body overnight (7 to 8 hours) if possible. The energy structure of the image will be absorbed by the body, and the cells will repattern themselves around the image in the crystal.

Headache Relief

Sometimes excessive energy gets directed to the head area, probably to protect the brain from something such as a sinus infection, stress, or even an overactive imagination. Well, that excess energy needs a way out! The closest chakra to the brain would be the top of the head, the crown chakra. If the crown chakra is open, the energy can rise and dissipate. If it is closed due to energy blockages, the energy backs up and you get a headache or, worse, a migraine.

Imagine having a gentle, easy, drug-free approach to getting rid of a simple headache. I'm about to give you one! You will need either a single-point clear quartz crystal (preferably in the transmitter configuration; see Chapter 10) or a single-point amethyst. A small, smooth, tumbled crystal in rose quartz, smoky quartz, or lapis lazuli can also be effective with the following technique to open up the crown chakra and kick that headache:

1. Take the crystal and hold it pointing upward on the top of your head in the middle of your skull.

2. Hold the crystal steady, touching your skull for a few minutes, to gather the energies. You might feel some pressure. Energy blocked at the neck will begin to flow upward toward the crown chakra.

3. When you feel enough energy has collected, slowly raise the crystal 1 to 2 inches above the center of your head. You should feel all that excess energy being pulled up and out, directed by the crystal.

4. Breathe deeply to help the internal energy pathways provide new energy to the head. When you feel the headache is gone, lower your hand.

Gem of an Idea

For additional healing effects, try rubbing a drop of lavender oil on the crystal and massage your temples with the crystal to remove headaches.

Cleanse the crystal in salt water overnight to remove the excess energies from the crystal. Recharge the crystal in the sun.

There are a couple of other ways to alleviate head pain. You can use an amethyst that is 1 to 2 inches in diameter or a clear quartz crystal ball and roll it across your forehead and temples. This will pick up excess energy and transfer it to the crystal. To ease sinus pain, place smooth unbroken pieces of golden rutilated quartz crystals over your eyelids and sinuses (generally speaking, on your forehead and cheekbones) and lie down with the crystals on for 10 or 15 minutes.

Breathe a Sigh of Relief

In yoga, different breathing patterns are taught to control the internal energies of the body. For example, when you're holding a difficult pose, your yogi will tell you to expand your breath into your limbs to help steady yourself or lessen discomfort.

You can use this practice in everyday life, too. Just focusing your breath on a painful or troubled area provides additional energy for healing. When a crystal is added, the healing gets an energy boost.

One of the most frequent types of breathing used in working with crystals is called the "circular breath." This breathing pattern involves imagining that you're breathing into and out of the crystal.

Ready to give this a try? Follow these steps based on an ancient meditation:

1. Ground yourself. Relax and breathe regularly. Hold a cleansed and charged clear quartz or an amethyst crystal 1 to 2 inches long to the area of discomfort.

2. Visualize the pain or discomfort as a mass of dark clouds over the area.

3. On the inhale, draw the dark clouds representing your pain or ailment into the crystal.

4. When you exhale, think of sending the clouds out from the crystals as white light.

5. Continue inhaling and exhaling for 5 to 10 minutes.

Cleanse and recharge your crystal afterward so it's ready the next time you need it.

A variation of this crystal healing process is to hold a clear quartz or amethyst 1 to 2 inches long in each hand. In the left hand, the crystal should be laying flat in the palm of your hand with the tip pointing toward your wrist. In the right hand, the crystal should be laying flat in the palm of your hand with the tip of the crystal pointing toward your fingers.

Here's an example of how this works. If you have ailments on the right side of your body, breathe in and visualize the breath gathering up pain along the entire left side of your body. At the heart, throat, third eye, or crown chakra, cross over with your visualization and exhale, feeling the breath carrying all that pain going down the right side of the body and out the crystal held in your right hand. Repeat the inhale and exhale to gather and transfer pain from the body. Do this circular breath 10 times and whenever there is a flare-up of symptoms.

Increasing Fertility

To attract the right energies for a baby soul, three karmic soul connections need to come together: the karma of the father, the karma of the mother, and the karma of the wee little babe who wants to come for an Earth visit on a life-time visitor pass.

For a woman to increase fertility, she should wear the following two crystals:

◆ **Garnet**—This red crystal gathers the physical and procreative energies and should be worn near the ovaries. A small, flat, ½-inch piece of tumbled garnet can be taped at the sacral chakra, about 2 inches below the belly button. Wear during ovulation.

◆ **Rose quartz**—It's called the Love Stone for a reason! It really tempers the heart and creates a full loving aura around the expecting mother for a soul to enter. Wear this crystal continuously as a necklace or pendant at the heart chakra, even during the pregnancy, to send your baby soothing, calming, loving vibes.

For a man to increase fertility, he can also wear garnet as noted previously, as well as either of the following two crystals:

◆ **Green tourmaline**—Tourmaline provides electrical impulses and can be worn as a pendant to strengthen internal chemistry and the procreative life force. Wear continuously as a pendant at the heart or throat chakra.

◆ **Lapis lazuli**—This deep blue crystal opens the higher psychic centers to connect with the emerging soul energies and offers fatherly protection. Wear continuously as a pendant at the heart or throat chakra or as a large ring.

Also, the energy in your home is important. Think about this from the perspective of the baby soul who is looking for parents. He or she wants to come into a soothing, nurturing, loving environment (wouldn't you?).

Gem of an Idea

Your home's bagua can help with baby issues. Add more yin crystals such as moonstone, rose quartz, or pink calcite in the children's section of the bagua to bring in a girl; use more yang crystals such as carnelian, lapis lazuli, or garnet to bring in a boy. See Chapter 9 for more on the bagua.

Timeline of Healing

When you first begin healing with crystals, you might actually feel worse. This doesn't mean the treatment isn't working—in fact, it indicates just the opposite! Energy is being released and is shifting around the body. This means it's working. This healing crisis usually passes within a few days.

In homeopathy, it is said that it takes one month of treatment for every year you have been ill for healing to begin. So if you have been sick for three years, you should expect to feel better after three months of treatment. Crystals seem to accelerate this rate, although there's no definite rule of thumb on how long healing will take. However, just opening the door (and your mind) to healing also opens the door for miracles to occur. A little crystal can go a long way toward improving health!

> **Yellow Flag**
>
> Symptoms of a healing crisis include increased pain, a flare-up of the condition, the release of strong emotions such as anger or fear, fever or other temperature changes, and flulike symptoms. Try getting more rest, and drink plenty of fluids to not only flush out the released toxins, but also allow the internal energies to flow more smoothly through your body.

List of Crystals for Physical Healing

The following sections are arranged by healing an organ or a body part. For body parts not mentioned, use the crystal for the chakra that is closest to the area. If you are uncertain, use one of the Five Master Healers discussed in Chapter 10. Meditate and let your inner vision show you which crystal is needed. You can also use your pendulum by holding it over the name of each crystal until you receive a response (also discussed in Chapter 10).

Body Part or Condition	Crystal/How It's Used
Adrenal gland	Sugilite
Arthritis	Chrysololla (strengthens tendons and muscles)
Asthma	Fluorite (opens congested airways), rutilated quartz
Bladder	Bloodstone, rose quartz
Blood and blood disorders	Amethyst, aventurine, bloodstone (oxygenates), copper (helps the flow of blood), fluorite (cleanses), garnet (circulation), gold (purifies), hematite (blood stream), jade (quality of blood), malachite, peridot, pyrite, rose quartz, ruby, turquoise (immunizes)

continues

continued

Body Part or Condition	Crystal/How It's Used
Blood pressure	Amethyst dioptase, kunzite, turquoise
Blood sugar	Rose quartz, malachite, opal
Bowel troubles	Black tourmaline, red calcite (stops diarrhea)
Bone strengtheners	Calcite, fluorite, kyanite, lapis lazuli, onyx, selenite
Brain	Diamond, gold (balances left and right brain hemispheres), tourmaline (neural pathways), pyrite, rhodochrosite (improves memory), rhodonite, sugilite
Ears, eyes	Amber (pain), Herkimer diamond (balance), agate (soothes), jade, kyanite, opal. Hold against ears on sides of temples to warm and transfer energy
Female organs	Garnet, jade, rose quartz, rutilated quartz, smoky quartz
Hair growth	Galena, unakite (rub to improve circulation)
Hormones	Female—Epidote (hold pieces in your hand to offset a hot flash), labrodorite (regulates metabolism)
Immune system revitalizers	Turquoise, amethyst, emerald, garnet, jasper, peridot, ruby, rutilated quartz, turquoise
Intestines	Pyrite (blocks the aggressive growth of bacteria and virus)
Inflammation	Rose quartz
Joints	Amethyst, chrysocolla, hematite
Lymphatic system	Fluorite, moonstone, rose quartz, sodalite
Lungs	Fluorite (colds/flu)
Heart	If you are attracted to dark green, try malachite for cardiovascular disease prevention; bloodstone (strengthens the heart muscle), dioptase (cardiovascular), emerald, jade, kunzite (a significant heart crystal), lepidolite, peridot, rhodochrosite, ruby, sugilite.
Kidney, pancreas healers	Amber, aquamarine, yellow or green calcite, carnelian, citrine
Liver, gall bladder soothers	Emerald, green fluorite, hematite, malachite (tugs at the liver, detoxifying it)

Body Part or Condition	Crystal/How It's Used
Spleen	Jade, jasper, malachite, peridot, rhodochrosite, rhodonite, rose quartz, smoky quartz, sodalite, sapphire, tiger eye, topaz
Lungs	Aventurine, turquoise, rutilated quartz
Metabolism	Apatite (suppresses hunger)
Muscles	Amber (pain), copper (rheumatism), hematite (increases magnetic activity), lepidolite, purple fluorite (for numbness)
Nervous system	Amazonite, aquamarine, azurite, dioptase, gold, onyx, rhodonite, selenite, sapphire, obsidian
Nose, throat	Celestite, kyanite, rhodochrosite (nasal tissues), turquoise
Pineal gland	Lepidolite, opal, clear quartz
Pituitary gland	Garnet, lepidolite, moonstone, opal, clear quartz, rhodochrosite, rhodonite, sapphire
Skin, tissue	Carnelian, gold, gypsum (wrinkles), peridot, rutilated quartz, sapphire, labradorite (emphysema)
Spleen	Bloodstone (strengthens), moonstone
Stomach, intestines	Chrysocolla (digestion), dioptase (nervous stomach), moonstone, obsidian, pyrite, tiger eye
Teeth	Fluorite, selenite
Thyroid	Amethyst, celestite, lapis lazuli, rhodonite
Urinary tract	Rose quartz, sodalite

Remember that your attitude, outlook, and determination are powerful tools in healing and recovery. You've probably heard of people who were able to use superhuman strength to help others—such as a mother lifting a car off of her child or a rescue worker moving huge pieces of rubble to get to a buried victim.

When you're sick, it can be hard to muster up the energy needed for healing—it might feel like a superhuman feat, in fact. But that power is there; it's inside every one of us, and we can use it to facilitate our own healing.

The Least You Need to Know

◆ Crystals can be selected for healing depending on the source of illness. Master Healers are helpful when the actual cause of illness is unknown.

◆ The easiest ways to effect a healing are to wear crystals or to place them directly on the area for healing.

◆ You can use imagery, programming of crystals, and breathing techniques to increase the effectiveness of healing.

◆ Fertility can be increased by wearing rose quartz, garnet, green tourmaline, or lapis lazuli.

◆ When you begin wearing crystals for healing, you may actually feel worse before you begin to feel better. This is your energy shifting around, and is to be expected.

◆ Selecting a crystal based on the color of the chakra closest to the problem can also help facilitate healing.

12

Crystals for Emotional Well-Being

In This Chapter

- ◆ Using crystals for emotional clearing and purification
- ◆ The love stones
- ◆ Gemstones to make you giggle?
- ◆ When you wish upon a crystal
- ◆ A list of crystals for emotional healing

No doubt you have been stuck at some point with some feelings that you didn't really want to express. Maybe you felt uncomfortable and that you would never be able to get rid of those feelings. Finding some relief from negative emotions such as anger, grief, and jealousy can be a learning curve. It takes a lot of awareness and some help from our crystal friends to provide a way through our emotional experiences.

Crystals take us to a new emotional level where feelings about ourselves and others become lighter, transforming our moods in the process. The mind is cleansed, the heart is free, and we feel open to a whole new way of living!

How to Use Crystals for Emotional Clearing

You might have heard the quote "I think therefore, I am" from Rene Descartes, the seventeenth-century French philosopher. That is so true! When you carry excess emotions such as anger or jealousy, biochemical reactions occur in your body that pump out more adrenaline, causing your heart to beat faster and nasty acids to churn in your stomach. So you feel bad in your head *and* in your body, and a vicious cycle begins.

Working with crystals gives your emotions a chance to restore balance before negative energy manifests at the physical level. Remember when I told you in Chapter 3 that one of the features of crystals is that they can make an erratic signal constant? That's the result of their transforming negative energy by modifying its energy structure.

Clearing Anger

There is no greater poison than anger, says Dalai Lama, the Tibetan Buddhist spiritual leader. Anger clouds your thinking and your ability to act in a reasonable way. If we have an opportunity to consciously manage our negative emotions before they turn into anger, our mental and social health will not suffer.

Because crystals can amplify energy, wearing a crystal when you are angry can make the feelings of anger feel worse and more intense. Is there an upside to this, you're wondering? Yes; it will make you more aware of your feelings and allow you to deal with them before they do any further harm.

Anger acts as an energy blocker, usually at the solar plexus chakra. Blockages due to anger often also occur at the throat chakra due to repressed speaking about our feelings. Anger is sometimes found in the root and sacral chakras if you have suffered abuse.

Yellow Flag

Anger is considered to be a negative emotion that has been repressed and is shuffled off to the shadow part of ourselves, an unwanted feeling that we don't know what to do with and that is stored often unconsciously. Eventually this feeling seeks expression as rage, a wild uncontrolled type of energy release, or it might be turned inward and manifest as physical or mental disease.

It has been said that if you have two or three chakras with blockages from negative energy patterns, your health is probably compromised, but if you have four or more, disease is likely. It is best to check in and see how your emotional health is.

Anger, as erratic energy, can be calmed and regulated by crystal oscillations. Now you may think if your anger is really big, you'll need a really big crystal. In fact, even a small one about an inch in diameter will help. Crystals that absorb negative energy work well for anger and are discussed in the following list. Try selecting a crystal from this list to help clear negative energy:

- **Hematite**—When you feel unsettled, hematite is a great grounder of emotions. Your anger will be more self-contained, and your thoughts will become gentler. Hold a tumbled piece 1 to 2 inches long in each hand. You might notice a feeling of heaviness as your emotional body sinks back into alignment and a sense of relaxation comes over you. The high polished surface of hematite is like a mirror, helping you move beyond your self-limitations.

- **Kyanite**—Do you get out of sorts with your thought processes and start to build a story that might or might not be true? Eventually even thinking about something you have little or no control over can lead to anger, but kyanite will cut through these mental illusions. Wearing a small piece as a jewelry item will help keep your mental fields aligned for a higher purpose.

- **Smoky quartz**—Wearing smoky quartz, one of the Master Healers, helps to unblock and open chakras to absorb negative energy. Its crystalline structure is able to take on the brunt of heavy emotions. However, it does absorb a lot of negative energy into its structure so you will need to cleanse it in salt water overnight every 48 to 72 hours depending on the intensity of your release. Recharge the crystal in the sun every second or third day. (See Chapter 7 for more on cleansing and recharging.)

If you find that you are truly having a hard time letting go of your anger, you might also want to try meditating with a love stone (discussed a little later in this chapter) or one of the Master Healers (see Chapter 10).

Gem of an Idea _____

Try one of the following anger-release affirmations to program your selected crystals:

- "I, [your name], love and accept myself for who I am."
- "I, [your name], choose to let go of anything that is not for my higher good."
- "I, [your name], embrace serenity and joy."

True Forgiveness

Forgiveness does not erase the wounds that have already occurred; it's simply accepting a limit on punishing those around us. It takes effort and courage to stay aware of your feelings and to intercept negative emotions when you have decided to forgive someone and move forward. Because, try as we might, those negative issues rear their ugly heads again when we least expect it, and we're left feeling like the victim. Even though we don't like it, somehow we can't let go. However, it's imperative that we do. Hanging onto grudges kills the soul.

The shadow parts of ourselves are whatever we have shoved aside to either ignore or deal with later. By knowing ourselves better and embracing the shadow parts, we bring love and light into all dimensions of our being. It is from this enlightened space within us that forgiveness can be found and expressed to others. If you are not there yet and have some forgiving to do, a spiritual cleanse would be a good way to prepare yourself. By cleansing yourself consciously rather than disassociating from the shadow, you will free yourself from negative feelings.

The following crystals are good to support a spiritual cleanse:

- **Blue lace agate**—A member of the agate family, the soft baby-blue color of blue lace agate will connect you with your spiritual gifts and provide nonjudgmental support and loving, unconditional energy.

- **Moonstone**—The ultra yin energies of moonstone provide a motherly, unconditional love and acceptance. It is best worn at the heart or solar plexus chakra but can be worn anywhere else on the body.

- **Rhodochrosite**—This golden pink crystal with white banding provides renewal and a way to turn self-criticism, anger, and loathing into compassion, love, and self-acceptance.

- **Rose quartz**—This Master Healer is a heart chakra opener. Taken at this level of healing, rose quartz provides self-support and asks you to move forward, leave the past, and step into your spiritual glory.

- **Rutilated quartz**—This quartz crystal with its fine "angel hairs" breaks up old energy patterns and promotes clarity on issues. Rutilated quartz helps move you past outdated thought patterns so you can embrace new values.

- **Selenite**—Selenite is like frozen white light and will offer support and a sense of purpose from your higher self. It is best used at the crown chakra overnight so you can receive higher guidance without interference from daily distractions.

◆ **Sugilite**—If you are holding onto old judgments, sugilite helps you become more sensitive to higher spiritual values and will support your alignment with them as you develop more conscious awareness.

To initiate an energy cleanse, it is best to spend some quiet time away from others and begin by holding one of the suggested crystals in your left hand at your heart chakra. Think of the occasion that caused you to seek or give forgiveness. Continue by visualizing everything that happened. Feel what you need to as deeply as necessary, whether it is pain, anger, or disgust. Continue to hold the crystal until you feel the energy clearing. If you experience a dramatic and often sudden release of pent-up emotional energy—what we call a *catharsis*—do not be too concerned. Breathe deeply and rapidly and it will pass.

You will know that you have cleared what is needed when you feel a sense of peace and are more relaxed and breathing more deeply.

Gem of an Idea

Use the following affirmation to program your selected cleansing crystals: "I, [your name], release all negative feelings to be transmuted by this crystal into loving, healing energy for myself and others." If you want, you can name the people you'd like to help instead of "others."

The Love Stones

For centuries, both women and men have used gemstones and crystals to attract their love partners. However, when our love needs are not being met, our expectations about life are left in an uncomfortable spiritual position. We begin to doubt, rather than be in wonderment with the process of relating to another person.

Crystals have magic properties that break through personal barriers and help to attune oneself to a higher love vibration. The easiest way to get crystal energy is to wear the crystal as a pendant near your heart for at least 21 days for the energy to work. The vibrations of the crystals will continue to affect areas of imbalance, restoring a positive state. The effects of crystal healing at the emotional and psychological levels are subtle, yet are often noticed more by others than by yourself. As your personal vibration changes to a higher, more positive

Gem of an Idea

If you exchange crystals with a friend, you will be forever connected to each other. So to make that life-long connection with someone extra-special, choose one of the love stones!

outlook, you will attract your soul mate to you. If you already have a partner, your love relationship will deepen.

Some key crystals are useful in healing relationship issues. If you wish to combine a few of the crystals for help with multiple issues, you can combine three or four crystals—but no more because your heart will be busy enough as it is:

- **Amethyst**—Known to heal the heart at the highest spiritual levels, amethyst purifies negative emotions and promotes feelings of flexibility, cooperation, and peace. Amethyst provides protection and balance during major personal transitions and reduces feelings of being victimized by others. It also supports all aspects of spiritual growth with peace and calm to fulfill one's mission on Earth; it helps you love again, and again.

- **Aquamarine**—Strengthens one's resolve to feel that life has purpose. This crystal is very protective emotionally and helps you remain centered through complex issues. Aquamarine is excellent for dispelling fear originating from one's weaknesses.

- **Bloodstone**—Dispels discouragement and gives strength and endurance to withstand endless difficulties. This crystal reduces stress and anxiety. Bloodstone revitalizes and encourages unselfishness in relationships.

- **Carnelian**—Eliminates feelings of inadequacy and low self-worth. This stone is especially good for recovery after rejection by your lover. It transmutes sadness in your heart into the initiative to do something positive about the problem. This crystal encourages enthusiasm and is good for giving vibrancy to one's sexuality.

- **Emerald**—A very ancient love stone, it helps to soften arrogance and promote cooperation. Emerald dispels negative thoughts and helps you hold onto what is practical. It cools an angry heart and promotes divine love and peace. This crystal is excellent for preserving love that is maturing into a long-term relationship.

- **Hematite**—Gives emotional support to new love and protects the heart from small "love wounds." The shiny surface reflects back negativity and helps reduce stress to the whole body. Hematite also helps to ground love energy so it doesn't fly away when challenged.

- **Kunzite**—Opens the emotional heart to the highest level. Because this gemstone has a high lithium content, emotional stress can be alleviated. Just looking at kunzite provides a sense of peace and stimulates sensuality. It allows you to surrender rather than resist.

- **Malachite**—Clears the heart of past experiences by unblocking and absorbing any negative energies. Malachite allows you to stay tolerant, loyal, and practical. It gives courage and helps dispel fear in the relationship. Malachite helps you break free of self-denial and repeating old love patterns and promotes responsibility and fidelity in partnerships.

- **Rose quartz**—The number one love stone, rose quartz opens the heart for love and gives love to the wearer who might otherwise have trouble giving love to himself or others. Rose quartz shows you the power of "love conquers all." This crystal brings softness to hardened hearts, teaching you to trust. It dispels negative emotional states, such as despondency and possessiveness, and promotes harmonious relationships. Rose quartz is very calming and loving.

- **Ruby**—Another ancient love stone, ruby encourages romantic love and promotes the ideal relationship. This crystal brings focus to the heart and releases disoriented and trapped love energy. It protects the heart from unnecessary love-suffering and promotes the attainment of love objectives: health, happiness, wealth, and spiritual knowledge.

If you need to attract a new partner, patch up your life to move on with a new relationship, or help heal the one you have, read the descriptions again and then select the crystal that best fits your situation.

Opening Up to Joy

If you have blockages in your chakras, you may not be experiencing a lot of joy. That's where crystals can really help, by gently releasing energy so that it flows more freely in your subtle body. Your heart opens to greater happiness and you experience a different quality of joy.

One time as a girlfriend and I walked around at a local gem and mineral show, we came across some small transparent pinkish-lavender and green clusters of a crystal called vesuvianite. Holding a piece each, we started to giggle uncontrollably. Thinking we were being silly, we put the crystals down. Realizing that the vesuvianite might be responsible, we each rushed to pick up another piece and once again giggled uncontrollably. No doubt we were getting quite a rush of delightful energy to chakras.

Crystal Clear _____

Vesuvianite is also called idocrase and is associated with a distant galaxy whose principle star is named Shakti Astri. There is a story that the goddess Isis lived there and at one time came to Earth to find Astarte, her sister and the goddess of fertility and sexuality. Astarte returned to Shakti Astri and brought her powers of fertility. Astarte was also worshipped by the ancient Greeks as Aphrodite and by the Romans as Venus.

Many crystals will modify your mood and give you feelings of upliftment. Some crystals seem so serious with their energy, focusing your mind on troubles, cleansing, clearing, and healing. Take a break once in a while to just feel really good and happy. Here are some more crystals to perk you up:

Gem of an Idea _____

Make a special "Stress Day" pouch of crystals to alleviate your mood. Pack a pouch with opal, rose quartz, moonstone, and citrine. Add a wrapped Gummi Bear candy to absorb the energies and eat it later when you need an additional perk!

- **Clear quartz**—A clear quartz crystal with a rainbow is also a mood-lightener. The rainbow neutralizes and dissolves grief and other sadness and restores feelings of joy.

- **Diamonds**—These are glittery and seem to dance in the light. They brighten and enliven your aura by clearing out stale energy.

- **Opals**—These are delightful for sour-mood interventions, providing a great display of colors. The colors provide a brightening of the colors in your aura.

Any crystal with the play of light or luminescence will generally light up your heart and your third eye to the special pleasures of life. Open up your heart chakra and your eyes and look around at the gift of living at this very moment.

Lucky You!

There are so many crystals for luck, but in this part of the book, let's focus on wishing. You've heard songs about "wishing upon a star"? You can wish with crystals, too. It's actually a form of programming, but if you use the right crystal, your wish might come true. How, you ask? The crystal amplifies the thought energy and lines up the universal energy for wish fulfillment.

Which crystal is best to use for wishing? A double-terminated clear quartz crystal provides one end for giving and one end for receiving energy. After you have programmed your crystal, hold it about 5 to 10 inches from your heart chakra with one end pointing directly at the center of the chakra. You can close your eyes if you want and visualize what it is that you're wishing for. See the request going out as white light from your heart center through the tip of the crystal and out to the other end of the crystal with your request. If the wish is in your heart's highest purpose, you should see some results. How soon is dependent on how long it takes the Universe to line up the energies.

Co-creating with the Universe is tricky business, so be very specific about what you ask for. Here are some crystals that can be particularly useful in this regard:

◆ There is a special type of crystal called a *manifestation crystal*. This is a rare form of crystal that has another crystal growing inside it. It is easier to find them in clear quartz, but many other types of crystals will combine, such as smoky quartz with garnets. To prepare, place a kyanite at your solar plexus to align all your energies. Take the manifestation crystal and place it at your third eye. If it is too large, place it in front and imagine a beam of white light coming from the crystal to your third eye and back. Use the circular breath technique between you and the crystal as described in Chapter 11. As you do, visualize what you wish to manifest. Your intention will be aligned with the universal laws of attraction.

◆ Rainbow moonstone has also been used for wishing. It is actually a form of colorless labradorite that looks like a miniature *aurora borealis.* Place the crystal at your third eye and project the image of what you wish into the crystal. See a miniature version of the image playing out inside the crystal. See yourself actually getting your wish fulfilled.

def•i•ni•tion

Aurora borealis, also known as the Northern Lights, is the display of light energy in the northern hemisphere. Electrons from solar winds interact with the magnetic and electrical fields of our planet. The colorful display looks similar to the energy glow from the aura around the human body.

◆ Take any seven small crystals of the same kind, preferably Herkimer diamonds or another double-terminated crystal. Prepare each one with a prosperity wish programmed into each crystal. Wear these seven "wish crystals" in a pouch and hold them from time to time to reinforce the energy of the wish.

◆ A clear quartz crystal with a rainbow configuration, as discussed in Chapter 10, is helpful to manifest wishes. First, prepare your crystal by programming it with your wish. Then wear the rainbow crystal so your wish goes into your aura and will attract the wish to you. This technique of programming a rainbow crystal can also be used to attract a soul mate.

Granting a wish for someone else is easy to set up. Have the person make a wish by writing it down on a sheet of paper. Place the paper inside a special wish box with a lid 3 or 4 inches square. Place the seven wish crystals on top of the wish sheet in the box, close the lid, and leave it in place without disturbing it for three days. On the third day, remove the paper and burn it so the message and the accumulated energy is sent into the Universe for manifestation.

Gem of an Idea

Here are some sample affirmations to program your crystal for wish fulfillment:

◆ "I, [your name], am open to receive all the abundance I create."

◆ "Everything that I create comes easily to me."

◆ "I, [your name], accept all that I create in my life."

Crystals for Emotional Healing

It seems as though more and more people are suffering from deep emotional wounds these days. The prescriptions for antidepressants are skyrocketing, and we all have a friend or two who's down in the dumps. Crystals can play a big role in evening out that negativity, even in severe cases. Depression, sadness, and anxiety can be caused by a blockage in the chakras. That's where crystals can really help, by gently releasing energy so it flows more freely in your subtle body.

The next time you're feeling blue, bring out some of these big guns:

◆ **Amazonite**—Soothes; is good for those undergoing emotional processes; and pacifies worries, fear, and aggravations. It's excellent for children, neurological problems, and nerves.

◆ **Amber**—Calms nerves, enlivens the body, and rekindles energy.

◆ **Amethyst**—Releases negative thought programming, clears emotional blockages, moves you into cooperation with other supportive forces, allows you to "sense" (use sensibility) with your emotions, and moves you into a more conscious state to see the cause and effect of your emotional responses.

◆ **Apache tear**—Good for sorrow, grief, and forgiveness, it removes self-limitation and emotional barriers.

Yellow Flag _____

Crystals can help convert negative energy into positive vibrations, but they are no a substitute for treating chemical imbalances or more serious mental health issues. For severe depression or anxiety, seek professional medical advice.

◆ **Aquamarine**—Quiets fears, phobias, and anxiety; releases expectation; shields, stabilizes, and eases discomforts and hiccups (caused by fear).

◆ **Aventurine**—Purifies the emotional body and tranquilizes nerves.

◆ **Bloodstone**—Grounds the emotional heart, alleviates distress and anxiety, used as a support tool.

◆ **Blue lace agate**—Alleviates spiritual tension and emotional intensity.

◆ **Botswana agate**—Soothes repressed emotions and moves you beyond limits; it's excellent for smokers whose nerves are on edge.

◆ **Calcite (all colors)**—Clears chakras by color. Calcite is a gentle cleanser of emotional upsets and helps you move forward after releasing emotional restrictions.

◆ **Carnelian**—Works with extreme negative states such as envy, fear, rage, and sorrow. Connects to the Higher Self for emotional clearing, to move negative states into states of love; it dispels apathy and encourages trust by connecting the lower chakras (base, sacral, and solar plexus) to the heart.

◆ **Celestite**—Known as a gentle emotional releaser, it dissolves unnecessary programming and transmutes emotional energy.

◆ **Chrysocolla**—Promotes emotional strength, stabilizes emotions, balances expression and communication, and releases distress and guilt.

◆ **Chrysoprase**—Used to alleviate alcoholism and provide ease to feelings of depression. It allows you to take one day at a time and build on successes through small changes, and it encourages patience with inner transformation.

- **Citrine**—Calms fears, promotes happiness, and frees energy for spontaneous expression energies.

- **Clear quartz**—Unblocks and transmutes negative energy. Dispels negative dispositions.

- **Emerald**—An emotional heart soother, this crystal provides peace at the heart level, especially about matters that trigger anxiety. Instead of falling into a deep emotional pit, emerald will help focus and guide your actions to stay centered on your life's purpose.

- **Fluorite**—All colors of fluorite calm the emotional body. Purple fluorite helps to break up emotional blockages.

- **Hemimorphite**— Protects self-esteem and purifies one's intentions. It is effective to reduce anger and hostility toward others.

- **Kunzite**—With its high lithium content, it settles emotions quickly. Promotes feelings of well-being and peacefulness at the emotional and mental levels.

- **Lapis lazuli**—Provides objective insight and mental clarity. Unblocks and releases emotions from the heart for self-acceptance. Reconnects the wounded parts.

- **Lepidolite**—Reduces stress responses, alleviates despondency, and provides grounding for "flyaway" emotions.

- **Malachite**—A heavy releaser of negative emotions, it's best used in conjunction with rose quartz to bring peace to emotions after releasing.

- **Moonstone**—Reduces emotional tension, provides for missing emotional nurturing, and helps to bring a sense of peace to the emotions.

Crystal Clear

Moonstone is believed to support one through life's emotional transition points (puberty, marriage, births, menopause, and so on) and, as such, it makes a very meaningful gift!

- **Moss agate**—Soothes self-esteem and battered egos. Strengthens positive traits and promotes emotional strength; it's used for women's healing and nurturing.

- **Obsidian**—A huge releaser of negative emotions, it is somewhat overpowering in releasing old energy patterns by piercing any resistance. Transmutes energy blockages into white light.

- **Onyx**—Alleviates mental confusion and absorbs grief.

- **Opal**—Brightens negative attitudes and dispels dark moods. Helps to discern the truth and brings hope and happiness to the wearer.

- **Peridot**—Targets jealousy and aims at releasing self-centeredness. Restores inner balance that is overpowered by self-destruction.

- **Petrified wood**—Very calming to jittery types and those who worry.

- **Rhodocrosite**—A soothing emotional balancer used after a period of intense emotional stress. Works well to dissolve and transmute feelings of guilt.

- **Rose quartz**—Soothes and purifies all emotions. Provides loving energy and comfort to those with raw emotional states.

- **Rutilated quartz**—Pulls apart complex emotional issues and unblocks chakras to allow negative energies to dissolve.

- **Selenite**—Allows you to reach beyond your emotional state to the higher psycho-spiritual centers such as altruism, compassion, and love.

- **Smoky quartz**—Excellent for stubborn people who refuse to let go of negative emotions. A powerful healer that dissolves and transmutes energy.

- **Snakeskin agate**—Promotes inner peace and cheer and dispels worries.

- **Sodalite**—Calms emotions and numbs mental chatter.

- **Tiger eye (yellow)**—Provides mental and emotional discipline for people who are unable to appreciate self-responsibility.

- **Tourmaline**—Green tourmaline is a major unblocker of emotional energy, keeping energy circuits open and energy flowing. Pink tourmaline activates and soothes the heart and provides feelings of intense beauty while preventing victimization.

- **Turquoise**—Provides emotional detachment and focus on self-accomplishment without entanglement with others.

- **Unakite**—The two colors of this crystal, pink and green, relate to the emotional (pink = movement) and the physical (green = grounding) parts of the heart chakra. This crystal supports moving on after disappointment.

- **Zoistite**—Powerful at the direct release of repressed emotions and amplified awareness about the issues.

The Least You Need to Know

◆ Crystals can be used to support the release of troublesome emotions that could lead to physical problems.

◆ Opals and rose quartz are among the crystals that can be used to enhance positive emotions.

◆ The intensity of emotional release can be controlled by the type of crystal selected and the length of your exposure to the crystal.

◆ Many crystals help with issues of emotional distress as a drug-free support for when you're feeling a little down in the dumps. For more severe anxiety and depression, seek medical advice.

Chapter 13

Crystals for Spiritual Healing

In This Chapter

- ◆ Achieving higher consciousness
- ◆ Accessing the crystal deva
- ◆ Contacting the angelic realm
- ◆ Learning about your past lives
- ◆ Two methods of distance healing
- ◆ A list of crystals for spiritual expansion

You've no doubt heard that crystals are great boosters in the search for spiritual wholeness. But if you are expecting your experience of working with spiritual crystals to go a certain way, you must release those thoughts and simply know that you will encounter exactly what is needed for your own healing and growth at this time.

You have your own journey to travel. No one else is experiencing what you are feeing and thinking because you are unique in all ways. Crystals are adaptable to your individual energy and are indiscriminate about your needs; in this way, they're the perfect unbiased helpers, assisting you on your journey by lightening the load you carry and providing a renewal of spiritual energy.

Think of crystals as a bridge to higher consciousness. They help you to transcend the ordinary and enter a greater awareness about yourself. That awareness will take you to a higher level of consciousness where it is possible to be in more direct contact with the sacred realms.

Deepening Your Spirituality

The microscopic details of a crystal are said to contain the same organization as the rest of the universe. Imagine being aligned with the same vibration that the rest of the universe responds to. Suddenly you realize that every cell in your body is in sync with All That Is!

Spiritual development encourages manifestation, inner peace, connectedness to the awesome beauty around us, and an awakening of consciousness. You can no longer slumber through life. You are alive and pulsating with energy. You can use this awakened energy and knowledge for healing, for communicating with other realms, and for learning about yourself. The question is, *how* do we do all this?

To open a channel of communication within yourself, you have to tune in to your energy and to the energy of the crystal with which you're working. When the word *spiritual* comes up, think *subtle energy*. Tuning in to spiritual energy is similar to what happens when someone whispers. You have to become more alert and focused so you can hear.

Crystal Clear

As our level of consciousness expands outward—like the universe—we are ready to take in more information about ourselves. Crystals help to create an energy bridge that brings us into alignment with that universal vibration.

Spiritual energy can hold various vibrational levels. Some crystals are already tuned to help you access certain levels, such as when you want to access past lives or angelic realms. Some energies are so refined, though, that we are not even aware they exist! But when we want to be part of that light, to be accessible to God's source and to enlightenment, we can be. When we hold a clear crystal in our hands, it's as if we are holding a way to make that sacred connection within ourselves.

Many specialized crystals help support the development of our spiritual connection. These types of crystals tend to be transparent or highly reflective of light. They also have a greater ability to hold light. When there is more light, there is more vibrational essence for bridging your consciousness to other realms.

Crystals used for spiritual attainment are often highly evolved. When using these "light tools," it is best to hold one in your hands for meditation. For a deep journey, place them on your third eye in the middle of your forehead or sleep with a selected gemstone taped to your crown chakra at night. They will provide you with a pathway of consciousness. What you bring back from your journey is worth writing in your crystal journal.

Some recommended crystals to get you started are apophyllite, celestite, labradorite, or moldavite. More details on each crystal are provided at the end of this chapter.

Connecting with Crystal Devas

The concept that there is spirit in all things is a belief shared by many faiths across the world. Among Amerindians—that is, Native Americans, Inuit, and other First Nations people—there is regard for the spirit in water, trees, rocks, animals—in all things. The *collective consciousness* for the realm or kingdom of these living entities is called a *deva*.

You can connect and communicate with, say, the geranium deva, which holds the collective consciousness of geraniums. Maybe you'd like to know how far back to trim the plant. Well, go ahead and ask! How do you know you have contacted the deva? You might suddenly realize that answers are just popping into your head, or you just have a feeling about how you're supposed to care for your flowers!

def•i•ni•tion

Collective consciousness is a shared belief that unifies a social group. **Deva** is a term used to convey contact with the awareness of a group of like-minded people or things.

Just as there is a deva of various plants, there are devas for crystals, and it's not difficult to get this information. How is this possible, you wonder, when we're different species? Take animals, for instance. They seem to understand our words and facial expressions. We understand theirs as well, whether it is the way a dog barks, the tilt of a cat's head, or a wagging tail. We use certain impressions to bridge the gap, so to speak. The same type of bridge is used for the communications with crystal devas.

I channeled some information from one of my Himalayan clear quartz crystal devas that went something like this: When I asked, "What is your purpose?" the deva's response was: "I am all that which matters to you on this plane. I open the centers from the heart to the throat chakras so you can speak the beauty from your heart. I provide a light blue color ray to your third eye to open your awareness to higher planes and to infuse this color into your aura for protecting a vibrational spectrum."

Crystal Clear

You might be offered a devic name by the crystal, which is the name of the crystal's consciousness. You might hear the name pronounced inside your head, or it might come spontaneously from your mouth. Use the name to summon the deva by calling the name three times before using the crystal. One of my crystal devas is named "Orca" because the crystal has a small whalelike fin and provides information about fluids within the body.

By contacting the deva or consciousness of a particular crystal, you can learn more about that crystal and the healing power it offers. So let's try an exercise to reach *your* crystal deva. Hold a cleansed and fully charged crystal in front of you. Program your crystal with the following affirmation:

> "I, [your name], am open and able to communicate with the deva of this crystal."

Gaze at the crystal and initiate a circular breath by breathing into and out of the crystal for a few minutes. When you want to access the devic energy, allow your mind to flow freely. Your thoughts and impressions reflect your contact with the devic energy. Write down your thoughts and impressions in your crystal journal so you have a record for future use. As you develop more personal meditative focus and conscious awareness, more information will be available from these other realms.

Asking an Angel for Advice

Making contact with an angelic presence can be a beautiful and uplifting experience. When you have spiritual validation from a source outside of yourself, your faith—if it was ever shaken—can be restored. And your heart is wide open to give and receive love and compassion.

Many world faiths believe in a guardian angel, a protector who is assigned to you at birth. I've known plenty of people who have been in touch with these other-worldly figures; every one of these people has been profoundly affected by the experience! If you have been aware of the presence of an angel, consider yourself fortunate because the channel must have been opened at that time. Working with crystals can help you keep the channel to that realm open.

Here are three crystals that help access the angelic realms:

◆ **Angelite**—This light blue crystal holds light angelic energy and provides a shield of light around the wearer. This crystal can provide a telepathic portal to the angelic realm. Use angelite for meditation, or tape it on your third eye for enhanced dreaming.

◆ **Clear quartz**—Use the seven-sided clear quartz channeling configuration with the seven-sided face that was described in Chapter 10.

◆ **Selenite**—There is a specific formation called a "fish tail," but really, it looks like an open pair of angel's wings. Selenite holds many mysteries, including the access codes to the angelic realms. When meditating with selenite, ask to be given access to the angelic realms.

Gem of an Idea

If you have no experience with angels, try inviting them into your life by thinking they are around you at all times. Look at pictures of angels or wear an angel pin or crystal pendant in the shape of an angel. And of course, use the appropriate crystals to make contact.

When you are looking for other crystals to help you gain access to the angelic realms, ask your angel guides, the angels that walk with you, to guide you to specific crystals that will help you access the angels. Many crystals that facilitate opening of the third eye and crown chakra also facilitate telepathy and clairvoyance—both skills that are helpful in communicating with the angels.

To make a "phone call" to the angel realm during meditation, use a cleansed and fully charged clear quartz channeling crystal with the seven-sided face described in Chapter 10. Program the crystal with the following affirmation:

"I, [your name], am open and clear to receive communication with the higher angelic realms."

Get grounded by visualizing roots growing from under your feet into the ground to anchor your energies. If you need to move around during the meditation, move slowly and gently so as not to shock the connection to the more subtle angelic energy realm. Then follow these steps:

1. Place your right thumb on the face of the channeling crystal. Relax your mind and your body. Regulate your breath so it's deep and evenly paced. Visualize white light coming in and out of the crystal to your heart chakra.

2. Now focus on your crown chakra and continue to breathe deeply, visualizing white light coming in and out of the crystal on your crown chakra. This helps open the higher centers for communication.

3. When you are feeling centered, bring your focus back to the crystal. You might feel some tingling at the top of your head and maybe some warmth at the heart. That's okay because it signals that your heart and crown chakras are activated and that you are ready and open for communication.

To capture the attention of an angel, try singing very sweetly. Let's say you wanted to call Gabriel, the Messenger Angel who is often depicted with a trumpet. Using your voice very lightly, sing into the crystal, calling the name Gabriel in long tones, "Gaaaaa-briiiii-ellll …."

Call several times, and then stop. Listen for a response. Call twice more and stop to listen again. Then just meditate, leaving your mind open to see images or hear messages. Do not be afraid to ask for your angel to provide you with something, such as comfort and advice or healing. I've heard it said that if you ask three times, you cannot be refused.

When you make contact, ask for the name of the angel. After you "meet" in this way, the two of you are bound together and you can call on this angel again when needed!

Recalling Past Lives

Many people believe in past lives, but belief is different from knowing that you have been here before. When you have a clear mind, you have the ability to reach quite far into yourself, perhaps as far back as your last life … or the one before that … or the one before *that*! As you expand your awareness using crystals for meditation and relaxation, your consciousness starts to enter into different realms of awareness, and they just might hold some surprises for you.

The exploration into these different realms can help you to access knowledge stored in the *Akashic Record* or to communicate with a spiritual entity. Information about a past life can be helpful for understanding your quirks in this life. It can also help explain why you might feel attracted to some things and repulsed by others.

If you want to give it a go and reach for past life knowledge, program a clear quartz rainbow crystal to help provide an energy bridge to the Akashic Record. Your statement of intention (or programming) might go something like this:

"I, [your name], am now open and able to access and retrieve information from the Akashic Record."

def•i•ni•tion

> The **Akashic Record** is said to exist on another dimension and holds information about the universe—including information about yourself, your past lives, as well as all past events. The Record is like a huge library of energy!

Now sit or lie down comfortably with the crystal at your heart chakra, and follow these steps:

1. Ground yourself very well, seeing roots growing under your feet into the ground.

2. Clear your mind and regulate your breath.

3. When you are ready, visualize a library of books or other electronic forms to access information. Find the book with your name on it.

4. Open the book at a point where you'd like to find something about yourself, such as what you were doing in the seventeenth century. You might start seeing images of yourself during that time period. Try to be aware of where you are, what your name is, what you do for a living, and so on.

5. Explore what you need; when it's time to return, close the book and come back very slowly into the awareness of your room.

Write down as much as you can recall in your crystal journal; add drawings of any-thing that might be relevant. I've had many people tell me they were able to confirm suspicions they've had about their past lives through this simple little exercise.

For a more complete understanding of and look into the Akashic Record, check out *The Complete Idiot's Guide to the Akashic Record* by Synthia Andrews and Colin Andrews (see Appendix C).

Yellow Flag

> You can also access your past lives through a medium, but I think it's better—and more reliable—to get this information on your own. After having met six people claiming they were John the Baptist in previous lifetimes, two women claiming lifetimes as Cleopatra, and two Beethovens, I must tell you to be cautious about what you hear from a past life reader.

Spiritual Healing

All crystals can provide an increase in awareness, healing, meditative peace, the release of energy blockages, and so on. The spiritual connections provided through crystals are a catalyst for your own development. By selecting different crystals to work with during your life journey, you can find it easier to move through various obstacles. For instance, if you need spiritual and emotional support, the right crystal can ease your distress and help you move past the sticky places.

Crystals for Distance Healing

Two methods of working with crystals are simple and effective for distance healing, which we first mentioned in Chapter 3. One involves using the photo of the individual who needs healing; the other method works without a photo.

If you have a photo of the person who has consented to distance healing, find a shelf or table where the picture can remain for up to three days. If there are other people in the photo, take a piece of paper and cover them. This will help you focus better on the one person to receive healing energy.

Yellow Flag

Distance healing should be attempted only when you have been given permission to do so because the other person must allow her energy fields to be open to the healing energy. If distance healing is against the will of the other person, regardless of your best intentions, you'll run up against a closed energy field.

Select up to three crystals, depending on the illness or the part of the body or the chakra that needs healing. Put them aside. You'll also need from six to eight small, cleansed clear quartz or amethyst crystals to arrange in a circle around the photo. Hold all the crystals in your hands to program them with the following affirmation (refer to Chapter 7 for programming instructions):

> "These crystals are now activated at highest intent to provide distance healing for [name of the person]."

If you want to include the specific healing issue, you can either write it on a piece of paper and place it under the photo or simply state it as part of the above affirmation. Hold the crystals and meditate, thinking of the person and her healing needs.

Place the clear quartz or amethyst crystals in a small circle around the photo with the tips pointing in toward the picture. (If you are using tumbled crystals, just arrange them in a circle.) Take the healing crystals you've selected and tape them onto the photo directly or to the glass in the frame. You can also leave them in front of a standing frame.

Leave the crystals in place for a few days and check in with the person to see how the distance healing is working for her. Once a day, you might like to sweep your crystals with some incense or smudge such as sweetgrass to clear any negativity from them. At the end of the healing period, cleanse and recharge all your crystals.

A friend told me she used a photo of her sister for distance healing and surrounded the portrait with six clear quartz crystals. She called me the next day, excited to see water on the tip of each crystal. Even though the face of each crystal was sloped, the water did not roll off. The water remained for over a week without evaporating. This uncommon experience with distance healing shows the manifestation of the healing energy!

Healing Is in the Air

For the second method of distance healing, you will coordinate a time to send healing to the person. The other person will need to remain quiet or sit in meditation for at least 10 minutes while you send the crystal healing energy.

Use a cleansed and fully charged clear quartz or amethyst crystal 2 inches long, programmed with the same affirmation outlined in the previous method. At the appointed time, ground yourself and hold the crystal in both hands, tip pointing up. Visualize the "target" person inside the crystal. See that person receiving healing. While visualizing, direct your breath into and out of the crystal. This will help direct your healing intent and charge the crystal.

Continue to focus and use the circular breath in and out from the crystal for about 10 minutes. It can seem like a long time, but it's worth it to send the highest form of vibration to a loved one, isn't it?

Don't forget to write in your journal what time your healing started and ended and note any thoughts, messages, or images you might have received while sending distance healing. Check in with the other person to see how he is feeling. You might find some interesting similarities of observations! And don't forget to cleanse your crystals afterwards.

Crystals for Spiritual Expansion

A crystal can provide healing at physical, emotional, psychological, and spiritual levels. Like veils being removed from your mind, crystals provide clearings to your consciousness so you can see truth and reality more clearly. They can allow you to communicate better, whether it is through mental telepathy, simply speaking about a topic, or producing something creative like music or drawing. They also provide deeper meditation where you will be less distracted and will find yourself immersed more deeply in the experience of emptiness.

Gem of an Idea

Use a uniquely shaped crystal to access information on past lives, future events, and metaphysics. These oddly shaped gemstones hold a lot of power!

In selecting a crystal for spiritual expansion, try to find one that is excellent quality; in other words, look for a crystal that has good color and is attractive in its shape and size. The piece should not be broken or chipped. It should be small and light enough to be used at the third eye without leaving a dent or bruise on your forehead. If you are using the crystal for holding during meditation, it should feel comfortable in your hand.

In general, the following crystals for spiritual expansion are used for meditation while being held in your hand, wearing them, using them in the suggested chakra, or being included in the crystal layouts discussed in Chapter 17. Give yourself lots of time to work just with one crystal, and remember to record your experiences in your crystal journal.

- **Amethyst**—Amethyst is a major crystal used as a crown chakra opener. It transmutes negativity and balances yin and yang forces. Amethyst facilitates expansion of the third eye and expands psychic abilities by connecting intuitive receptors to the crown chakra, which provides a link to a truth. Use amethyst on any chakras to unblock and transmute negativity and to remove limitations to spiritual growth and awareness.

- **Apophyllite**—This crystal is an awesome third eye and crown opener. Apophyllite facilitates *astral travel* and helps to initiate a person to new levels of intuition. This crystals acts as a bridge to cross time dimensions.

def•i•ni•tion

Astral travel is an event marked by your subconsciousness leaving the physical plane (also called an *out-of-body experience*) and traveling to a nonphysical astral realm where you can visit loved ones who have passed on, talk with spiritual teachers, and enjoy countless other freedoms.

- ◆ **Aquamarine**—To augment spiritual awareness, aquamarine can be held in the hand and asked to provide information stored for your knowledge from other dimensions. This crystal helps your attunement to be of service to others and diminishes the self-centeredness that often gets in the way of genuine spirituality. It works best at your truth center, the throat chakra.

- ◆ **Azurite**—Azurite provides an opening to a deeper level of consciousness and cleanses and prepares the mind to work on a higher spiritual level to provide deeper understanding and acceptance. It works with the throat chakra to purify the intent behind one's spiritual activities.

- ◆ **Azurite-malachite**—This is a blend of two types of crystals that grow together; they provide a powerful sense of getting to core matters by probing and penetrating past the masks we bear. The truth is exposed by unlocking the past. Use this crystal at your third eye or throat chakra.

- ◆ **Bloodstone**—This crystal provides grounding for going deeply into spirituality and mystical matters without getting lost. Bloodstone is a great anchor or safety net and can be used with other crystals to provide safe-keeping of subtle energies. Hold this crystal in your hand or place it at your solar plexus.

- ◆ **Blue lace agate**—This crystal is very calming when used at the throat chakra. It helps to speak your truth, to channel your higher thoughts, and to facilitate expression of spirituality. Wear it as a necklace or place it at your throat chakra.

- ◆ **Calcite**—Pink or white calcite provides an opening of the higher chakras where a direct channel is needed for communicating with your Highest Self. Use it in your hand during meditation, or place it at your throat, third eye, or crown chakra.

- ◆ **Carnelian**—Carnelian restores trust to spiritually jaded people and keeps the focus on a higher level rather than physical or emotional levels. Wear this crystal at your heart chakra or hold it in your hand during meditation.

◆ **Celestite**—Used at the throat, third eye, and crown chakras, celestite provides a pathway for consciousness to enter the higher realms.

◆ **Charoite**—This ray of purple light dispels fear and connects the third eye to the mental plane to help loosen the need for attachments.

◆ **Citrine**—The golden rays of citrine provide a complex energy structure that energizes the crown and sacral chakras. Citrine transmutes physical vibrations into higher spiritual aspects and provides protection for the aura. Use it at your heart chakra, or hold it in your hand during meditation.

◆ **Diamond**—Diamond provides spiritual confidence and activates the crown chakra. The brilliance of light from the diamond dispels brain fog and gives clarity to meditation.

◆ **Dioptase**—This brilliant green crystal provides attunement for the third eye. Dioptase can be a wake-up call for those still so attached to worldly problems that entering into higher states of consciousness is impossible.

◆ **Emerald**—Emerald balances the heart and crown chakras. It provides peace and calms the emotional heart for higher spiritual attunements.

◆ **Golden topaz**—This builder of faith is also a crown activator and helps you recharge with golden light. It opens and reconditions the third eye to see at a higher level.

◆ **Iolite**—Iolite provides an ability to open the third eye for clarity of visions and other intuitive work. It is a protector while entering higher states of consciousness and provides unconditional love.

◆ **Kyanite**—An initiator of moving the upper chakras into more subtle levels of awareness, it helps you see how spiritual and physical bodies reflect each others' needs for healing.

◆ **Labradorite**—This crystal operates on and unifies the upper chakras (heart, throat, third eye, and crown). It helps with detachment from situations so clarity of spiritual purpose can be seen.

◆ **Lepidolite**—An excellent crystal to reach past lives, it improves intuition and helps with the perseverance of the spiritual journey.

◆ **Moldavite**—Moldavite is a major transformer and tool of consciousness. Wearing even a small piece will augment your abilities for interdimensional communication. Moldavite provides a channel for other light beings to contact you.

◆ **Purple fluorite**—This crystal holds intense white light and activates the third eye and crown chakras. It clears out what is not needed for your highest good.

When you select your crystals for spiritual expansion, look for lighter, transparent crystals with good structural shape, because these relate most often to the higher chakras. Opaque, darker crystals, whether they have clearly defined structures or not, often work best in the lower chakras. You can always use your pendulum to check out the use of crystals or contact the deva of the crystal for more information.

The Least You Need to Know

◆ The bridge to higher consciousness can be accessed using crystals in meditation.

◆ The consciousness within a crystal is called a deva and is part of a larger collective consciousness of crystals.

◆ Access to angelic realms requires a light touch, some singing, and lots of listening.

◆ Access to the Akashic Record can shed some light on your past lives.

◆ Distance healing is a way to send healing regardless of where a person lives.

Chapter 14

Crystals for the Whole Family

In This Chapter

- Crystals for men's health
- Smoothing out women's issues
- Easing the teen years with crystal energy
- Children use crystals—naturally!
- Quick results for pets

Our minds and bodies are under so much stress these days. It comes at us from all kinds of sources: mental stress from financial or workplace issues; psychological stress from events such as elections, natural disasters, or civil unrest; and physical stress from illness, injury, or emotional distress. And we adults are not the only ones suffering—I don't know how many times I hear people say, "I would not want to be a kid growing up in today's world." Life can be tough on all of us!

It is essential to find a means to alleviate stress without putting out a huge investment. And guess what? Crystal therapy meets those requirements and is a drug-free natural means of healing.

Yellow Flag _____

Check the authenticity of your crystal accessories! Unfortunately, the use of gem synthetics has slowly replaced the use of genuine gemstones in popular jewelry, so wearers are not receiving genuine benefits.

Even Tough Guys Need Healing

Crystals and gemstones have often been worn by men as jewelry or to decorate formal suits to signify their official or regal status in society. In ancient times, polished crystals were embedded in shields for protection during battle. Carved crystal amulets have offered protection from enemies and poisoned wine.

If you are a man in an urban setting, you might feel awkward about wearing crystals dangling down in front of your chest in public. If you are not inclined to be an "urban shaman," here are some suggestions:

♦ Wear your healing crystals in a medicine pouch (a pouch on a string) tucked down inside your shirt. Try to select crystals that are relatively flat, so your pouch will go unnoticed. Place your crystals inside a small pouch or drop it into your breast pocket to help heal your heart, either physically or emotionally.

♦ For the office or workplace, leave your stones out as decorative objects. If anyone asks, you can say you are a mineral collector, or you are buying stones for your kids as part of their geology class!

♦ Keep your crystals loose inside your front pants pockets, and hold them in your hands for a while several times during the day.

♦ At night, leave the crystals next to your bed or under your pillow while you sleep. Remember to cleanse and recharge your crystals at least once a month using the techniques in Chapter 7.

The following crystals and gemstones are useful in healing men's issues. Some of these issues address stress, health, increasing power, and improving self-esteem and communications. Of course, these crystals can be used by anyone with these issues:

♦ **Amethyst**—Amethyst is not only a Master Healer, but is also called the "royal stone." Amethyst's most noted healing quality is its ability to purify and transmute all forms of negativity. Get a large amethyst crystal cluster for your home or office to protect yourself from hostile energies around you. If anxiety causes shortness of breath, put the cluster on or near your chest and breathe slowly for a few minutes to lessen the symptoms. Consider a large, well-set amethyst gemstone ring to enhance your personal magnetism and provide mental clarity. Amethyst is also helpful for migraines, arthritic pains, and connecting to one's spirituality for guidance.

◆ **Jade**—Jade is known as a "crystal of tranquility" and as the "sport stone," promoting agility and swiftness. Many men from the Far East know the benefits of wearing jade. Some will tell you that it is for their health and how the color of the jade gets darker with good health and lighter with declining health. Jade soothes the emotions and provides emotional detachment and restoration after various traumas such as minor surgery, divorce, funerals, or loss of job. Some say jade is for good luck. Jade is easily obtained and can be worn as a pendant, bracelet, or ring.

◆ **Lapis lazuli**—The "stone of the pharaohs," lapis lazuli is well-known as a favorite stone used in the courts of the ancient Egyptian kings. *Lapis* means "stone," and *lazuli* means "blue." This deep blue stone is used for stimulating mental strength and intellectual precision. Lapis is a consciousness elevator, raising one's awareness to new heights and to greater expansion. It brings feelings of success, connectedness, and protection. For intuitive people, lapis intensifies psychic power.

◆ **Malachite**—A "man's stone," the deep forest green of malachite is symbolic of the deep healing and cleansing this stone provides. It can aid in breaking old patterns, whether emotional (stuck patterns of behavior) or physical (tumors, swollen joints, muscular, and so on). Malachite promotes business relationships and the increase of wealth by removing obstacles to one's growth. The most important aspect of this crystal's healing ability, however, is for the preventive health of the physical heart and liver. If you are attracted to this crystal, chances are you have a family history of heart-related problems and probably need a heart check-up.

◆ **Moonstone**—The "feminine balancing crystal," moonstone provides for a depth of perception, feelings, discernment, creativity, intuition, and self-expression. This crystal is used to soften and balance dominant male attributes and provide some feminine qualities. Other properties of moonstone include increased awareness and focus, rejuvenating qualities for the skin and hair and protection for travelers by letting them see possibilities ahead. Moonstones are known to increase their powers before and during the full moon, so leave them out at night to soak up the moon's rays.

◆ **Rose quartz**—The "love stone," rose quartz is a Master Healer that specializes in transmuting emotional negativity at all levels. It enhances one's ability to give and receive love, by opening the heart chakra and stimulating greater flexibility in communications. It mellows out a reluctant heart and provides peace in relationships through harmony. Rose quartz is used for meditation because it stills one's aggressive thoughts and provides mental tranquility. It can heal a broken heart very quickly, too.

◆ **Smoky quartz**—The "emotional balancer crystal," smoky quartz is another Master Healer and is a very specialized crystal for negative emotional energy. This crystal is excellent for mood swings, aggressive actions, ill temper, and generally nasty thoughts. It grounds all kinds of negative energy. This stone is helpful for burnout, fear of failure, reluctance to take risks, or wanting revenge, as well as for tendencies to overeat, smoke, or drink due to stress. It helps you accept responsibility for yourself and to broaden your capacity for effective communication by dissolving self-limiting perceptions.

If you have reservations about wearing (or using) gemstones, set them aside, just for a month or so. Try the appropriate crystals for your specific needs and see what happens. I'm willing to bet you'll be singing a different tune in four weeks' time!

Crystals for Women's Health

Crystals can be used to assist women of all ages and in all stages of healing. The awakening of the self to a spiritual journey is not an easy task. It can demand much time and resources to achieve self-development and growth. Some choose not to undertake the risks and perils of peeling off our defenses to become fully human and alive and to experience the full wealth of life.

Crystal Clear

Isis is an Egyptian goddess of the feminine, healing arts, resurrection, and rebirth. She is also a protector. *Isis Unveiled* is a term that refers to the Egyptian goddess whose face and form was covered with a red cloth, symbolic of the ignorance and emotionalism that stood forever between a person and truth. To the wise, Isis lifts her veil of ignorance, dispelling and revealing the mysteries of the universe. The inner journey becomes sacred to those who can withstand the intensity of full consciousness.

Crystals have a healing role to play in this fantastic journey. Like the mysteries of a woman's consciousness, crystals help to prepare the unveiling of female consciousness through healing all levels of her being. Crystals provide protection and give sanctuary for the deep healing a woman does within herself.

The following crystals and gemstones are useful in healing women and in addressing women's issues:

◆ **Amber**—A "gentle stone," amber is very soothing and calming to the nerves. It can uplift a negative disposition and encourage you to take life less seriously. It promotes fidelity in relationships. As a self-healing stone, amber guides the emotions into a clearer mental outlook and to take greater responsibility for one's choices in life. It is also excellent for soothing emotions during post-operative care.

◆ **Amethyst**—A Master Healer, amethyst purifies and transmutes negativity. Amethyst provides protection and balance during transition periods. It reduces the feeling of being victimized, giving you a spiritual perspective on life's circumstances. The lavender-pink color amethyst relates to the heart chakra, to open and lighten up a betrayed heart and to heal the sense of loss of life and innocence. The blue-red color amethyst promotes a deep spiritual connection between one's self and one's life challenges, supporting the challenge one has taken on and giving patience and calmness despite overwhelming odds. The chevron amethyst (banded white and purple) helps peel away old karmic patterns to promote self-love and the ability to get along with others, especially with one's soul mate or family members.

> **Gem of an Idea**
>
> Wear the healing crystals discussed in this section as necklaces or pendants. Earrings and bracelets are nice as part of a set, but the real healing comes from the heart chakra level.

◆ **Apache tears (obsidian)**—Known as the "grief stone," Apache tears allow for tears to be shed, stimulating emotional spontaneity and the release of barriers that prevent you from experiencing deep sorrow. This stone is excellent for transmuting one's own negativity under stressful situations. The Apache tear is a dark black stone of obsidian and, when held up to the light, appears transparent. However, it has been noted that the grief one feels goes into the stone and can turn it opaque.

♦ **Jade**—The "crystal of tranquility," jade soothes the emotions and helps keep the peace for community relations. It provides a sense of self-worth and self-sufficiency and capability in dealing with any situation. Jade promotes harmony, balance, and tranquility through emotional detachment. Like amber, jade is excellent for recovery after an unpleasant experience (minor surgery, divorce, funerals, loss of job, and so on).

♦ **Jasper**—Known as the "nurturing stone," jasper makes it easier to use one's own power and to know that it cannot be taken away. It calms aggressive energy and facilitates safety and protection during recovery periods (such as from stress, operations, and other life traumas). Red jasper provides lively fresh energy and reduces feelings of being victimized. Yellow jasper balances hormones and protects the wearer during travel. Green jasper restores energy and focus during recovery from burnout.

♦ **Red coral**—Red coral is known as a "woman's stone." It quiets the emotions and dispels feelings of despair and despondency. It encourages a passionate energy and stimulates and strengthens female reproductive organs through tissue regeneration. This stone relates well to the spleen meridian for blood circulation and to purification of the kidneys and bladder. Red coral is considered to be the blood of Mother Earth by Native Americans and is considered particularly precious by Tibetan women for menstruation, fertility, and blood disorders.

♦ **Rose quartz**—The "love stone," rose quartz is a Master Healer and transmutes emotional negativity at all levels. It enhances healing by balancing energy and hormonal fluctuations. Rose quartz embodies the expression "love conquers all." It is excellent for calming the heart and solar plexus chakras after situations involving emotional upheaval, chaos, trauma, or crisis. Rose quartz allows love to come to wearers who have trouble finding love within themselves to give to either themselves or others. This is also a great friendship stone to give to someone you care for.

♦ **Smoky quartz**—Another Master Healer, smoky quartz is the "emotional balancer crystal" and clears and transmutes negative emotions. This crystal is an excellent stabilizer for mood swings and grounds all kinds of negative energy. It is an excellent crystal to use in times of stress and to rebuild emotional burnout by offering protection during the healing period. Smoky quartz reduces the fear of failure, unblocks self-limitations, and lets you risk trying some new experiences.

Gem of an Idea _____

Need a crystal to ease the monthly physical and emotional tension that accompanies PMS? Smoky quartz is it—and it also works well to quell general crankiness!

◆ **Sodalite**—A "stone of peace," sodalite helps alleviate insomnia caused by overactive mental chatter. It helps to dispel irrelevant thoughts, provides mental focus, and maintains logical reasoning with regard to emotional upsets. Sodalite promotes issues of trust and enhances companionship and the commonality of goals with others. It is excellent for busy women who need to relax and restore their mental energies.

Health, harmony, and hormones all in balance ... you can't argue with that! Just be sure to use your chosen crystals with consistency and intention for best results.

Health and Harmony for Teens

There are five issues where teens might need some healing tools to deal with certain issues that are relevant to personal health and harmony. (Adults, children, and even seniors might also benefit from these crystals.) Here are some suggestions on how to use the crystals as well as a listing of recommended crystals that can be used to alleviate symptoms. You can also wear up to five of these crystals at the heart, throat, and/ or solar plexus chakras:

◆ **Trouble sleeping**—Sleeplessness often comes because our minds are troubled by what has happened during the day. We lie awake still running the activities through our brains like an endless movie. Crystals help to regulate mental activity and calm extra energy. Select one of the recommended crystals below and place the crystal on your chest for about 10 to 15 minutes before sleeping, or sleep with the crystal tucked under your pillow.

Recommended crystals: Sodalite, blue lace agate, rose quartz, amethyst

◆ **Unsettled feelings/feeling off-center**—Feeling weird or unbalanced is not uncommon among teens with hormonal and emotional fluctuations. The teen brain also makes many changes. Teens will often need the recommended crystals to center themselves and to help ground their energies so they can be used more effectively in day-to-day living. Wear one of the recommended crystals by itself at the heart chakra for best effect.

Recommended crystals: Lapis lazuli, selenite, Herkimer diamond, clear quartz cluster, double-terminated clear quartz crystal

◆ **Fears**—There are many reasons people have fear. There are many types of fears such as fear of being in a closed space (claustrophobia), stage fright, fear of failure, fear of rejection, and fear of the unknown. Crystals can help reduce the severity of fear and nervousness. Wear the crystals for several days before engaging in a known event that scares you. Hold the crystal in your hand for deeper effect. Put your fears into the crystal and let the crystal energy work with you.

Recommended crystals: Petrified wood, aquamarine, sugilite, sodalite, amber, Apache tears

◆ **Self-esteem**—Low self-esteem is caused by thinking of yourself in a negative way such as being a failure or as having self-doubt in your own abilities. A number of crystals help support a person and provide both nurturing and healing at many levels. Orange carnelian is an especially powerful crystal for self-esteem. It is also good for skin complaints such as acne and rosacea. This crystal is best when worn at the heart chakra to provide nurturing to a depleted energy system. Others might notice your brighter outlook even before you do!

Recommended crystals: Carnelian, amethyst, rose quartz

◆ **Memory and logic**—Who wouldn't want a crystal to provide improved mathematical abilities and increase memory? The recommended crystals help to provide precision, the ability to see relationships between things, and a coordinated response to problem solving. These crystals aren't usually worn on the body because they aren't suitable as jewelry. The best way to use them is to hold them in your hand and gaze at them, sleep with them near your head, or keep them on your desk when you study to enhance your recall of information. The crystals will help declutter and restructure your left brain where logic abilities reside.

Recommended crystals: Pyrite, purple fluorite, geodes

You can't skip through the teen years altogether, but the right gemstones can make them a heck of a lot easier on you and your adolescent!

Crystals for Children

Crystals are truly gifts from the earth. Children seem to have a natural attraction to pick them up and fully explore any kind of stone or crystal. They will often use all their senses, seeing what the crystal looks like, feeling the texture with their fingertips, or even rubbing the crystal against other parts of their body. They are curious to know what it smells like, and what it sounds like when the crystal drops on the ground or plops into water.

Yellow Flag

Some children use their psychic senses, "hearing" what the crystal is saying to them, or they will mysteriously use the crystal for healing without any instructions whatsoever. Children can respond very quickly to the healing energy of crystals. However, please consult the best available qualified medical help on the care of your children, and use your common sense in regards to your children's health and wellness.

Some children suffer from many different physical ailments at different times as they grow up. Having a crystal such as amethyst can help remove pain when properly directed. At the emotional level there are crystals to help with feeling afraid or lonely, such as rose quartz, turquoise, or sugilite. Some children seem to be very spiritually advanced and need to have a crystal like lapis lazuli that protects their energy fields or their minds from the thoughts of others. Children are part of the mosaic of Earth and can't often speak for their spiritual needs, because they lack an adult vocabulary. That does not mean, however, that they don't have spiritual needs. They do.

The following crystals can help in your child's healing at the physical, emotional, and spiritual levels. Let your child carry the crystal in her pocket, or place one or two in a small medicine bag around your child's neck. Let your child even sleep with her special crystal. Crystals often get lost or misplaced by children, so you might want to have a few extras on hand.

◆ **Amethyst**—Amethyst helps children in transition, whether it be a growth spurt, a major disappointment such as failing a grade, or even hearing the devastating news of divorce or death. Amethyst accepts all negative emotions and provides comfort through spiritual acceptance. For children with various physical or emotional disabilities, an amethyst cluster in the room will help clear unwanted discharged energies, bringing the room back into a balanced state. For pain on the body, hold an amethyst directly on or over the area for up to 20 minutes.

- **Aventurine**—The "leadership stone," aventurine strengthens and restores the heart energy, providing a balance of male and female energies. This crystal is green, loving, embracing, and protective of the heart. Many children who are shy, timid, or suppressing their leadership qualities need a crystal like aventurine. This stone helps the individual to become active and initiate action on her own accord. Asthmatic children seem attracted to this stone because it opens up the lungs, so they experience a sense of relief.

- **Carnelian**—Carnelian, the "self-esteem crystal," is used to help restore feelings of inadequacy and low self-esteem. The deep orange colors relate well to strengthening and blending the first, second, and third chakras, promoting self-security and self-love. The pinker shades relate to enhancing love between child and parent through self-acceptance. This crystal is also used for dermatological ailments such as acne by holding the stone over the skin and moving it in circles for several minutes several times a day.

- **Lapis lazuli**—A "psychic balance stone," lapis lazuli is an incredible stabilizer for children who show psychic gifts early in life. The deep blue color stimulates expansion of consciousness in a supportive way, promoting purification and clarity of spiritual insight. Lapis lazuli provides self-acceptance of one's given gifts and encourages openness of one's spiritual awareness. This stone is highly prized for its protective powers and stimulation of all psychic senses.

- **Pyrite**—Iron pyrite, a "protection stone," comes in many shapes, from sun discs to cubes. Children are attracted to its shiny brassy surfaces. Pyrite is like a small mirror; negative energy is reflected away. The terror of being unprotected is reduced. There is also a feeling of physical empowerment, that life in the physical form is perfect, and love is abundant.

- **Rose quartz**—Rose quartz is another terrific general healing crystal for children, especially for those who have a lot of hurt feelings or aggressive tendencies. Rose quartz can soothe a broken heart shattered by seeing raw reality—the ways things are, rather than the way one wants them to be. For hyperactive children, rose quartz soothes erratic emotional states, anxiety, fear, compulsions, and many other mental disorders. Some neurological benefits have also been noticed with muscle spasms relaxing when rose quartz is guided over the nerve centers. For young hearts, rose quartz helps to keep the heart chakra open, vital, and protected, filtering in good energies and keeping out the bad.

♦ **Tiger eye**—Tiger eye is a "grounding stone." When rocked back and forth, the light reflects in a certain way as if the tiger's eye were winking at you. Let your children explore this fascinating stone and help them find the flashing tiger's eye. This stone is excellent for grounding psychic energy and providing security for opening up the psychic centers. Sometimes children get carried away and get lost in their dream worlds. Tiger eye helps to pull them back into their bodies (after astral travel). This stone is useful in putting action to one's thoughts. Tiger eye is about being practical. Perhaps every parent needs one for their child before trips to the shopping mall!

You can help with your child's interest in the mineral kingdom. Take your children to a rock shop, gem and mineral show, and museums, as well as to land areas of high mineral content (check a geological survey map) such as quarries, caves, and mines. Let your children pick crystals for themselves. Often they will select a crystal that is helpful to their healing process.

One four-year-old girl I met selected an Apache tears, which is typically used for the grieving process. The little girl, clutching it in her hand, remarked, "Oh, I want to wear this all the time!" I asked the mother if there had been a death in the family recently. Astonished, she replied, "I just lost my brother four weeks ago, but we didn't tell her." The girl was obviously sensitive to the family's sorrow and needed some protection from the feelings of others around her.

> **Yellow Flag**
>
> Don't let children put crystals into their mouth; some, like malachite, contain high levels of copper.

Healing Animals with Crystals

Using crystals for healing pets and animals can produce quick results. A few years ago I was using crystals for healing at a horse farm when one horse was severely bitten over the eye by another during exuberant play. The horse owner immediately brought the injured horse to me; it was profusely bleeding from a 4-inch gash above its eye. I had just been demonstrating the use of a crystal wand to my students.

The wand was made of a large amethyst crystal fixed to a 2-foot copper wand.

> **Crystal Clear**
>
> Not all crystal healings are as spontaneous as the horse whose injury was healed, but crystals generally provide an acceleration of the healing process.

I pointed the wand to the area above the horse's eye and held it several inches away, holding it steady. Within 30 seconds the blood flow had stopped. Over the next few minutes, we were amazed to see that scar tissue was starting to form. The owner, Lorna, was delighted because she said the crystal healing had saved her an emergency visit by the vet to sew up the gash.

Getting Started

Some very simple crystal healing techniques can be used to help your pet or animal friend be more comfortable during times of stress or illness. Healing animals requires the healer to have a strong and centered mind. An animal's mind is not like a human's. Humans *relate* to pain; animals *react* to pain.

In other words, when you work on your pet, know when enough is enough. Watch for tell-tale signs: tail swishing, foot stamping, laying the ears back, teeth-baring, hair-raising, attempts to flee, and other warnings. Crystal healing can sometimes be too fast for the animal to integrate, or it can be too intense and might cause pain and other discomfort. As crystal energy promotes rapid healing, easing off might help alleviate the stress caused by a healing crisis. When the healing is good, the animal will show signs of comfort and affection, such as eye-lids drooping, teeth gnashing, drooling, general softening of muscle tissues, and sighing.

Healing Pets

The following are some suggestions for using crystals for healing pets and animals. It is not intended that this information replace the advice of a professionally qualified veterinarian. As always, seek the best available competent medical advice for your pet or animal. If you are attending an animal in pain after being hit by a car, for example, the animal is not going to be receptive to being handled and will probably bite or strike out. In such cases, they should be attended to with proper emergency veterinary care.

For best results, remember to use fully cleansed and charged crystals for animal healing sessions, and cleanse them after each use:

◆ Place amethyst or rose quartz underneath your pet-friend's bed or pillow for up to two weeks. Be cautious of sharp edges, and position the stones to be comfortable and safe for your pet. If the crystal energy is too intense, your pet will be agitated and might not want to rest in his bed. If your pet likes the crystals, you will see an improvement in his health within a few days.

◆ Choose a crystal from the list in the next section. Hold it in your hand, and starting a few inches away from the affected part or injured area, rotate the crystal clockwise. Take your time, go slow, and breathe gently and evenly. Animals express their emotions with movement, so watch to see if your pet wants more or tries to move away.

◆ Get a small pouch that can attach to a collar, and place up to three small crystals inside it. If you put too many crystals in it, your pet might feel disoriented. Be careful that the pouch does not interfere with movement or cause it to be caught on anything.

◆ Warm up crystals in the sun before your healing session. The sun gives masculine, active yang energy to the crystals. Apply the warm crystals to injured areas. If you are using an ice bag to reduce swellings, try a few tumbled smoky quartz with the ice to help unblock overactive or inflamed areas.

You can also add a rose quartz or amethyst to your pet-friend's water bowl or bucket. The crystal will leave its energy signature in the water and, when your pet drinks, the energy will go where it is most needed. (Just make sure your pet can't chew on or swallow the crystal!)

> **Yellow Flag** _____
>
> Malachite should only be used externally. Never put malachite in drinking water because the high copper content is poisonous. Do not permit your pet or animal to lick or eat this crystal! Even consuming small amounts can lead to serious or fatal blood poisoning. And just for safety's sake, leave *all* crystals out of your pet's reach when you aren't around.

Crystals for Animals

The following is a list of generally available crystals and gemstones and their associated physical healing focus. Use as recommended in the previous section in a water dish (except for malachite; see the previous sidebar), for direct healing by holding the crystal over the area, or in pouches.

◆ **Amethyst (Master Healer)**—Use for all healings: pain, fear, disorientation, and healing the head area.

◆ **Black onyx**—Bowels, parasites, protection from diseases.

◆ **Calcite**—Skeletal strengthening and bone mending.

- **Carnelian**—Skin, boils, lesions, bruises, scrapes.

- **Clear quartz (Master Healer)**—Effective for all conditions.

- **Coral**—Kidneys, bladder.

- **Fluorite**—Use blue for bones; blue/green or clear for respiration; green for blood purification or lymph; and green/yellow for digestion.

- **Garnet**—Reproductive system and physical stamina.

- **Hematite**—Muscular system; it reduces pain.

- **Kyanite**—Alignment of all chakras (yes, animals have chakras, too!), tendons, and bones.

- **Malachite**—Blood and liver cleanser, for heart problems, liver detoxification.

- **Rose quartz (Master Healer)**—Use for injuries, for wounds, and to reduce stress.

- **Smoky quartz**—Nervous system, swellings, hostility.

- **Sodalite**—Calming, for nervousness, and for settling down during travel.

- **Sugilite**—For comforting a lonely or dying pet.

- **Turquoise (Master Healer)**—Use for healing and protection from illness.

It is important to be balanced, centered, and grounded and to have good intentions and no distractions before you attempt these crystal healing techniques. Crystals tend to amplify the effects, and you will need to be cautious until you determine how your pet will react.

The Least You Need to Know

- Men can use crystals for healing and support by wearing them in pouches or pockets or using them overnight.

- Women can find solace in crystals for physical healing and emotional support.

- Teens can use crystals to improve their studies and to find comfort in physical and emotional stresses.

- Children have a natural attraction for crystals that can provide them with a means to meet their special psycho-spiritual needs.

- Animals respond very quickly to crystals due to their highly sensitive natures, so use care until you know how an animal will react.

Chapter 15

Crystals for the Curious

In This Chapter

- Crystal water
- Gem essences
- Make up a crystal power pack
- Using crystals in other crafts

As a crystal healing therapist, I regularly talk to people about which gemstones are best to hold while meditating, which crystals calm and soothe the chakras, or how to do a whole-body crystal layout. Now I want to share some different uses for crystals with you—techniques that are practical, fun, and easy to do! You might even make some gifts for your friends from these suggestions.

Healing with Crystal Water

No doubt you have heard of special places where you can drink natural spring water coming from a sacred site like Lourdes or from the holy wells in England. There have been many claims of healing from drinking sacred water. These healing waters are available throughout the world.

When water travels through the underground, it becomes electromagnetically charged by piezoelectric energy emanating from the bedrock, which, interestingly, contains various crystals. The water also picks up an energetic field unique to its location. When we drink this water, we are actually getting crystal-charged water!

Because our bodies are approximately two-thirds water, the electrolytes contained within each cell can be manipulated and changed by the crystal-charged water. Electrolytes are responsible for carrying nerve impulses and muscle contractions, so if they are out of balance or in poor condition, the ramifications could be quite serious.

When we drink crystal water, the crystal energy will work its way into each cell and transfer light in the form of ions to the body's systems. An electrolyte conducts electricity and works with piezoelectric energy introduced from a crystal. So just as we can program a computer and make it faster and stronger, we can program the crystal water through intention to create healing energy structures. Imagine that!

Mixing Up a Batch of Crystal Water

The traditional way to create crystal water from gemstones is to place a few cleansed crystals, such as clear quartz or rose quartz, in a clear glass jar and fill it with spring water. Why spring water, you ask? Well, spring water already carries a universal life force and electromagnetic properties. When this combines with the power of the crystals, you have a regular life-sustaining elixir on your hands!

To infuse your spring water with crystal power, place the crystals in the jar with a clear glass lid in direct sunlight for 4 to 7 hours. (Be sure the jar is in a safe place and won't tip over or be hidden by an approaching shadow.) After crystallizing the water, remove the crystals using a slotted metal spoon, and transfer the crystallized water to an airtight bottle. Drink the water within a few hours because the potency decreases rapidly over time.

Yellow Flag

Malachite, also known as copper carbonate, has a high copper content and reacts with acids so it should not be used for making crystal water. It should especially not be given to animals. Also avoid azurite, orpiment (contains arsenic), and cinnabar (contains mercury). Commercially prepared essences of gemstones or homeopathic doses that use dilution methods are generally safe.

When you sip your crystal-infused water, you will find that the plain old spring water will have changed its quality. It will feel different, more full or thicker in your mouth and less watery. This is because it has started to take on the properties of the crystals and become heavier.

What kind of benefits can you expect from drinking crystal water? They're similar to wearing crystals, except you will feel them at a subtle level within your body tissues as the chi or prana gets reenergized. If you are sensitive to your external energy, you might also be aware that your aura is brightening.

You can use different combinations of crystals in your water for special concerns. For example, tiger eye and azurite help you to focus on school studies, while carnelian and opal help to rejuvenate the skin. For skin issues such as eczema or rashes, infuse the water with the colors yellow or orange by using an orange- or amber-colored glass to make the crystal water. Try making and using the crystal water three days in a row for amazing results.

Because the crystal water has to be consumed within a rather short period of time to receive its benefits, I recommend using a small-ish jar to steep it in. Another nice thing about this process is that you're killing two birds with one stone—making a wellness energy drink for yourself while recharging your crystals in the sun.

Other Uses for Crystal Water

Remember that crystal water must be used within a few hours or be disposed of. If you happen to have some crystal-infused water left over, or you want to find more uses for this amazing liquid, here are some ideas for putting the extras to good use:

♦ Pour any remaining water into your flower pots to energize your plants. Crystal water is especially excellent for seeds and starter plants. If you have an ailing tree or shrub, pour a circle of crystal water around its base a few times a month.

♦ Use a natural fabric such as cotton or a sea sponge to soak up crystal water, and then place the damp cloth on sore muscles or on the forehead for headaches and sinus issues.

♦ Pour the water into an atomizer, a plastic sprayer, or a misting machine, and spritz the room and your bed linens. Add a few drops of essential oils for increasing subtle effects. Clary sage and frankincense are cleansing and neutralizes negative vibrations in a room. Geranium, mandarin orange, and peppermint create an uplifting and joyous environment. Try combining crystals and essential oils such as amethyst and lavender for peace and relaxation prior to meditation or yoga.

My favorite room blend of crystal water is rose quartz, amethyst, and blue lace agate with a combination of clary sage, lavender, and orange essential oils. The room becomes warm and welcoming, imparting a brighter, lighter, and higher vibration in the room.

◆ Spritz yourself, too, and be sure to get a dab in each chakra.

The Healing Power of Gem Essences

Have you ever wondered why there are so many medicines to do the same thing? Well, what works for one person doesn't necessarily work for someone else. Each one of us may need a different type of medicine for healing. The same is true to some degree with crystals simply because each crystal is different and so is each person's energetic field.

What if there was a method of getting a standard dose of crystal healing power? There is! A *gem essence* provides the same jolt of energy to everyone because it provides the vibrational essence of the gem. A gem essence is a method used to preserve the special essence of crystal water. Our human systems accept the essence and can fully integrate it as part of our own energy. This type of subtle material used for healing is called *energy medicine*.

def•i•ni•tion

A **gem essence** is a homeopathically prepared solution made by using sunlight to infuse spring water with the characteristics of specific crystals. **Energy medicine** is a method of healing that restores balance to the body's energy field to bring about health and wellness.

A gem essence is like crystal water, except it has longer-lasting healing power. Start the same way as making crystal water, but to hold the gem essence within the water so it can be stored for a longer time, you'll add alcohol to stabilize the energetic properties. That's common for stabilizing homeopathic solutions. Here's how to make a gem essence:

1. Place a few cleansed crystals, such as clear quartz or rose quartz, in a small- to medium-size clear glass jar, and fill it with spring water.

2. Set the jar in the sun and ensure it is exposed to full sunlight during the peak hours of the day when ultraviolet light is at its strongest. Place a clear glass lid over the top. You can also use a quartz crystal singing bowl to make the gem essence so there are no energetic obstacles.

3. If you can, stay by the water jar or bowl with the crystals soaking up the sun for a little while, focusing on positive thoughts, prayer or meditation; this will help to bind the pattern for healing in the water. Remember Emoto's findings about the water crystals being structured through thought from Chapter 3? Your prayers and focused intent will be magnified by the crystal and the water will take on the healing properties of the crystal.

4. After 7 to 9 hours of sun exposure, pour off the water into a sterile pitcher without touching the water to keep the gem water pure. You can use another crystal to prevent the crystals from falling out as you pour.

5. To stabilize the gem essence, a homeopathic method is used by mixing a good VSOP (Very Special Old Pale) brandy in with the crystal water. Using a sterilized 2-ounce amber-colored bottle with a glass dropper, fill the bottle halfway. Pour in brandy to fill. An amber-colored bottle is used because the gem essence is light sensitive. Shake the bottle 32 times to disperse the alcohol and activate the ingredients.

6. Label the gem essence with the name of the crystal used and the date it was made.

The usual gem essence dose is 2 to 4 drops, 3 to 5 times a day as needed. A course of treatment should not exceed six weeks because sensitivity to the formula decreases when the energy is integrated over time. There are no known toxic effects to gem essences. However, you might notice some effects over the first few days of taking the formula. You can also add up to 8 drops to plain bath water to soak your entire body (and chakras!) for 20 minutes in the gem essence.

The gem essence will keep for several months. It's okay to keep the essence in the refrigerator if you want to store it for up to six months, but the constant vibration and electrical circuitry of the fridge may lessen its potency. Use of the amber bottle prevents contact with sunlight, which would definitely decrease its potency.

Some gem essences can be applied topically for physical healing. Add 4 to 8 drops of gem essence to an 8-ounce bowl of water. Soak some cotton batting in the solution and apply the gem essence externally. Here are some suggested gem essences for topical application:

◆ **Amethyst**—To ease headache or stress, apply to the forehead and temples.

◆ **Carnelian**—For skin complaints such as rashes, pimples, or redness, apply over the area.

- ◆ **Hematite**—Apply to sore muscles and painful joints and bruises.

- ◆ **Rose quartz**—To alleviate inflammation in the joints, place batting soaked in essence over the joints.

- ◆ **Tiger eye**—Apply to the stomach area to calm a stomachache and aid the digestive organs.

- ◆ **Turquoise**—To cool a fever, apply to the forehead; to reduce a sore throat, apply over the throat.

Crystal Power Packs

Small crystals have great benefits when grouped together in a bag. You can create your own power pack of crystals from chipped gemstones or crystals that are too small for big healing issues. Remember that *all* crystals, regardless of their size, have piezoelectric characteristics.

Here are some ideas for using the power of many tiny crystals:

- ◆ Find a little bag—cotton, silk, or another natural fabric—and place your crystal pieces inside. Place the bag in the refrigerator and use it to cool irritated eyes, sore sinuses, and headaches.

- ◆ Placing a crystal pack at the top and bottom of a bone (for example, at the wrist and elbow or knee and hip) for 3 to 5 minutes will help clear the meridians of stagnant chi.

- ◆ Add some herbs to the crystal pack, such as lavender for relaxation or peppermint to perk up your energy. (It is not recommended to use herbs *in* crystal eye packs because dust and particles from the herbs can cause eye irritation.)

- ◆ To enhance dreaming, make a dream pillow using rainbow-colored crystals. Select some brightly colored crystals, but limit the crystals to seven; otherwise, your head will be too "buzzy" to sleep. Place the dream pack under your pillow, or if your body needs to relax, place it on or under your belly. Some crystals that enhance dreaming are mookite, the Australian dream crystal; labradorite; and moldavite. Place these crystals under your pillow or tape a small piece to your third eye chakra.

How about some special help for insomniacs, those of us who are so plugged into work and other stresses at the end of the day that nighttime relaxation is all but impossible? A different kind of sleep pack is helpful for chronic restlessness and anxiety. Try these ideas:

- **Hematite**—It is physically and mentally calming and will help to deflect and transform unwanted energies into universal light. If you are physically uncomfortable at night, tape pieces onto your body at the joints or around sore spots.

- **Kunzite**—It has a high lithium content and helps a whirling, neurotic, obsessive mind to calm down and relax. Wearing the crystal at the heart chakra throughout the day provides the most help. For people who wake up earlier than expected without full rest, you can actually use this crystal to reduce anxiety over not requiring enough sleep! Many people sleep less than five hours a night with no ill effects. In fact, I sleep less than six hours a night surrounded by crystals. They provide me with energy and help me maintain a higher vibrational rate.

- **Lepidolite**—It can be used during the day to help offset the build-up of muscle tension so you are more relaxed by bedtime. You can also use the crystal if you wake up during the night to settle an overactive mind and reduce a build-up of physical tension. Holding one loosely in each hand will help you drift back to sleep.

- **Moonstone**—It is a very old remedy for calming emotional distress that activates insomnia. It helps to reduce emotional tension. Moonstone is the yin energy, the feminine. It helps to stimulate self-composure and self-confidence. I keep pieces of moonstone by my windowsill during the full moon to absorb the lunar rays. When needed, place the crystal on the solar plexus or heart chakra against bare skin and focus on the crystal to activate it before sleeping.

Gem of an Idea

Make a baby dream pillow, about 4 inches square, to place under a baby's bed (it's safest there!) to help her relax and align her subtle bodies as she goes through rapid growth. Some calming and soothing sleep crystals that babies and young children like are rose quartz, sodalite, amethyst, and moonstone.

- **Sodalite**—It is a crystal of peace that helps to calm mental chatter and confusion. Putting the crystal under your feet will calm your whole body. Placing the crystals around your head or in your pillow at night will also promote mental relaxation. You can also program the crystal with an affirmation such as, "I am now relaxed and sleepy."

You can also try a layout of these crystals around your bed placed under the bed sheets, under your pillow, in your pillowcase, or taped onto your chakras.

To cleanse a crystal sleep pack, smudging is best. When you are finished using your pack, recycle the crystals by giving them a good cleanse in salt water and letting them recharge for at least a few days in the sunlight. (Review Chapter 7 for details on cleansing, recharging, and smudging your crystals.)

Other Crystal Crafts

When you incorporate crystals into crafts, you're getting more bang for your buck, so to speak. First, you're creating something that's lovely to look at or that has a specific use; second, you're harnessing and using positive energy in a new, fun way! If you happen to be very crafty and need lots of gemstones to work with, you can buy crystals in bulk. Ask your local gem seller for assistance.

Blessing Salt

There is an ancient tradition of using salt to provide a blessing and clearing of negative energy. Remember that salt is also a crystal: rock salt is pure sodium chloride. However, for blessing salt, sea salt is preferred because its composition is more highly organized and has higher ion content to carry white light used for healing purposes.

The blessing salt is generally consecrated by a priest; you can do your own salt blessing through prayer, such as the following, by invoking any source (for example, a saint, an angel, or a deity) you wish to do the job:

> "Bless this salt with your loving energy and with all your power to remove all obstacles, and any ill intent, misdeeds, or bad influences, and help me to create a space where evil thoughts cannot dwell and disease is repelled. Where sprinkled, no harm or wrong doing may occur. No enemies to body, mind, and spirit may take hold. All is cleansed in the pure white light of your compassion."

Ways to use a blessing salt include:

♦ Add a small amount of blessing salt to water and use the water for cleansing crystals.

♦ Toss a few grains onto new crystals to cleanse and bless them before using them.

- Sprinkle some salt in the four corners of a room to bless and purify the room.

- Sprinkle some salt across doorways and at windows to help keep your home safe.

- Add a few grains to drinking water or add to a salt shaker to season food for increased personal benefit.

- Mix some dry rice with salt to prevent clumping in shakers.

- Sprinkle salt over popcorn or other food.

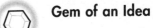

Gem of an Idea

A small sachet of sea salt, dried lavender, and sage leaf can be used as a blessing salt, and it makes a terrific and thoughtful gift. Add a few sprinkles of metallic paper stars and crescent moons to add to the alchemy. Add a card of instructions for cleansing crystals (soak crystals overnight using 2 teaspoons of the salt in 8 ounces of water).

This is an easy and versatile way to include the healing energy of crystals in almost any activity. Even Japanese sumo wrestlers come into the ring and throw handfuls of salt around to purify the ring because they know salt clears negative energy.

Pet Crystals

Pet rocks were all the rage in the 1970s. Smooth rocks with plastic doll eyes were packaged and sold in cardboard pet crates as a marketing gimmick. The instruction booklet instructed that pet rocks required no feeding, walking, or grooming. No wonder they were so popular! Well, we're going to create a pet crystal. Any crystal will do, but clear quartz, rose quartz, and various agates are particularly appealing to the eye. Sodalite is another good choice; it's a popular crystal that promotes peace, provides restful sleep by reducing mind-chatter and worrying, improves communication, and soothes the emotions.

You'll need supplies to create a face, such as doll eyes, paint for facial expressions, and maybe some cloth to glue on to resemble a hat or clothing. You'll need a container to put your "pet" in, maybe a small basket or a plastic eggshell, if it's very small. Use your imagination. Give it the personality you'd like to see in the crystal.

When you choose the crystal for your pet, consider its characteristics and what it's most commonly used for. (See Appendix A for complete information.) Then place your pet on your desk or in a place where you will see it often and draw energy from it. Although it doesn't need walking or feeding, pet it every once in a while to make a physical connection with it! This can be a fun way to introduce children to crystals.

Mosaic Art

Did you ever have one of those mosaic art kits, using crushed, colored stone glued to a board with a design stamped on it? They are a lot of fun to work with, and the end products don't have to be perfect—they're interesting even if they have flaws. Well, guess what? You can make your own mosaic kit.

> **Gem of an Idea**
>
> You don't have to destroy your own crystal collection to make pieces small enough for a mosaic piece. Many gem and mineral shops sell crushed crystals in small bags—perfect for this project.

Create your own design from whatever you find spiritually inspiring; perhaps you feel compelled to create an angel, symbols from tarot cards, or a tree of life. Draw the design on a board. Paint the design with the colors of the crystals you will be using to provide a background. Glue white or colored cord onto the board, outlining each block of color to add definition. The cord will also help to keep the colored stones separate and will provide added dimension to your stone work!

Working one section at a time, add a thick layer of transparent glue to the board. Carefully sprinkle the crushed crystals into the section of the design, and press the crystals into the glue. Turn the picture upside down and gently tap it to remove any loose or excess crystals. Now work the next section in the same way, and the next, and the next. Let it dry overnight.

Frame and hang the board so you can receive the continual healing benefits of the crystals and the spiritual inspiration. Cleanse the board using incense, and recharge the crystals in the sun from time to time.

Crystal Kits and Gifts

All kinds of science kits are available for people of any age. Crystal growing kits are especially popular, providing all the materials needed for home-grown crystals, usually from chemical reactions. They are a lot of fun.

If your youngster needs a science project (or just wants to learn more about crystals), you can easily put your own crystal science kit together. Use a plastic tray with multiple sections, and add a card with the name of each crystal, where it was found, along with any other details such a Mohs hardness scale or lattice structure (see Chapter 2 for more information on these topics).

You can build a collection of stones and crystals representing each of the igneous, sedimentary, and metamorphic rock classifications we talked about in Chapter 2. Why not create a collection of crystals with different samples from each of the Mohs classifications? Use a Herkimer diamond or a clear rhinestone for Mohs #10 instead of a real diamond.

How about creating a chakra crystal kit with a crystal for each chakra? (I discuss the crystals that are recommended for each chakra in Chapter 6.) A rainbow pack of crystals along with a meditation CD would also make a lovely gift.

For someone who could use some healing, it's easy to put together a healing kit as a gift. Here's a sample kit:

- Hematite (muscle pain)
- Malachite (internal organs)
- Rose quartz (reduce inflammation)
- Carnelian (skin ailments)
- Calcite (bone)
- Green fluorite (digestion, colds)
- Amethyst (headache)

Add instructions on how to use the gemstones, such as placing the crystal on the area for up to 10 minutes or taping it on the area overnight. You can also create a kit for emotional healing and another kit for spiritual attunement. Personalize the kits with a special selection just for the recipient—one for a co-worker for his work stress, one for your sister to help with her pregnancy, one for an elderly person for aches and pains, and so on.

Crystals help stimulate creativity, so I'm sure once you get going, you will think up some more ideas on how to use crystals!

The Least You Need to Know

- Drinking crystal water brings additional crystal healing into the body. Other uses include mixing crystal water with essential oils and spritzing rooms and linens to refresh stale energy.
- A gem essence is a homeopathic mixture created with crystal energy.

◆ Crystal packs filled with gemstone chips can help soothe sore muscles and tired eyes and even alleviate insomnia.

◆ Making crafts with crystals is a fun way to include them in your everyday life and to absorb their positive energy.

Part 4

Crystal Healing Techniques

Working with subtle energies in and around the body requires some special techniques. Anyone can use these techniques and with practice can be very efficient using crystals for healing.

A crystal layout is a slightly more advanced way of using crystals. Crystals are laid on and around the body to increase the energy connections and healing potential of the crystals.

Part 4 gives you all the information you need to set up a relaxing crystal healing session for another person. It is recommended that you have a crystal healing session first to understand the nature and power of crystal energy.

Chapter 16

Crystal Clearing Techniques

In This Chapter

- Understanding vortexes of energy
- Clearing congestion in the chakras
- Aligning and balancing the chakras
- Aura cleansing with a partner
- Using a crystal wand

Sometimes you might feel sluggish, grumpy, lousy, and maybe even nasty toward other people. Or sometimes you become inactive because your lack of energy doesn't move you to do anything. What's really happening is that your energy is blocked somewhere in your subtle body. After you are cleared of blockages, your emotions and moods are lighter and you have oodles of energy.

To clear these blockages, some intervention is needed. With the right techniques, you can clear energy from yourself as well as others. Some of these methods are active; some are pretty passive. But all of them will get things moving along the energetic pathways, making you and/or your partner feel like your old selves again!

Vortexes of Energy

In Chapter 6 we talked about chakras, or the "wheels" or centers that help distribute energy throughout the body. Before we go any further into cleansing techniques, I want to make sure you have a clear idea of what we're talking about.

Think for a moment of a sink full of water. When you unplug the sink, a funnel of water slowly swirls in a counterclockwise rotation and zips down the drain, creating an *energy vortex*. Chakras are a little bit like that, taking in energy and pulling it into the central channel—the *sushumna*—that runs parallel to the spine and links the other chakras and subtle energies (the nadis) of the body.

When a crystal is placed near a chakra, it influences the subtle energy of *all* the chakras. The whirling chakras pull the energy modified by the structure of the crystal into the sushumna and nadis for distribution by following the programming in the crystal and intent of the healer.

def•i•ni•tion

An **energy vortex** is the rotation of energy that swirls around its center. The speed of energy is faster at the center than at its outer boundaries. The **sushumna** is the central channel in the chakra system to which the chakras are joined.

Obviously, the chakras are quite sensitive to crystal energy. Even if you are not fully aware of changes in your own subtle energy, it is best to start out slowly with the crystal exercises in the next section. As your subtle body becomes more energized and your awareness expands, you will become more and more sensitive to small changes. For this reason, I recommend that you always ground yourself very well before beginning this type of work, using the techniques in Chapter 6. No good can come from overwhelming the subtle body!

Clearing Chakra Congestion

Like a magnet, a crystal has the ability to pick up and absorb energy of all kinds. When a crystal absorbs negative energy, you can easily cleanse it by smudging it or placing it in an overnight salt water bath. But sometimes our chakras get cluttered with negative emotions and need a good cleaning, too. Up until now, you've done this by either wearing a crystal or placing one on your body or specifically at a chakra. Now you are going to learn another way to clear unwanted energy quickly from centers of energy.

Please note: When using a crystal for healing in the chakras, you need to be very gentle and move in slowly. Chakras are as delicate as tissue paper. Although they are a bit more elastic than paper, you need to be respectful of their capacities for change (some chakras do *not* like to be thrown for a loop!). Slow and steady wins the race here when it comes to transforming negative energy to positive.

Crystal Therapy System

Let's try an easy exercise using a more advanced crystal healing technique, just so you can see the effects of clearing a chakra using crystal therapy. Whereas holding a crystal or wearing one is a passive way to work with crystals, this technique, which is part of the *Crystal Therapy System (CTS)*, is a more dynamic way of working with crystals, meant to speed the opening, clearing, calming, rebuilding, and rebalancing of the chakras and other areas of energy distortion to affect a healing response.

def•i•ni•tion

Crystal Therapy System (CTS) is the crystal healing methodology I teach at the Crystal Alchemy Academy, a crystal healing school. The methodology is based on energy medicine and dynamic techniques for opening, clearing, calming, rebuilding, and rebalancing energy using crystals. The training program consists of four levels of instruction on crystal healing.

We'll use the throat chakra for this exercise because many people seem naturally more sensitive in this area. Later, you can try this with your heart or solar plexus chakra. Please read through the instructions first to make sure you understand and are comfortable with the entire process.

Your intent for this session is to clear any blockages in the throat chakra. Follow these simple steps:

1. You'll need a clear quartz crystal 1 to 2 inches long that has been cleansed and is fully charged.

2. Program the crystal with this affirmation: "I, [your name], now gently release all that is not for my highest good."

3. Before you go any further, you'll need to ground yourself very well (think of roots growing from under your feet). Relax your body by taking some deep breaths and checking for any tension.

4. Spend a few minutes in meditation and focus on your throat chakra. This will help to bring your energies to a ready state.

Hold your crystal in your right hand and slowly bring it up to your throat chakra, positioning the tip about 4 inches away. Hold the crystal still, pointing the tip into the center of the chakra. Let the chakra and the crystal unite in their energies. You might begin to feel a heaviness, a tingling, a gagging response, or some other sensation as the crystal starts to work in your energy field. If you do not feel your energy start to stir, continue to hold the crystal in position and allow your mind to relax. (Be patient—there's no right way or exact time frame for this!)

As the crystal bonds energetically with the area, the throat chakra will begin to open. Any negative energies that are ready to be released will be attracted to the crystal and be pulled from the chakra. Some of these negative energies will be transmuted into white light by the energy of the crystal. Other energies (such as blockages) will start to break up and stick to the crystal. Gather these energies from the chakra by slowly moving the crystal in a clockwise circle 3 to 4 inches wide. Now you are creating an energy vortex with the crystal to pull out unwanted energies.

Intense Release of Energy

To reduce the intensity of the session, reground yourself. You can also use a smaller crystal or hold the crystal farther away. Move it 10 to 15 inches away from your chakra, and hold it steady instead of moving it around the chakra.

As you feel the energy intensify, you can use the crystal to scoop the unwanted energy from the chakra and flick it away where it will be transmuted into white light. Continue to scoop and release the energies until you feel some lightness or clarity in the chakra (about 3 to 5 minutes).

Crystal Clear _____

If you feel an intensity building up during this process, it's okay; it's just your own unwanted energy that has been stuck trying to release itself. Breathing deeply and quickly can help alleviate any discomfort. Stay with the feeling. It's like exercising a muscle. There are bound to be some cramps along the way, but it's worth it for the end results.

Your breathing will probably change into a deeper cleansing breath as you relax further. This will be a sign that you have finished clearing. As the clearing happens, you might also experience related energy releases such as yawning. Just think, all that energy was stuck there! Clearing it now helps to reduce the possibility for disease or emotional issues later.

Put the crystal aside for cleansing later with a salt bath or smudging and recharging the next day. This type of crystal energy work runs down the crystal's internal battery, but your own energy should feel lighter because you have cleansed energy that might have been dragging you down.

Aligning and Balancing Your Chakra in Seconds

Chakras not only need to be cleansed, but also need to be aligned every so often. As humans, we encounter many bumps along the road, both emotional and physical. Reassessing and realigning energy keeps us moving at a steady clip and prevents major breakdowns. The use of kyanite for chakra work is not known or practiced by many, yet it is very effective.

So what does a chakra alignment actually do? The chakras are fragile yet substantial enough for almost everything we experience throughout our lives, including falling off bicycles, falling in love, walking down grocery aisles, or walking down *the* aisle. Chakras respond to everyday stresses by floating around a bit in their positions. They are structured like a flower with petals that open and close to protect subtle energy from damage.

Some shocks are just too much and can cause a misalignment of the subtle body energy. Take, for example, a car accident that results in a whiplash injury. The rapid extension of the head forward and back can snap the third eye and crown chakras out of place. So in addition to the physical injury to the neck muscles, some of the shock you feel is your subtle body being yanked out of alignment. Doctors and physiotherapists work on your physical body, but the subtle body also needs repair.

For this exercise, you will need a piece of kyanite, which has a natural alignment in its structure and can align energy sideways as well as up and down. (That's perfect for the throat chakra because it balances like your head on your neck.) The crystal should be a length no less than 2 inches long and ½ inch wide. Hold the crystal with one end pointing directly into the center of each chakra for a count of 7 or 21 seconds each, depending on whether you need a minor adjustment or a bit more work.

Crystal Clear

Kyanite is sometimes called a kyanite *wand* because the crystal is often long, flat, and split like a wooden stick. Kyanite is recommended as part of the crystal toolkit in Chapter 7.

You can confirm how aligned your chakras feel by using a pendulum to ask if all chakras are aligned. If you get a "no," ask which chakra should be redone. When you are in alignment, you will find yourself standing and sitting tall and your response to every-day stress will be minimal. Chakra energy changes throughout the day, so some people like to wear a small piece of kyanite to keep their energy in align-ment and flowing freely longer.

Another nice benefit of this crystal is that you do not need to worry about cleansing or charging it because it's one of the few crystals that is constantly charged and never needs cleansing! Placed close to other crystals, it helps align their energies as well.

Aura Clearing with a Partner

Now how would you like to do some more crystal healing, but this time with a part-ner? The following exercise is part of the aura balance and clearing techniques taught in my crystal classes. The exercise helps to warm up the aura by circulating energy and activating the subtle energies. You will be using the crystal to sweep the aura of impurities. The aura will be balanced, meaning that the energies will flow smoothly. The exercise also helps to open the hand chakras for even more sensitivity to crystals.

Yellow Flag

As with any crystal work, grounding is important. Both you and your partner can stand facing each other. Each of you should visualize roots under your feet anchoring you deep into the ground for a couple of minutes before beginning this exercise.

(Yes, even your hands have energy centers, although they are not as powerful as the major chakra centers discussed in Chapter 6.) Your partner in this exercise needs to be willing to participate and remain open-minded to experiencing crystal energy work.

As the healer in this case, select a cleansed and charged quartz crystal point 3 to 5 inches long in either rose quartz, clear quartz, or amethyst. These Master Healers already know how to work with the human aura and are gentle balancers of energy.

Before you begin, inform your partner that you can stop at any time—and be sure you do stop if you're asked to. When a person closes up his or her energy, there is no point in continuing anyway. Even if your partner says nothing but seems uncomfort-able, offer to stop. Checking in from time to time is standard practice among healers.

Now follow these steps:

1. Stand facing each other. As the crystal healer, you can call in your own healing spirits or those of your partner for help in this session. Recite a simple prayer request, such as:

"Masters, Guardians, Teachers, and Guides. I ask for your protection and assistance during this healing session. Please provide for conscious awareness and direction for healing [name of the partner]. Let all activity be conducted for the highest good of [name of the partner]."

2. Hold your crystal in your right hand close to your heart chakra to receive its energy and to warm up the crystal and connect with your energy at the heart level.

3. Visualizing white light radiating from the tip of the crystal, point the crystal at a spot between the arches, about 6 to 12 inches below your partner's feet. This is the earth chakra and represents the person's anchoring point to the earth. It's the place to start clearing the aura. See the Chakras/Meridians illustration in Chapter 6 for the location of this center of energy.

Now …

1. Starting in the middle and moving your right hand to the left, visualize sweeping up under your partner's feet. In a continuous flow, continue to visualize a white light coming from the crystal. Draw the crystal up, following the right side of your partner's body about 2 to 4 inches away from the side of the body. You are drawing an outline of the person's aura. Move very slowly.

2. As you draw the crystal up, you might feel tugging or pushing or pulling. This is resistance in the energy flow of your partner's aura. The crystal is working very hard to remove impurities, negativity, and imperfections from the aura, so you need to go slowly to not only feel what's going on, but to also allow your partner to make adjustments in his or her energy.

3. If you feel the crystal becoming saturated with negative energies, gently withdraw it from the person's aura and gently shake it free of negative energy. You can also breathe in, think the word "release," and visualize white light streaming out over the crystal and transmuting the negativity into white light. Return to the point in the aura where you left, and then continue.

4. Continue to move your crystal in a clockwise direction around your partner, slowly tracing up and over the person's head and down on the right side. Stop when you feel a sticky area and focus on clearing the patch before moving on. If you find that the hand holding the crystal gets tingly, shake your hand out to remove excess negativity.

You can't go wrong with this exercise because the crystal is doing all the work and you are not actually working in the more sensitive chakras. Your partner might experience tingling and some feelings of pressure as the crystal encounters blockages in the flow of the energy in the aura. He or she might also feel some swaying back and forth with the energy flows. These are all typical responses to energy activation and clearing. It can be a nice experience, and at the end, you'll both feel relaxed from sharing in the healing.

If you and your partner are going to switch places, be sure to go through the grounding exercise again and have your partner use his or her own cleansed and charged crystal to work on your aura.

Gem of an Idea

If you have been the healer, make sure you cleanse your hands of any negative energies picked up from your partner. Wet your hands in cold water and rub the skin lightly with sea salt to purify the energy and cleanse the hand chakras. Rinse again in cold water. Cold water is used to help close down sensitivity in the hand chakras after handling crystals. Be sure to cleanse your crystal before using it for other healings.

Wand Wonderment

In ancient traditions a wand called a *scepter* was used as a symbol of authority. In more recent times, during a British monarch's coronation, two scepters are used. One scepter has a dove at the top and is held in the left hand. This scepter symbolizes the spiritual authority of the monarch under Christian authority. The Cullinan I diamond, also known as the Star of Africa, is one of the largest diamonds in the world, weighing in at 530.20 carats, and it is mounted in the dove scepter. The other scepter has a cross and is held in the right hand. This scepter represents temporal or lay authority.

Just holding a wand generates a lot of energy. When crystals are placed at the tip, the energy generated can be amplified and directed to disperse in a very powerful and focused way. The wand can be moved around to direct the flow of energy.

If you have a crystal wand, use it in place of the crystal in the exercise from the previous section for clearing auras. Before you begin, it is best to have cleansed it by using the smudging technique and to hold it in your hand to warm it up for several minutes to excite the molecules and generate an energy charge. The energy charge will find its way to the tip of the wand where it can be used for healing.

Test the wand on yourself first to ensure the energy is activated. (The test can be as simple as pointing the tip at the opposite hand to activate the hand chakra.) And although the resulting healing might feel magical, please resist the urge to refer to it as magic!

The Least You Need to Know

- ◆ All of us experience blockages of energy from time to time. A good cleansing of the chakras is in order to make us feel well and balanced.

- ◆ Energy blockages can be cleared from chakras by scooping negativity out with a crystal.

- ◆ With a clear quartz crystal and a partner, you can cleanse your aura and put your energy back in balance.

- ◆ Using a wand helps to balance and clear the aura of energy around a person.

Chapter 17

Crystal Layouts

In This Chapter

- ◆ Why place crystals in a pattern?
- ◆ The geometry of crystals
- ◆ Crystal layouts for meditation
- ◆ Activating the layout

Crystals are beautiful to look at on their own, but when you start putting them into geometric layouts, not only does their appearance become even more dazzling, but their power also magnifies!

Layouts have been used for thousands of years, going back to BC times and, as such, are obviously nothing new. We can't be sure what our ancient ancestors used these techniques for, but *we* can use them for meditation, healing, or connecting with the spirit world. Anything is possible when crystals start communicating with each other!

Patterns of Power

In this chapter, you're going to learn how to lay crystals on the body for optimum healing power. But why, you might be asking, do gemstones have to be positioned in a pattern? How does this affect their healing power?

def•i•ni•tion

Sacred geometry refers to formations used in the construction of sacred architecture and in the design of sacred art. The ratios of sacred geometry are believed to be found in music, light, and the cosmos.

Sacred geometry and the use of stones in special geometric patterns is as old as the hills. Actually, ancient civilizations were building structures like the famous Stonehenge, near Amesbury, England, before 3,000 B.C.E.

These types of geometric formations are found in other locations as well, although no one really knows what they mean or why they were built. We do know that grouping of stones is astrologically significant and that these sites seem to amplify energy and healing.

When crystals are laid out in a pattern, they also start to speak energetically to each other. The crystalline resonance is amplified by the pattern, making it possible to enter into a higher state of awareness. Maybe in creating your own crystal geometric patterns, you'll rediscover an ancient secret!

Crystal Geometry

In Chapter 3 we talked about Platonic solids and sacred geometry and how these concepts relate to the idea of crystal healing. The harmonics and proportion of geometric designs are thought to be a means to communicate with the sacred and are thought to provide the powers of healing through their mathematical significance with the laws of the universe. Although geometric designs can be intricate and artistic, there's much more to them than beauty. When certain crystals are laid on or around the body in a very specific manner, they begin to resonate with each other and connect interdimensionally.

When you sit or lie in a *crystal layout*—a structure created using sacred geometry—it becomes a living *mandala* of energy where your mind can become more focused for dimensional access and where healing can be more effective. You can create a crystal layout for yourself or for a partner.

def•i•ni•tion

A **crystal layout** is a geometric arrangement of crystals placed either around or on the body to create and augment crystal resonance for meditation and healing. A **mandala** is an ancient diagram of geometric patterns symbolizing the universe and the cosmic order of all things. By viewing the diagram, subtle energies are invoked.

Rosemary's Regression

By changing the geometric pattern of the layout, different resonances can be achieved. Some of these vibrations provide deeper meditation and gateways to other macrocosms. For example, communication with deities and the development of psychic abilities are possible with an oval layout. There will be more about this coming up, but here's a teaser: the oval layout was used during a past life regression that was filmed at my home by some college students. (Apparently, I beat five other entries to have a documentary made as part of their class project!) I invited Rosemary, a friend, to be the client for the filming session.

After setting up the oval layout using 10 large crystals that were 4 by 8 inches each, Rosemary settled into the oval, lying on her back. I added crystals at her chakras and began the regression. The camera crew and a sound person were patiently filming when Rosemary started to relate images about being back in ancient Middle East. Her body suddenly arched upward with only the back of her head on the pillow and her heels on the floor. The sound person was so scared, she dropped her equipment and ran into the kitchen.

As we were still in the regression, I asked Rosemary where she was. Rosemary said she was in a healing cave where citrine was embedded in the walls of the cavern and there was golden light everywhere. This is where the Essenes, Jewish mystics, brought people to heal, she said. Rosemary said she was aware that her body was arched but said she was comfortable and felt the energy of the crystals in the cave was healing her. After a bit, Rosemary's body relaxed and the film crew finished up and went home. (The sound lady never did make it back into the living room!)

So now that I have your interest, let's start talking about layouts and what they can do for your own healing processes.

A Crystal Crown

Need more intensity on your meditation sessions? Want deeper interpersonal communications? A crystal layout called a crystal crown is just what the crystal healer ordered! This is a nice beginner layout, and the suggested pattern works well to provide relaxation and an opening of the crown chakra for spiritual expansion.

To set up your crystal crown, select some of the spiritual expansion crystals listed in Chapter 13. Try to use two of the same type of crystal because you'll put one on each side of the head to balance the left and right brain hemispheres, as well as create a yin/yang balance within the subtle energies.

To balance the upper and lower chakras, you'll need extra grounding. You already learned in Chapter 6 to visualize roots growing from under your feet for grounding. This time, you can place a dark crystal 2 to 4 inches long, such as black tourmaline or obsidian, between your feet about 6 inches to anchor you to the earth. Set this grounding crystal in place before you lie in the crown.

You'll need an affirmation for programming the layout. Here's one suggestion:

> "I, [your name], am able to receive and accept All That Is."

Crystal Clear

Crystals in a layout should not actually touch your body. That way, you are getting subtle energy directed for spiritual expansion rather than for direct physical or emotional healing.

Now we're ready to get down to work! Set up your pattern of crystals in a semicircle on the floor; then gently lay your head in the semicircle. (If you want to align the crystals on top of a bed, gently place a pillow over them; then lay your head on the pillow. You will be staying in the crystal crown as a meditation for about 10 to 20 minutes.)

After a basic layout is set up, you can hold additional crystals in your hands or tape a crystal onto your third eye for increased awareness. For extra meditation focus, you can listen to a meditation tape or use one of the meditations in Chapter 20. If you have some healing to do, focus on that area and the crystalline energy structures will work with you on the problem.

The layout should look like this:

- At each side of the temples, place a 1-inch piece of sodalite to provide for stress reduction and calm the mind.

- On each side of the throat, place a 1-inch piece of azurite, lapis lazuli, or dioptase to release worldly concerns and enter into a deeper level of awareness.

- At the top of your head (about 2 inches above the center), place a large amethyst with the tip pointing away from the head. The crystal will provide protection as well as a crown chakra opening.

- On each side of the amethyst, place a piece of clear or white calcite or selenite. This will open the communications channel for telepathic messages and images.

- Place a third eye crystal such as topaz or lapis lazuli on your forehead. This will expand your awareness and provide mental clarity.

- At the heart chakra, place a crystal such as rose quartz or kunzite to balance the physical, mental, and emotional levels and to open the heart chakra for healing.

When you are settled into this layout, you can ground yourself further by imagining that you have roots under your feet growing into the earth, anchoring you. If you want to set up this type of layout for a partner, have the person lie down first and then place the crystals around the sides and top of his or her head.

> **Yellow Flag** _____
>
> Grounding yourself too strongly means you will deaden the flow of subtle energy and numb sensitive receptors. You'll end up not feeling much energy flowing. To resolve this, shake out your arms and legs and jump up and down a few times to stir up your vital energy. Try grounding yourself from the solar plexus chakra by visualizing roots growing from your midsection into the ground. Imagine the roots for grounding as cords of white light instead of heavy thick roots.

Now you are all set to breathe deeply and relax your body. Activate your third eye by focusing on the middle of your forehead. The crystals at the crown will make a connection with the third eye as they open the crown chakra. You can direct your own visualization or meditation or simply ask for a healing and see what happens.

Some people report seeing images and even colored lights in the room as their upper chakras open. The important part is to not fall asleep while you are in an energy circle or other layout so you can be aware of the energy shifts. When you are aware of what you see through the veils of time and past the material plane of existence, there are lessons to be learned. If you are asleep, there is little value. You are training your mind to see to other parts of the cosmos. Holding on to your consciousness takes time to develop.

When you have completed your meditation, disengage your energy by mentally projecting the word "Release!" to cease all energy connection with the crystals. Take off your heart crystal and dismantle the crystal crown layout. Write any thoughts or inspirations you have in your crystal journal. Cleanse your crystals and tuck them away. Try a different assortment of crystals for your next crystal crown layout.

A Ring of Crystals

Why do we want to wear rings (wedding rings), put things in a ring (a circus ring), and see a ring (ring around the moon)? Well, for one thing, rings can contain things. A ring is a circle and can also rotate. It represents perfection and the blissful void. It is the beginning and the end. Rings are also an alchemical sign of completion and wholeness. When crystals are arranged into a circle, we are containing the energies of the crystals and can direct that energy for healing and meditation. If you have never been in a circle of crystals, you are in for a treat!

One of the first crystal formations I tried was a basic circle. I got every crystal I could find in the house, all 34 of them. After cleansing them, I took them outside and put them in a wide 5-foot circle in the grass to soak up the sun's rays for recharging. Later that afternoon, I entered the crystal circle and sat in meditation for what seemed like hours, connecting with the earth, the crystals, the lovely welcoming energy, and my inner spiritual place. It was a wonderful initiation, and I recommend it for anyone who has more than a few crystals or for someone who is developing a crystal toolkit to establish a connection with their crystals.

How do you make a perfect circle of crystals? Don't worry—you don't need to acquire a huge compass or the equipment that roadside surveyors use. All you need is a length of string and an eye for detail:

1. Place a heavy crystal in the middle of the floor or ground where you want to make your circle.

2. Cut a length of string that will be one half the diameter of the circle you want to make.

3. Place one end of the string under the crystal in the center, and stretch out the string. Place a crystal at the other end of the string.

4. Position the crystal with the tip pointing in to the center of the circle. (If you are using a tumbled crystal, just place it according to your intuition at the end of the string.) Swing the string to the next position a few inches from the first crystal, and place the second crystal.

5. Continue to move around the circle following the length of the string. Each crystal will be exactly the same length from the middle of the circle.

If you have only 4 crystals, they can be placed using the string length at the north, east, south, and west positions. If you have, say, 12 crystals to use in a layout, place the first 4 crystals in each of the four directions and fill in the remaining spaces between the directions with the rest.

The most important part is to stand back from the circle and be sure that you see a good alignment and spacing between your gemstones. Read the section about activating the layout later in this chapter, and you'll be all set for a new experience every time!

The best use of a ring of circles is to sit in it. Before you enter the ring, remember to activate the layout (as described later in this chapter). As you step into the circle, visualize a ring of white light rising up like a column around you, enclosing you. Once you feel this powerful energy connection, you can direct healing to areas of your body or to emotional issues. You can also hold the thought of sending healing to a person. When you are surrounded by crystals and are making that crystalline connection, you are linked with all things. Saying a prayer or a positive affirmation is very beneficial, as it will be amplified and transmitted by the ring of light.

When you have completed your healing or meditation session, disengage from the energy by mentally projecting the word "Release!" This will cease all energy connection with the crystals. Gently get up and step outside of the ring. You do not need to dismantle the ring and can reuse it later. However, you should clear the energy by smudging the area with sage or incense. You can use the ring up to three times before cleansing the crystals in salt and recharging them for the next session. Also, you might want to keep track of the number of crystals you've laid out. I've lost a few to the vacuum cleaner from carelessness!

Crystal Clear

Animals seem to benefit from circles of stone, too. While traveling in Nepal, I came across a street dog that had been in a fight and was a bit banged up, bleeding and limping. The villagers thought I was crazy when I directed the dog back to my room and he waited outside while I got some crystals. I set up a circle of quartz crystals around his body and put an amethyst cluster under his bleeding neck. He stayed there for over an hour and then left of his own accord. The next day, the dog seemed perfectly all right.

Star of David

The Star of David is an ancient symbol that is rich in symbolism. It consists of two interlocking equilateral triangles forming a six-point star. In Judaism, it was used by kabbalists for protection against evil spirits. In Hinduism, it is called the *shatkona*, representing the union of Shiva and Shakti, godlike energies that form all of creation. The Star of David formation is used for unifying and integrating energy. It's a terrific layout, but it can be a little tricky to get the crystals aligned properly.

To build the Star of David layout, you are going to set up two triangles of crystals.

The first triangle will be the Shakti triangle (female energy) with the point of the triangle facing down. First, put a crystal as a marker in the center of the area where you want the layout set up. Using a length of string, measure the placement of the first crystal from the central marker directly below. This crystal should point up toward the center crystal. For the second and third crystals, use the string above the marker to create a *V* formation where the crystals are placed at the tips of the *V*, pointing toward the first crystal.

The second triangle will be the Shiva triangle (male energy) with the point of the triangle facing up. Using the string, position the first crystal above the center marker. This crystal should point down toward the center crystal. For the second and third crystals, use the string as above to create a *V* formation where the crystals are placed at the tips of the *V*, pointing toward the first crystal you laid as part of the Shiva formation.

Gem of an Idea

For the Shakti crystals, you can use the yin crystals mentioned in Chapter 6. For the Shiva crystals, the layout will be more powerful if all the crystals are the same type. Try boosting the energy flow of the Shiva-Shakti layout by holding a clear quartz crystal in your left hand with the tip point inward and a clear quartz crystal in your right hand with the tip pointing out.

Stand back and ensure that each crystal tip is aligned and pointing in the right direction. If not, adjust them. Now you have two triangles in union and can remove the marker crystal from the center. Read the section later in this chapter on activation of the layout, and you're good to go!

When you enter the Star of David, try to think of the formation as two interlocking three-dimensional triangles and that you are going to sit in the middle where they interlock. This sacred geometry will provide a gentle alignment to your subtle energies that will open your energies for higher meditation and communication with the cosmos. Ask for a chakra alignment, or an alignment for your highest good.

See the suggestions in the earlier section, "A Ring of Crystals," for other ideas on working with the energy in a crystal layout.

When you have completed your meditation, you can dismantle the star, cleanse and recharge your crystals and smudge the area or leave the layout set up for a second meditation.

The Obliging Oval

The alignment of crystals in an oval pattern is the most versatile of layouts. An oval doesn't take up much space; any size crystals can be used; and the layout is effective for chakra balancing, physical healing, and past-life recall. Ovals help to contain energy, provide protection to the aura, and aid in the circulation of energy throughout the subtle body.

For the oval layout, you'll need six large clear quartz crystals. If you can find some crystals that are 3 to 6 inches long and 2 to 4 inches wide, you'll find they carry the right type of energy to hold the geometric structure together. Try to select ones that feel heavier than they look. Remember that the larger the crystal, the more energy it can hold. The placement of the crystals is as follows:

- ◆ One crystal pointing up at the head and one at the feet

- ◆ One crystal on either side of the body at the lower hips to catch the lower chakras

- ◆ One crystal on either side of the body at the upper arms to catch the higher chakras

Oval layouts feel protective and provide a deep meditative experience. Don't forget before you enter the oval to activate the layout (described later in this chapter). You can ask for communications with a spirit guide or angels while in this type of layout. See the suggestions in the earlier section, "A Ring of Crystals," for other ideas on working with the energy in a crystal layout.

If you are working on physical healing, place additional crystals on your body while in the layout. You can add more crystals—at the third eye and heart chakras, for example—to boost the subtle energies. After the session, smudge the area and cleanse and recharge your crystals unless you are reusing the oval for another meditation. Write any impressions in your crystal journal.

Gem of an Idea _____

Your crystal layout can remain on the floor to reuse at a later time. To keep the energy fresh between your meditations, place a bowl of salt water in the middle of the layout to absorb any negativity in the environment. Use a silk cloth to cover the crystals for dust protection and to help retain the energy of the crystals.

Activation of the Layout

Just setting out the crystals will provide some energy connections between the stones. When the crystals are properly aligned, the crystalline structure actually takes its shape from the geometry of the layout. To realize the dynamic energy activation of the layout takes a further step.

You can activate the layout simply by using your mental intent. Visualize the layout as a three-dimensional structure. In a circle layout, for instance, think of a ball of light. In an oval, think of an egg-shaped light structure.

Adding a further ritual to the activation creates a sacred space for the layout and protects it from vibrational intrusions. Using strong intent and visualizing the three-dimensional structure of the layout, point a kyanite wand at the center of the layout for at least 21 seconds. This will allow time for the structure to adjust and align on the more subtle side of things.

You might like to experiment with various types of formations, such as a spiral of life. The spiral of life is made of a line of crystals that spirals into a center. The right-hand spiral is considered to be sacred. Walk gently following the spiral. You can stand at the center of the spiral and feel a wave of energy rushing toward you. Breathe this energy into your body, focusing on the chakras or any areas that need healing. Consider investing in a 1- to 2-pound bag of smaller, 1-inch crystals to use in more complex layouts. Cleanse and charge them before placing them into a layout.

The Least You Need to Know

- Stone layouts and sacred geometric structures have been around for thousands of years and mimic sophisticated astronomical alignments.

- Proper alignment of the crystals used in a layout increases the crystal resonance and power of the layout.

- Different geometric formations provide dimensional connections to other planes of knowledge.

- Activating the layout ensures the layout is empowered and for your intended purpose.

Chapter

18

Student, Become a Healer!

In This Chapter

- ◆ Clearing negative energy from a room
- ◆ Assembling your crystals
- ◆ A system for crystal analysis
- ◆ Your first official crystal healing session
- ◆ Ending a session

By now you know that crystal healing is a versatile form of purifying energy, whether that energy is in the air, in your mind, or in your body. You've come a long way in a short time, and you might want to try what you've learned in an official healing session with a friend or client.

Before you begin, you'll need to cleanse the area you'll be working in, you'll need to arrange your crystals, and you'll need to know which of the gemstones you'll be using. We'll cover all the groundwork in this chapter.

Oh, just one more thing you'll be needing for this session: confidence!

Clearing the Space

When you prepare an area for a healing session, you need to take great care to prepare a sacred and clean space. Why? Whenever harsh words are spoken in a room, or when someone has heavy emotions such as grieving, or an accident has occurred in a home, there is a residue negative energy signature. In any event, when you purify the environment using a room clearing technique, you are changing the negative structure back to white light, which is what you want surrounding you and your client during a healing session.

Singing Crystals

What the heck is a singing crystal, you wonder? Does it perform at Madison Square Garden with backup dancers? Hardly! Singing crystals are long, tapered pieces of clear quartz that chime when tapped gently with another crystal. To clear a room, tap the crystals together while walking around its perimeter. The crystal resonance is released into the room to disperse negative energy. You can find singing crystals in metaphysical shops or online.

> **Crystal Clear**
>
> You can also use singing crystals to clear a chakra. Simply hold the crystals over the energy center and tap gently. The first time you try this, you'll notice that the first few taps aren't particularly melodious. This is because the sound is meeting a discordant energy. Continue to tap gently until you hear a pure sound.

Ting Cha Ring Tones

Tibetan chimes, called *ting cha* or *tingsha*, look like two small 4-inch metal cymbals. Ting cha are traditionally made from gold, silver, copper, brass, nickel, tin, or lead. Ting cha are rung at the beginning and end of meditation sessions and at other practices in Buddhist temples. Ting cha help to clear energies, pacify local spirits, and bring the mind to the central focus of the meditation.

To clear crystals of unwanted energies and refresh them before using them for healing or meditation, set your crystals out. Using the following instructions for ringing the ting cha properly, sound the ting cha about 4 to 6 inches away from the crystals, imagining the sound waves washing over each crystal, purifying it. Imagine the sound going through each crystal, aligning its internal crystalline structure. Ring seven times without letting the sound fade away. This will sustain the clearing vibration.

To clear a room of unwanted energies, seat yourself in the middle and ring the chimes at least seven times until you note the change in tone that signals clarity. Wait until each ring has faded completely before striking the ting cha again for clearing. Anything in the room will be cleared of negative energy, including other crystals. If your crystals have been programmed, the ringing will not affect the programming.

To ring them properly, do the following:

1. Hold one of the ting cha horizontally (like a flying saucer) in your left hand, holding the leather cord a few inches with your thumb and forefinger.

2. With your right hand, grasp the leather string where it joins the metal cymbal and turn the cymbal vertically, like a plate standing on its edge. Strike the edge of the right cymbal against the left.

3. Let it ring until you can no longer hear the chime; then ring it again.

The first few rings will sound like they are hitting negativity in the air. After about the fourth ring, you should hear a definite clarity to the ringing. Experiment and see if you reach a point where the ring is so clear that you can hear it bouncing off the walls. That's when you *know* you have a cleared room!

If you're looking to purchase ting cha, you'll find them in a Tibetan arts and crafts shop or on the Internet under "Tibetan chimes" or "prayer chimes."

Salt Water Bowl

In Chapter 16, I talked about using a crystal to scoop and flick negative energies from the chakras. Although you can certainly let that energy dissolve into the air, you can also flick it toward a salt water solution, which will absorb it in a more visual way. This is purely a matter of preference; some people just like to have something physical to pour into the earth after a healing session.

Set up an 8- to 10-inch bowl of salt water to absorb negative energies. When flicking unwanted energy off the end of your crystal, simply aim toward the bowl. A bowl of dry salt can also be used to absorb unwanted energies in the room. Add a few teaspoons of lavender and sage to keep the bowl fresh for a week at a time. However, do not reuse the salt water or the dry salt because it will be filled with negativity. Pour it into the earth and be done with it.

Aromatherapy

An aromatherapy diffuser releases essential oils into the room and disperses unwanted energies. Adding a few crystals to the mix can assist with any particular concerns you might have. For example, adding some tiger eye will help students focus on their schoolwork.

My favorite cleansing blend is frankincense, rose, and orange oils. The frankincense grounds unwanted energy; the rose oil transmutes negative energy to a higher vibration; and the orange oil imparts a clean, antiseptic vibration to the room.

> **Gem of an Idea**
>
> You can pick up a prepared mix of aromatherapy oils, mix your own, or locate an aromatherapist who can prepare a blend just for you and your specific needs.

Assembling Your Crystals

Although you might have many crystals—too many to keep track of, you might think—it's important to keep them assembled in a certain manner. The way you treat your crystals will influence their subtle energies. By protecting them from negative vibrations, especially after they have been cleansed, you'll keep them in tip-top order and ready for use during any healing session.

It's worth the time to know your crystals by name and to memorize what their healing powers are because, although you'll prepare before a session and have a good idea of which gemstones you might use, things can sometimes turn on a dime and you don't want to be searching for a crystal you didn't think you'd need! Having your gemstones handy and arranged for practical use will save you time and frustration.

"Old Pal"

After your crystals have been cleansed and charged, they should be kept separate from gemstones that are still carrying negative energy. That's where a toolbox or tackle box comes in handy. I have a plastic one with various compartments—interestingly, it has a curious sticker on the outside that says "Old Pal." I find that very fitting—certainly crystals are some of my best old pals! Keeping them all together means the crystals will resonate and learn from each other's experiences and vibrations. Do they actually speak to each other? Well, you might not hear actual voices coming from inside the box, but their various resonances certainly do affect each other!

Because crystals can get heavy, select a sturdy box with a handle for easy transportation. You should be able to safely pick up the box and set all your gemstones in the sunlight at once for recharging. Now isn't that convenient? To protect your crystal tips when storing your crystals in a tackle box or toolbox, stuff cotton batting at the ends of each compartment to prevent them from knocking against their storage unit.

Tools of the Trade

After you have selected a toolbox, consider how to arrange the crystals inside of it. Here are some suggestions:

- Chakra tune-up kit (see Chapter 6)

- The Five Master Healers (see Chapter 10)

- Layout crystals (see Chapter 17)—these are the smaller 1-inch crystals to lay along arms and legs and use in layouts

- Grounding crystals, such as black tourmaline or garnet

- Kyanite, selenite, or clear quartz wands

- A place for your crystal pendulum

Yellow Flag

Keep aromatherapy bottles and supplies away from crystals because they will absorb the various scents. This can be a serious issue when using the crystals in healing. The third eye, for example, will pick up any smells—and if they are stale and impure, the chakra will shut right down.

Keep your toolbox away from electromagnetic sources such as TVs, computers, radios, wiring, microwaves, and other home appliances. These can all cause crystals to vibrate unnaturally, and the results will be unpredictable at best! You might start to notice that none of your crystals are working like they should or like they used to, even after a thorough cleansing and charging.

If you are still learning which crystals are which, label the sections in your toolbox. If you forgot the name of a crystal, add it into a mystery pile and take these gemstones to someone who can identify them for you such as a gemologist, geologist, or jeweler.

Crystal Analysis and Selection

Working with a partner can be fulfilling in that you can see the effects of crystals on someone other than yourself. Still, it can be overwhelming to research hundreds of crystals. Starting with just a few in your toolbox, such as the Master Healers and the chakra tune-up kit, is a good way to develop some healing skills.

Having a system handy to use with your partner or others will save you time and reduce the chaos of determining which crystals to use. A system provides an approach to analyzing which crystals might be needed in a session.

When you are first working with a partner, don't just dig into your crystal toolbox and start choosing gemstones for her. It's much better if you can take the time to find out about what she'd like to heal during the session—and I mean in more than just a general sense. Really get down to the core of the issue if you can. Ask probing questions that can help you determine which crystal to use. For instance, if someone is feeling uncertain about her job, is it because of a mean boss, new responsibilities, or a general lack of passion for the work? The specific information you glean could mean the difference between using a carnelian in the second chakra for self-esteem issues or a lapis lazuli at the third eye for clarity on seeing her spiritual direction!

Gem of an Idea

Have your partner select a few crystals to which she is attracted. Interpret the crystals for her, telling your partner about the uses of the crystals she's chosen and why she might have chosen them. Use them during the session in the appropriate chakra. Record any responses from your partner to these crystals in your crystal journal.

Use the following analysis worksheet to collect information from your partner for a crystal healing session. If you're working with more than one person, it's a good idea to keep some sort of written record of your sessions for easy recall and referral. You might want to make several copies of the blank sheet so you'll have them handy.

For general physical health, record what the person says about her current health issues; this will provide indicators for selecting crystals and a way to measure progress in a follow-up after the session. For general emotional/psychological health, ask what's been on her mind or what has been causing her stress. For psycho-spiritual issues, ask who or what has been spiritually inspirational and where she could use more peace in her life. Remember, your own intuition is important. What crystals you sense are needed are also very helpful to the healing process.

Music is an important part of the healing session, as it can relax, soothe, or energize your client. Allow your clients to bring their own music to the healing session, or allow them to choose them from your selection of healing CDs.

Ask your client to select any essential oils to be used at the beginning of a session to create a relaxing environment or at the very end of the session to help integrate all the healing energies. Some good choices might include the following:

- **Clary sage**—Clears the aura and grounds energies.
- **Frankincense**—Purifies and removes negative influences.
- **Geranium**—Creates a sense of joy and happiness.
- **Peppermint and rosemary**—Refreshes and reenergizes.
- **Rose**—Opens the heart chakra and soothes the emotions.

For chakra analysis, determine which chakras are blocked by noting any ailments in the location of a chakra. You can also ask your client if she feels blocked anywhere in particular, or you can ask your pendulum which chakra to work on. Also examine your client's own selection of crystals to determine which chakra she seems to be targeting.

You can also record any affirmations you programmed into the crystals.

Analysis Worksheet for Healing Session

Client's name: _____   Selected music: _____

Essential oil(s): _____

General physical health

Problem area(s): _____

Crystal(s) selected: _____

_____

General emotional health

Problem area(s): _____

Crystal(s) selected: _____

_____

General psycho-spiritual health

Problem area(s): _____

Crystal(s) selected: _____

_____

Chakra analysis

Crystal(s) selected:

1 Root _____   5 Throat _____

2 Sacral _____   6 Third eye _____

3 Solar plexus _____   7 Crown _____

4 Heart _____

Spiritual attunement

Support affirmations: _____

Crystal(s) selected: _____

_____

General notes: _____

_____

Putting Your Lessons to Use

Before beginning work with a partner, ensure that the room where you will be working is cleared of negative energy, as described earlier in the chapter, and that your crystals are cleansed and fully charged. You can use soft music, candles, flowers, and/or aromatherapy to energize the room and provide a pleasant and relaxing atmosphere.

You have already learned how to cleanse an aura in Chapter 16. That's a great place to start and to make note of the areas on your partner that seemed "sticky" so you can follow up during the session. Using the analysis worksheet, select the crystals you will use during the session and put them on a table so you can access them easily.

> **Gem of an Idea** _____
>
> During your first session, it might seem awkward finding your way around so many crystals, as though you don't know where to start. That's where taking a crystal course will help. You can practice in a classroom situation and use the techniques on another student. You would also receive a crystal healing so you'll know what to expect. Putting it all together is what makes the crystal healing session so special. (See Chapter 20 for more information about further training.)

In this session, we focus on going through the steps of grounding, putting crystals on any physical areas of concern your partner might have, and working in the chakras to provide a clearing and end with a chakra balance. It will take about 30 minutes. How's that sound? Let's do it!

1. Have your partner lie face up on a massage table or a comfortable mat on the floor. Place a dark grounding crystal such as obsidian or garnet 4 to 6 inches below your partner's feet. If he is lying on a table, place the crystal between his feet at the ankles. You can say a protection prayer and go through your own grounding exercise.

2. Consult your analysis worksheet; if your partner has any physical symptoms to be addressed, bring out the crystals you selected for those issues and place them at the correct points on the body. Don't forget that you can also tape them onto your partner's clothing so they don't slide off. (Review Chapter 11 for a reminder on the techniques used for physical healing, such as infusing energy.)

3. Using your analysis worksheet for reference, place the chakra crystals you selected gently onto each chakra. You can also add a crystal crown layout around the head as detailed in Chapter 17. Use the techniques for clearing chakra congestion as outlined in Chapter 16.

4. Use your kyanite wand to center and balance each chakra. See Chapter 16 on aligning chakras in seconds.

So far, you've placed crystals for the physical system, for the emotional and mental subtle energies, and for spiritual guidance or healing in the chakras. You've been busy placing crystals on and off and doing some programming, clearing, and chakra balancing. Now it's time to let the crystals do the rest so you can take a break:

5. Leave all the crystals in place on your partner and leave the room to allow all the healing energies to integrate. If you can't leave, then sit quietly at least 3 feet away from your partner to let the energy of the crystals and the energy of your partner integrate. This last step is important to affect a healing response. It is also a time when your partner might seem to take a nap because he is so relaxed.

6. After about 5 minutes, rouse your partner gently and remove the crystals. (See the following section so you don't damage subtle energies when you remove the crystals.) Put your crystals aside for cleansing. Let your partner get up when he is ready. Offer him some water for grounding.

Congratulations! You completed your first crystal healing session. The debriefing with your partner after a session is important. Write in your analysis worksheet any notes as a record for following up later if needed.

Closing the Session

Ending a session takes finesse and skill. You don't want to suddenly cut off the lovely flow of crystal energy by yanking the crystals off your partner and telling her to get up. There should be no sudden movements, nothing that will startle the other person out of her blissful state. Instead, gently remove the crystals, one at a time. Remember that the crystals have been sitting there for a while and the energy structures are still in place around your partner. Pulling the crystals off too rapidly can cause discomfort and even tears in a person's energy fields. Place the crystals aside because you'll want to cleanse them properly. Your partner might need some help getting up. Tell your partner to take her time because the subtle body energy will need a moment to get resettled after they are up.

After a crystal healing session, you'll notice the person looks more relaxed and has an interesting glow of light around her face. Keep a mirror handy for your partner to see some of these facial changes. Ask your partner about her experience with the crystal healing and write her impressions in your journal.

The Least You Need to Know

- Clearing a room of negativity is an important step before a healing session.

- Gathering your crystals into one area helps to protect them and to keep the healing vibration pure.

- Analysis of a person's physical ailments and state of his chakras helps to determine the selection of crystals to use for healing.

- There are several steps in a crystal healing session, including grounding; using crystals for physical, emotional, and spiritual healing; and working on chakras. The final step is the integration of all energies.

- At the end of a healing session, remove the crystals one at a time to allow for your client's soothing transition back to the real world.

Part 5

Personal Development

The more you work with crystals, the more benefit you receive. As you become committed to learning more about crystals, your interest might expand to taking classes or having private sessions and instruction. Crystals combine well with other healing modalities and are used in creative ways in the arts.

Meditation is important for training the mind. Crystals work regardless of the state of your mind, but when the mind is empty, there is true awareness and the energy of the crystal is able to work better. When the mind is at peace, there is room for healing to expand!

In Part 5, guided meditations are provided for addressing personal issues, increasing creativity, and general relaxation and healing.

Chapter 19

Advanced Meditations

In This Chapter

- ◆ Guided meditation and useful set-ups for relaxation
- ◆ Enter the garden and receive a gift
- ◆ Earth-star standing meditation
- ◆ Conquer whatever is holding you back
- ◆ Infuse your being with light
- ◆ Getting instruction in meditation

By now you've learned all about crystals, their various healing powers, how to use them, and how to tune in to their frequencies to learn the mysteries that they—and only they—have the answers to. Because crystal healing is dependent on quieting the mind, we're going to wind down with a chapter on advanced meditations. This way, I know you will have plenty of visualizations to keep you occupied and working toward even greater healing!

When it comes to meditating with crystals, the fewer you use, the better. You don't need a huge outlay to experience a crystal meditation. Even one single crystal can be used with effect. A typical crystal collection would include at least one or more specialized crystals for meditation, usually to open the upper chakras: the throat, third eye, and crown chakras.

These crystals will help maintain your focus during meditation and can provide portals to enter higher levels of consciousness where you can get teachings on psychic development and other topics, meet friendly spirits, and ask for healing for yourself or others.

Meditation Starting Line

As you learned in Chapter 3, when we meditate, energy moves from the stress-prone right frontal cortex to the calmer left frontal cortex where the alpha state is activated. Fortunately, not much is needed for meditation except a quiet place. The benefits of meditation are incredible and are drug-free. Here's a sampler:

> **Crystal Clear**
>
> Prop up your legs and back with cushions if you need support for a sitting meditation. If you lose your focus, bring your attention back to your breath to stabilize your mind. Move very slowly in and out of meditation so you do not disturb the energy you have around you. Try to stay in a meditative state even afterwards.

- Reduces stress, worry, and anxiety

- Increases the rate of physical healing

- Reduces the effects of aging (such as wrinkles) and prolongs the health of organs

- Unblocks energies constricting functions of the senses (hearing, sight, smell, taste, and touch)

- Increases mental clarity, memory, and logic

- Enhances the bonding of physical, emotional, and mental planes with one's own spiritual aspirations

Some of the meditations in this chapter require that you lie down so you can place the crystals on your body. For a seated meditation, sit in a straight chair where you are not leaning back and your spine is straight. The traditional meditation pose is to sit cross-legged on a meditation cushion; however, not everyone can maintain that position for very long, so assume whatever position is most comfortable for you.

Try to meditate every day at the same time and place. When you meditate in the same place, the energies stay in the area and help to harmonize your environment. Next time you meditate, it becomes a little easier.

Flower Power

Let's try a warm-up exercise to get your mind in gear for a deep meditative state. Find a flower and gaze at it. Note all its petals, color, stem, and leaves. See the inside and the outside. Relax your mind and let your eyes and hands wander over the flower.

Note its aliveness, its scent, and the space around the flower. As you do this, notice how absorbed you are in the process. Now close your eyes and re-create the image, scent, and feel in your mind. Pay special attention to all the details you found in the flower when your eyes were open. Note that your concepts of all these attributes of the flower rises in your mind.

How are you doing with this meditation so far? Okay, so maybe you need a little practice. That's what meditation is for—practicing your mind!

Guided Meditation

Guided meditation is a great beginning point for entering into the mind. It's sort of like going into a maze but being able to know where to go as if guided by an instructor. As a new meditator, there's a feeling of security when you listen to a soothing voice. You begin to relax completely and let yourself be guided to visualize images for a specific purpose.

Guided meditation is usually a two-step process. The first part is learning to relax your body of any tension. Usually the muscles are relaxed and breathing is regulated. Soothing music or soft natural sounds, such as sea sounds, helps to focus your mind away from the day's stresses and into the present moment.

def•i•ni•tion

> **Guided meditation** involves a facilitator or healer leading you through the stages of relaxation. This is a method of physical relaxation that stimulates various centers in the brain related to visual, auditory, or other sensory faculties.

The second part of guided meditation is guided imagery, a widely accepted practice that has been well researched for its healing benefits. There are several types of guided imagery. Some types are focused on problem solving or obtaining a desired outcome, such as a successful business deal or sports competition. Other types can include healing visualizations, such as seeing healthy cells getting messages from your subconscious or even contacting spirit beings that live on more subtle levels.

The meditations offered in this chapter will help expand your awareness. When you focus your energy, not only will you believe the message to be true, but the energy will line up to make it a reality. If you think, see, and feel yourself to be successful, you will! The crystals help to focus and align energy as well as to amplify your thoughts. So you can absolutely believe what you think and just watch what happens next.

Music in Meditation

If selected properly, music can enhance a meditation. While your ears are busy listening, the busy-ness of your mind is distracted and soon you can settle in and relax more. Also, the vibration held by the music is going through the crystals and, if the tones are similar to the ones resonating in the crystals, the energy is enhanced. You will feel the difference if you meditate with music and crystals than if you meditate with crystals alone. Try it!

Sound is energy medicine because it is the light from crystals. Some incredible healer-musicians understand altered states, cosmic consciousness, and how sound is used for healing subtle energy. Even the human voice can be tuned to vibrate certain pitches for healing and therapy. Gregorian chants from the tenth century, for instance, are not only magical, but have also been shown to increase endorphins (those "happy" chemicals in our brains) and induce the same neurological effects as meditation, such as easing pain.

Gem of an Idea

Sound healers such as Steven Halpern and Jonathan Gold produce music recordings that can help activate chakras and initiate deeper inner connections for healing. If you can attend a live sound healer's performance where crystal singing bowls are played, you will probably find this an exciting experience. Don't forget to bring your personal crystal with you to the concert so it can be attuned by the vibrations in the room.

When you meditate with music, make sure it's nonvocal. You don't want someone else's voice coming into your mind. Using head phones is a great idea if they are comfortable. If you get too comfortable, though, you might fall asleep because your mind is too relaxed. Do your best to stay alert enough to remain focused on the task at hand.

Garden Visualization

Now we're ready to get into some fun journeys of the mind! Prepare to relax and go where these roads lead you ....

This first meditation is also called Alice in Wonderland. You are going to be Alice, and using crystals and some visualization techniques, you are going to go into a garden and have some fun. You will need your full set of chakra crystals from your chakra tune-up kit (see Chapter 6) plus a grounding crystal such as black tourmaline, obsidian, or garnet. You'll need to set aside 15 to 20 minutes for this meditation. When you are ready, follow these steps:

1. Be sure your crystals are cleansed and charged. Lie down with the grounding crystals a few inches from the bottoms of your feet. Start your grounding exercise by imagining treelike roots growing into the ground. Place your respective chakra crystals at each chakra. Relax your body and breathe regularly, and try not to fall asleep!

2. In your mind's eye, imagine that you are looking down at the floor of your room. You notice a tiny 2-inch door with a door handle. Now become very small, like Alice in Wonderland, and put your hand on the doorknob. Unlatch the door, swing it open, and go through the door. As you step through the door, you will see a path leading to a very beautiful garden full of wondrous flowers.

3. Follow the path in front of you. Notice there are wild flowers on each side of the path. As you see each color of the flowers, breathe in its scent to activate each chakra:

   Root chakra = Red flowers that smell like cedar

   Sacral chakra = Orange flowers that smell of gardenia

   Solar plexus chakra = Yellow flowers that smell of cinnamon

   Heart chakra = Pink flowers that smell of rose

   Throat chakra = Turquoise flowers that smell of frankincense

   Third eye chakra = Indigo flowers that smell of patchouli

   Crown chakra = White flowers that smell of sandalwood

   Use your imagination by making the flowers look spectacular, like nothing you have ever seen before. Determine if each type of flower provides a special power such as calmness, good luck, or healing.

4. Continue to follow the path until you come to a small fountain. There is a bench in front of the fountain. Sit and listen to the water trickling from the spout. You see a figure approaching and are joined by a spirit guide who will introduce herself to you. Ask any questions you feel comfortable asking. Listen well so you will remember everything you hear and have been shown.

5. Your guide will give you a gift inside a magic box. Lift the lid and look inside. Remember what you see, and either take it with you or leave it behind for later. Thank your guide for the gift and bid her goodbye. When it is time for you to leave, go back through the garden to the door and, after passing through, return to your normal size in your normal dimension.

6. To leave this meditation gently, open and close your hands a few times to bring you back into this dimension and open your eyes when you are ready. Move slowly to keep your energies at peace. Drink some water for grounding.

In your crystal journal, write down any details you recall and a description of the gift. Did you bring the gift back with you?

Earth-Star Energy Layout

In this meditation, you will be standing. What a great way to get your energy going! In this case, your energy is going to get a real workout by connecting to the earth chakra, that point about 4 to 6 inches below your feet that anchors you to the earth, and to the star chakra, the point about 4 to 6 inches above your head that connects you to the stars above. You will feel energized by this meditation and should set aside 20 minutes for best effect.

Crystal Clear

We're used to hearing the term "chakra" associated only with the energy centers on the body. But you also have a connection to the earth and the sky through their own chakras! This makes perfect sense, since we are all connected to the universal energy and are one with it. See the Chakras/Meridians illustration in Chapter 6 for their placement.

You will need four to eight single-tip clear quartz crystals that are each about 1 inch wide and 2 to 4 inches long. Set these on the floor in a small circle $2\frac{1}{2}$ to 3 feet in diameter. Use a string as described for spacing a circle layout in Chapter 17 to be sure the crystals are spaced properly. All the tips of the crystals should be pointing in toward the center of the circle. Activate the layout as described in Chapter 17.

You will also need two clear quartz crystals with single points, one for each hand. When you are ready, follow these steps:

1. Step gently inside the circle and center yourself. Hold one clear quartz crystal flat in the palm of your left hand pointing up toward your wrist. Hold the other clear quartz crystal flat in the palm of your right hand pointing toward the floor. This will help with the energy flow in your body for this meditation.

2. Start your grounding exercise by imagining treelike roots growing into the ground. See them reach your earth chakra 4 to 6 inches below your feet. This time the roots are going to continue to grow deeper, reaching deep into the earth. See the roots growing faster heading toward the core of the earth itself. The roots eventually reach the molten red-hot core of the earth. Now see the red energy from the core of the earth coming back up the root system, traveling very fast. Bring the energy into the bottoms of your feet, up your legs and torso, and into your heart chakra. Feel the warmth radiate throughout your body for a few minutes.

3. When you are ready to initiate the star energy, send a cord of white light out the top of your head up past the ceiling, rising up quickly through the layers of the sky, reaching a star. Now bring the cold white light energy of the star back down along your chakra system, through the crown chakra, through your third eye and throat chakras, and into your heart chakra. Feel the coolness and send this energy throughout your body.

4. As you breathe in, bring the red-hot energy up from the core of the earth, up through your feet, through your body, and out the top of your head through your crown chakra.

5. With your next inhalation, bring the white-cold energy from the star down through your crown chakra through your body and out through your feet.

6. As you pull the energy from these two centers, your body might sway a little. That's okay. You are getting a dose of energy that your body probably has never encountered before. This meditation helps to unblock subtle energy channels in your body and will help your circuitry open so you can take on more energy.

To end the meditation, gently bring your focus to your heart chakra and, when you are ready, open your eyes (if they were closed) and gently step out of the circle. Don't forget to cleanse and recharge your crystals, or smudge the area if you plan to reuse the circle for another meditation. Write down your impressions in your crystal journal.

Overcoming Obstacles

The trouble with obstacles is that they are always getting in the way of our happiness! And they seem solid even when they aren't! That means we can usually visualize them as something solid, even if they are not actually physical obstacles, and then use meditation to destroy the other options.

For this exercise, you'll need some purple fluorite for your crown chakra, rutilated quartz for your heart chakra, and two pieces of smoky quartz (preferably with single points, one for each hand). When you are ready, follow these steps:

1. As with the other meditations, find a quiet place to lie down. Do your grounding exercise. If you're having a particularly troublesome emotional issue, add a black tourmaline, obsidian, or garnet under your feet for additional grounding if needed. Set up the rutilated quartz and fluorite crystals at your crown and heart chakras; then hold a smoky quartz in each hand (with the tips pointing away from your body). Relax and breathe normally, releasing tension in your body as you exhale.

2. Envision the issue or problem you'd like to clear. It can be negative feelings toward a spouse, an issue at work, a dispute with a friend, a flat tire, or an over-due bill. Try to see as much detail as possible so you are also able to feel some emotion behind it, too.

3. Visualize a rope between you and the problem. See it thrashing you around, dragging you against your will. Now call upon the spirit energies such as a guardian angel or other being to help free yourself of this burden. See that being as having a sword, a crystal wand, or another instrument or weapon that will cut the rope cleanly. If the rope is not severed in one blow, go back and redo it until the rope is severed. Now visualize the rope shriveling up and melting to the point where there is nothing left. See the problem disappear as well. The rutilated quartz and fluorite will help break up the energy, and the smoky quartz will help with the grounding and transmutation of negative energy.

To end the meditation, gently bring your focus to your heart chakra and, when you are ready, open your eyes. You have broken free of your own negative feelings. Because positive energy is now no longer restricted, a resolution should be forthcoming!

Healing with Light

To make a healing meditation effective on the physical level, you need to truly believe that meditation will help. Take the time to visualize and feel the problem, whether the condition is throughout your body or a localized issue. The cause of illness might or might not be something you can see.

By focusing intently, you are reaching deeply into the layer of consciousness where the illness resides at its subtle levels. As you modify the image to a healthy state at the subtle level, the illness will recede. When the illness dissolves at the subtle level, the manifestation of the illness on the physical level is influenced. Throwing white light at the illness is one way to transmute the illness.

So as you must gather by now, intent medicine and meditation work together to formulate a new reality. Believing in the effectiveness of what you are doing helps to guide the energy to create something new at a subtle level. Meditation empowers your healing process and provides a positive energy influence.

A Body of Light

In this next part, you'll need a clear quartz crystal, preferably with a channeller or trans-channeller configuration (as discussed in Chapter 10), to act as an amplifier and oscillator for refining energy and making it more subtle for this type of meditation. The crystal should be about 1 to 2 inches wide and 2 to 3 inches tall, either polished or raw. Be sure it is cleansed and fully charged. The point of this meditation is to focus with a high level of concentration and intensity so you can activate intense but subtle healing energies. You can initiate this meditation for 10 minutes if you need to have immediate relief. For a major healing session, try to stay with this meditation for 20 minutes.

Remember the meditation in Chapter 5, where you had a look around inside your crystal? If you still haven't completed the crystal initiation exercise, it might be wise to try it before this meditation, just as a warm-up.

Crystal Clear

Light is a vital source for receiving healing energy and blessing from a higher source of power. Spiritual beings use light as a carrier for healing energy because it is the utmost of subtle energy in our cosmology. You can awaken this power in your body and direct it for healing purposes.

To get started, do the following:

1. Find a place to sit or lie quietly. Do your grounding exercise. Place the crystal in your left hand, the hand that gives out energy. If it's comfortable for you, place your left hand holding the crystal at your solar plexus. Place your right hand over the left hand. This pose will provide for energy to recirculate in your body.

2. Close your eyes, or keep them open and gaze softly out into space. Begin relaxation of your body. Note where there is physical tension, and with every breath exhaled, send out any tension. Breathe regularly but naturally. As any thoughts come up, send them away in the exhale as well. Take up to 5 minutes to just relax.

Crystal Clear

You might find that your body twitches and jerks a bit as you relax your muscles. The energy from the crystals will send signals to your neurological system to balance the energy load, taking off excess energy to even out the energy flows on a subtle level.

3. Imagine that your skin is glowing with white light. If white light is hard for you to imagine, try golden light or a glow like the aurora borealis. Go into every nook and cranny on your body to ensure the light is there. Next, envision that your flesh and muscles are glowing with light, even the skinny bits like your fingers. Then light up the nervous system and light up the pathway of nerves throughout the body. Next, light up all the organs and glands and other fleshy parts. Finally, look at the bones, and light them up. Now your whole body is one big golden vibrating mass of light.

4. Feel your body, lit up as it is! This light body contains vast amounts of positive energy. There is no disease here because it is very resilient and indestructible. This light body can handle everything, including radiation, nuclear destruction, and anything else you can name. Go ahead and name some. See? The light body is totally indestructible.

Power Cell

Now we are going to get even more serious. Imagine one cell in your body. Just like the crystal initiation, you are going to enter that cell and feel its vitality and how it moves around. Maybe it's as vast as the universe in there. Follow these steps:

1. Touch the cell and feel its aliveness. It pulses with energy. Feel its light and maybe imagine its tone and color. Feel its energy and maybe its peacefulness.

2. Expand the feeling, take in two or three cells, and feel their energies. Slowly expand your imagination, taking in more and more cells teaming with light and vitality. Feel how wondrous this is and that you can feel the warmth of the light.

3. As the glow reaches to all cells in your body, feel the glowing light energy reaching to places that need this healing and expand the light into dark cells and to where illness and negative emotions dwell. Replace the negative energy with light and feelings of bliss. See your entire body light up, and see light pouring out of the cells of your skin. See this light radiate around you as an aura. See this light reaching out to all beings and filling them with light and healing. Remain in this blissful state of awareness of your light body as long as you can.

To end this meditation, pull all the radiating light back into a ball at your chest and absorb the ball of light into your solar plexus chakra. Your crystal will be very happy from this experience and will remember what to do for next time.

Meditation Education

Knowing what to do to meditate is not hit and miss. You wouldn't want to do yoga without some instruction because you'd end up looking like a pretzel! That's why formal instruction for meditation is recommended. The how to's are to help you understand what to expect and how to avoid pitfalls. Because your mind is endless, having some boundaries is actually a good thing. As your mind progresses with meditation, there are road maps or markers along the way that knowledgeable meditators have also encountered. They can help you past the hurdles.

And of course, crystals are also great to help with those mind hurdles. Used in meditation, crystals create a crystalline structure as a container to help maintain your energy focus. They make you more aware, provide mental clarity, and can remove energy blockages. Meditation takes practice, and the more you do it, the more healing value it will have for you!

The Least You Need to Know

♦ Meditation provides many benefits, including mental clarity, improved memory, and less stress.

♦ Crystals can enhance meditation by regulating energy.

♦ Using music can enhance your crystal meditation because sound and crystals are both part of energy medicine.

♦ Meditation can be used to direct positive outcomes such as resolving problems and providing healing.

♦ While you can certainly meditate on your own, you may want to seek out a professional facilitator or healer to learn new or advanced methods.

Your Personal Path

In This Chapter

- ◆ Making the commitment to work with crystals
- ◆ Welcoming crystals into your everyday life
- ◆ Begin to see yourself as a healer
- ◆ Crystal healing schools
- ◆ Assessing your signs of progress
- ◆ The blending of science, medicine, and spirituality

By the time we reach adulthood, we're all but numbed to the mystery of life. The one bright spot in this is that when people feel their soul is empty, they often go looking for ways to fill it. As a seeker who has found crystals, you'll discover that they give something back. The very energy of crystals reconnects you to Earth, your spiritual home. Your energy becomes revitalized, and your subconscious awakens. Healing abilities become activated. Spiritual development becomes a natural truth to live by.

Once you get started, the journey is endless. And it is not determined by the crystal or by me. You choose your own life, and the quality of it is up to you. If you are already living a joyous life, crystals will be welcome companions on your journey. If you feel like you are living your life in fear, crystals will help see you through whatever has made you a fearful person. There is a way through the pain using crystal therapy for self-transformation.

Commitment to Working with Crystals

When you make a commitment to working with crystals, they make a commitment to you, too! The beauty of working with crystals is that they are always there for you—anytime, anywhere, under any circumstances. They will comfort your emotions when you feel raw and exposed, and they will open your eyes to what you are missing in life.

We all fall into ruts from time to time. Your crystals are like the rescue rope pulling you out. Think of it this way: If someone told you he could give you a pill that would help you meditate more deeply and be more at peace with yourself, would you take it? A lot of people would, and yet they think twice about working with the natural source of the same sort of energy. If someone handed you a crystal and said, "Here you go. Hold this sodalite crystal every night before bedtime, and you will sleep better and feel more calm during the day if you wear it," wouldn't that be a better option than taking a pill?

When people realize something new has come their way, they sometimes become very afraid that they are doing something they "shouldn't," either for religious or societal reasons. Negativity is so built in to our culture that newfound spirituality is often dubbed as "dabbling" and implied to be dangerous or just plain wrong. Well, I believe that if your intent is pure, then your deeds will be, too. That's all there is to that.

It's really a shame that so many people end up with closed minds when it comes to exploring new areas of the mind and soul. After all, when we were children, exploring new things was not only encouraged, but was necessary and meaningful for development on physical, psychological, spiritual, and emotional levels. So why should we believe that limiting that same type of growth as adults would be a positive step?

Crystal Comments

Here are some comments I've received from people new to crystals whose belief in them seems strong, if not a little humorous!

♦ I started working with rose quartz and kunzite and noticed their effects on my sleep. I have moonstone as well. This practice is a little bit scary for me because of its dramatic impact. However, I do realize the need for change.

♦ I have been working with crystals, and I have to say that I think that my bladder and kidney problems have resolved completely. I have also found that working with crystals for my foot problem brings amazing results.

♦ When programming crystals, I have read that one should be as specific as possible. Does this then indicate I can state the amount of money I require and the date that I need it?

♦ My brother-in-law had Ross River Virus (a type of flu common to the South Pacific area) awhile ago. I gave him petrified wood to put in a grid under his bed, and he was healed almost overnight. His friend got the same virus. He passed along the crystal to his friend, who had great success with them, too. So now two skeptics are big believers, which is great.

♦ I like crystals because they are attractive, although I'm a skeptic as to their healing properties. However, I liked what you said. It makes sense.

♦ I currently own a blue lace agate bracelet, and I have been trying to connect with it to heal the goiter associated with my thyroid problem. Usually I only put the bracelet directly on my thyroid gland for a few minutes before I sleep. As I do so, I would also "talk" to it to ask for healing.

♦ Crystals are truly amazing. Recently I came across snowflake obsidian chips in a shop. I reached for them without a thought. Almost immediately I felt their energy. When I finally released them from my hand, the crystal shop owner who then picked them up remarked that the obsidian were pretty warm.

You can see that people just like you reach out for crystals and that for many the experience is intuitive. None of these people have had crystal healing training, yet each one has found his or her way to a healing experience because of crystals.

Natural Stress Relievers

Along the way, using crystals will help to align your subtle energies and protect you from energy chaos, or what we commonly refer to as *stress*. Stress plays a huge factor in our daily lives, our health, and our well-being. Being well requires time and effort, and more and more, it takes creativity and imagination. When we are under stress, we are not always very creative. And when we're really feeling the effects of pressure, we suffer from not being able to visualize wellness. Crystals are terrific interceptors and facilitators because they have the ability to sneak right in and work with the natural healing system we already have—our own crystalline structure.

Gem of an Idea

Make time to meditate—it's not just "zoning out time" or "nap time." It's really something you are doing for your health. Meditation induces an alpha brain wave. Entering the alpha state is essential for relaxation and health.

One of the wonderful by-products of crystals is the enhancement of the meditative state, which is itself a huge weapon in the fight against stress. By simply holding a crystal, we get more value from our time sitting on a cushion gazing at nothing while waiting for emptiness to arrive. And if you haven't started the practice of meditation, or you find it hard to achieve the state of nothingness, you'll find a crystal can help you slip into that state of mind more easily.

Imagine the Possibilities!

Because crystals provide mental clarity, I'd really like to see our aging population take advantage of crystal therapy. Crystals such as tourmaline could specifically be used for offsetting Alzheimer's, dementia, and other geriatric diseases.

Crystals are also helpful to increase awareness and consciousness. The development of psychic abilities is cumulative, meaning the abilities build slowly over time. Let's say you've been wearing crystals and your extrasensory perception has become razor-sharp. If you remove the gemstones from daily wear, these powers won't disappear, but your awareness of them might diminish. Starting back again with crystals will reactivate your power and you will continue to build on top of what you already started.

Due to stress, our emotions and thinking are sometimes in jeopardy. Crystals help to provide insight into emotions and into what drives our thinking. Using the various crystal-healing techniques discussed throughout this book can actually transform negative emotional states and help us to become happier people. Now that's a convincing crystal argument if I ever heard one!

Work with Crystals Every Day

If you have a crystal collection, don't let it sit there gathering dust—use it! And if you can't think of any good reason to pull those gemstones out, look back through this book. If you are not personally experiencing physical or emotional trouble, perhaps someone you know could benefit from some healing. Maybe you need to balance the energy of your home or clear negative energy from a particular space.

If you don't already have a crystal collection, I hope by now you've read and learned enough about the healing power of crystals that you'll be inspired to go out and bring some home!

At first you might be planning to buy only a few crystals to see what crystal healing is like. But before long, I'll bet you'll want to expand your collection, especially if you see healing in action. You'll realize that although the Master Healers (clear quartz, amethyst, rose quartz, turquoise, and smoky quartz) work well, specific crystals for specific purposes can produce amazing results.

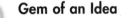

Gem of an Idea _____

Make it a point to drop in and see museum and mineral collections. The "real deals" will provide you with a good visual reference point for selecting top-quality crystals.

So go ahead and add to your collection as you find necessary. But remember that a balanced crystal collection isn't just about having a range of different colored stones. It's about having a range of power, including the different-shaped crystals I talked about in Chapter 10. That way, you'll have some gentle releasers of energy and some that are more active with their power.

Remember the many, many ways to include crystals in your life:

- ◆ Wear them as jewelry or collected as an assortment in a pouch.

- ◆ Sleep with them under your bed, at the top of your head, in your pillow, or taped to your body.

- ◆ Put them in your bath water or shower with them.

- ◆ Drink crystal water or create a gem essence.

- ◆ Place clusters of crystals on your desk or around your home.

- ◆ Use crystals to enhance the energy of your home using the principles of feng shui.

- ◆ Tape crystals to appliances to regulate their energy and extend their life cycle.

Gem of an Idea

Ideally, when a new crystal comes into your life, you will want to spend some time with it and learn about what it has to offer. The crystal in turn will help to attune you to a new, higher frequency. Sometimes you have to let go of old energies to bring in the new. That's how crystal transformation happens!

The possibilities are almost endless! Just don't forget the important practices when you bring a new crystal into your home and life:

♦ Cleanse your crystal and recharge it before using it.

♦ Spend some one-on-one time just gazing at the crystal. What are its features of color, texture, or inclusions? Does it have any special characteristics such as extra crystals clinging to it? This is a time when a transfer of energy and information is likely to occur. You might suddenly feel an electric pulse.

♦ Communicate with the deva of the crystal to learn more about the crystal's mission and purpose.

♦ Meditate with your crystal. Even the small ones can pack a lot of power. When your mind is relaxed and open, communications from other realms can be heard more clearly.

Finally, if you already have a collection, introduce your new crystal to its new pals. Remember that while it takes some time to integrate your energy with the crystal, the crystal is also making connections with its new home, including its new buddies in the toolbox. It's sort of like bringing a new puppy home. It has to sniff all the corners and get to know its playmates!

Gaining Confidence as a Healer

In Chapter 18, I went over the guidelines for a crystal healing session. Don't forget what they say: "Practice makes perfect!" How do you practice becoming a crystal healer? With a little help from your friends. Some of my students have volunteered to act as guinea pigs when I'm conducting a private healing class. In this way, we can learn from each other, both as a healer and as a client. But I also use new crystals on myself. If we do not know the effects a crystal will have on our own bodies and minds, we can't recommend it for others.

Getting More Training in Crystal Healing

Feeling the subtle energy of crystals interacting with your own energy is not easy to do on your own unless you are already fairly sensitive, so attending a class is a great idea. Formal crystal training is available to anyone who wants to advance in their work and perhaps become a healer. For example, a consortium called the Affiliation of Crystal Healing Organisations (ACHO) in England provides accreditation to crystal healing schools teaching a core crystal curriculum. (Some of the information provided in this book would probably qualify under such a program.) In countries where complementary therapies are formalized, certification from a holistic arts institution is often a requirement before treating clients.

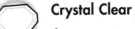

Crystal Clear _____

If you are interested in learning more about crystals and you live in a remote area, you might have to travel to find a good class or instructor. Also remember that crystal devas will teach you what you need to know if you just ask. (And this requires no travel at all!)

Community colleges often provide courses in crystals, usually through health and wellness programs that offer other practices such as Reiki, reflexology, and aromatherapy.

Although some municipalities in North America require certification to acquire a special annual licensing for holistic practices, private crystal training courses are unregulated and are dependent on the instructor being knowledgeable about the topic. Many people who use crystals know quite a lot about them—but that won't necessarily make them good teachers. A good teacher is not only able to know about the crystals and how to use them, but also is quite intuitive. As an *empath*, he can sense how a crystal is interacting with another person's energy and can guide that person in her healing experience. Word of mouth is the best way to find a great teacher. If you don't know anyone in the crystal community, ask holistic healers or the proprietors of metaphysical or gem shops if they can recommend someone.

def•i•ni•tion _____

An **empath** is a person with psychic abilities and emotional intelligence allowing him to remotely sense or feel what another person feels.

As for Internet courses, you'll find quite a few are available, but you really can't learn about crystals unless you have a willing partner for hands-on experiences. Plus, it's difficult to get feedback from an online instructor because often there isn't one. Of course, the Internet is a great resource to find an in-the-flesh instructor or school.

Signs of Progress

Continual handling of crystals has its benefits, one of which is having a brighter complexion. Skin seems to clear up first, followed by increasing good luck, enjoying feelings of happiness, and noticing that other people want to be around you.

Not only will you develop greater sensitivity to the energy of crystals, but you'll also inherit some of their powers. You'll be full of energy, maybe even literally shocking people, such as when you rub your feet over a rug and then get an energy discharge when you touch metal. People will feel your expansion of energy. They might say that they feel your power. (Try to react modestly when this happens!)

You might find that if you meditate frequently with crystals, some interesting extra-sensory perceptions develop, such as clairvoyance, precognition, or heightened sensory abilities like acute sense of smell or hearing. Your eyesight might become sharper, and you may be able to see and be more aware of things. Your intellect and memory will be clearer, especially if you have remembered to do your grounding exercises. You'll feel that you know things for which you have no prior knowledge or education. This is impressive, but not really surprising—this is a spiritual opening, after all!

def•i•ni•tion

A **siddhi** is a spiritual power achieved through meditation, such as flying through the air, being in multiple places at once, moving objects with your mind, and manifesting one's wishes.

As you progress, you might find what East Indian yogis call *siddhis* or psychic powers, which usually develop from spiritual practices such as meditation, prayer, and energy exercises like yoga. For a Western person new to extraordinary spiritual abilities such as levitation, you will think these are remarkable, but really it's just a mark of spiritual evolution.

Remote seeing, the ability to see something without having been present, is another psychic gift. If you ask a psychic about how he knows about future events, he'll tell you it's just his ability to let the natural gifts we are all born with through the barriers we place there. And yes, crystals can help in breaking through those barriers to a new level of awareness.

Compassion for All

Perhaps you picked up this book because you heard crystals can help with meditation and relaxation. But now you know that there is a huge component to using crystals for actual physical healing as well as emotional clearing and spiritual development.

Crystals in the form of silicon dioxide are everywhere—we even breathe in the dust of crystals! So doesn't that mean we are all living, moving crystals? Maybe it means we need crystals to help align ourselves with a bigger consciousness to find cures for what ails us. Those big crystals in the earth are holding us together. The closer we are to the vibration, the more aligned we are to our own oneness of being—our source energy.

You don't need to be shy about wearing or using crystals. Crystals are not associated with any religion or faith. They grow naturally in the earth and are already used in many industries, including pharmaceuticals, computer technology, and manufacturing. You are just using a more subtle aspect of their power for working on the more subtle energies of your body—the human aura, the chakra system, the nadis, your internal organs and external body, your mind and emotions, and of course your own spirituality.

You are part of the new millennium with hope that emerging technologies will provide a greater quality of life for all. You understand that science, medicine, and psychology are blending now and a whole new sacred science is being born. Medicine will work alongside with spirituality where the goal is compassion for all human life.

Please experiment with the crystals because each one has a different purpose for each type of person. Let your intuition guide you to select the right one. Remember to periodically cleanse your crystals and to recharge them in the sun. May you enjoy the healing benefits of all crystals!

The Least You Need to Know

- Making a commitment to work regularly with crystals can lead to personal transformation.

- Don't let your crystals gather dust! Use them to balance the energy in your home, to make an energizing beverage, or wear them at the chakras that need a little balancing.

♦ When you are comfortable working with crystal energy, don't be afraid to start looking at *yourself* as a healer.

♦ Private instruction and classes on crystal healing are great options for people who want to know more.

♦ Some signs of crystal progress include a brighter complexion, greater awareness, and even psychic powers.

♦ The healing power of crystals combines the physical with the spiritual, opening the door to greater compassion on this earth.

Crystals A to Z

agate   Agates are a general class of crystals that includes bloodstone, carnelian, chrysoprase, onyx, jasper, and petrified wood. Agates generally help to balance yin-yang energy on the physical level and the extremes of emotional and mental energy.

amazonite   Amazonite is very soothing emotionally and is particularly good for those undergoing emotional trials such as cancer treatment, divorce, or grieving. It pacifies worries, fear, and aggravations. It's excellent for children with behavioral disorders, for those with neurological problems, or for those with "bad nerves." It is best used at the heart or solar plexus chakra.

amber   Made from the resin of trees, amber is a semiprecious substance and is used in crystal healing for its emotionally soothing energy. It is also excellent for soothing emotions and physical stress during post-operative care. Amber calms nerves, enlivens the body, and rekindles energy. It can uplift a negative disposition and encourage you to take life less seriously. It also promotes fidelity in relationships. As a self-healing stone, amber guides the emotions into a clearer mental outlook and encourages taking greater responsibility for one's choices in life. It works best at the solar plexus chakra.

amethyst   One of the Master Healers, amethyst has the ability to transmute negativity and provide an improved outlook on life by promoting flexibility, cooperation,
and peace. As a transformer, amethyst's job is to take lower dysfunctional vibrations
and clear them by transmuting them to a higher vibrational level. Amethyst facilitates
expansion of the third eye and expands psychic abilities by connecting intuitive
receptors to the crown chakra. For physical healing, amethyst is used to regulate
thyroid conditions and alleviate the pain of arthritis. It heals all things at all levels.

ametrine   Due to heat-treatment, one half of the stone is shaded amethyst and the
other half is citrine—hence its name. Ametrine acts as a catalyst and speeds up intellectual recognition of spiritual ascension. This would be a good crystal for initiating
a quickening.

angelite   This crystal holds light angelic energy and provides a shield of light
around the wearer. Like celestite, it activates the subtle energies of the upper chakras
providing communication paths and clarity for channeling and telepathy.

Apache tears   This crystal stimulates emotional spontancity and the release of
barriers that prevent you from experiencing deep emotions. This stone is excellent for
transmuting one's own negativity under stressful situations. The Apache tear is a dark
black stone of obsidian and, when held up to the light, appears transparent. However,
it has been noted that as the grief one feels goes into the stone, it can turn it opaque.
It is best used in the hands or solar plexus.

apatite   This crystal provides relief for overeaters by helping to normalize one's
appetite (apply named!). Apatite comes in a variety of chakra colors. It also helps to
access the devas and opens up the upper chakras to seekers of truth.

apophyllite   This crystal is an awesome third eye and crown opener. Apophyllite
facilitates astral travel and helps to initiate a person to new levels of intuition. This
crystal acts as a bridge to cross time dimensions and provides access to spiritual
dimensions. It is best used in the third eye or crown chakra.

aquamarine   This crystal is very protective emotionally and helps you remain
centered through complex issues. Aquamarine strengthens one's resolve to feel that
life has a purpose. It is excellent for dispelling negative emotions originating from
one's weaknesses: fears, phobias, and anxiety. Aquamarine releases false expectations.
This crystal helps in your attunement to be of service to others and diminishes the
self-centeredness that often gets in the way of genuine spirituality. It works best at
your truth center, the throat chakra.

aventurine   Aventurine purifies the emotional body and soothes nerves. Aventurine strengthens and restores the heart energy, providing a balance of male and female energies. This crystal is green and very loving, embracing, and protective of the heart. Many children who are shy, timid, or suppressing their leadership qualities need a crystal like aventurine. This stone helps the individual to become active and initiate action on her own accord. Asthmatic children seem attracted to this stone because it opens up the lungs and they experience a sense of relief.

azurite   Azurite provides an opening to a deeper level of consciousness and cleanses and prepares the mind to work on a higher spiritual level to provide deeper understanding and acceptance. It works with the throat chakra to purify the intent behind one's spiritual activities.

azurite-malachite   This blend of two types of crystals that grow together provides a powerful sense of getting to core matters by probing and penetrating past the masks we bear. The truth is exposed by unlocking the past. Use this crystal at the third eye or throat chakra.

barite   Barite, the "relationship crystal" is one of the crystals that can be used to stimulate friendship and loyalty. It can be used to soothe emotions and remove toxins from the body as part of addiction recovery programs.

black onyx   Used for psychic protection, it is so black that it shields the wearer from attack. It allows the wearer to be sensitive to negative energies but not be harmed by them. Onyx alleviates mental confusion and absorbs grief. It is best used in your pockets or at the root chakra for grounding.

bloodstone   Has masculine yin qualities and a tremendous ability to heal organs in the middle torso: liver, stomach, pancreas, gall bladder, large intestine, and heart. Bloodstone dispels discouragement and gives strength and endurance to withstand endless difficulties. This crystal reduces stress and anxiety. It revitalizes and encourages unselfishness in relationships. It is grounding to an emotional heart and provides a support tool to those in distress or who suffer from anxiety. It also provides grounding for going deeply into spirituality and mystical matters without getting lost. Bloodstone is a great anchor or safety net and can be used with other crystals to provide safe-keeping of subtle energies. Hold this crystal in your hand or place it at your solar plexus.

blue lace agate Connects you with your spiritual gifts and provides nonjudgmental support and loving, unconditional energy. It alleviates spiritual tension and emotional intensity. This crystal is calming when used at the throat chakra. It helps you to speak your truth, channel your higher thoughts, and facilitate expression of spirituality. It is calming whenever a major opening has occurred in a chakra. Wear it as a necklace or place it at your throat chakra.

Botswana agate Soothes repressed emotions and is excellent for smokers whose nerves are on edge when used at the throat chakra. It can move you beyond self-limits. Used at the third eye, it provides communication access to the devas of the animal and plant worlds.

calcite Clears and optimizes the energy in chakras, by color. Calcite is a gentle cleanser of emotional upsets and helps you move forward after releasing emotional restrictions. Pink or white calcite provides an opening of the higher chakras where a direct channel is needed for communicating with your Highest Self. Use it in your hand during meditation, or place it at your throat, third eye, or crown chakra.

carnelian Effectively heals skin, acne, herpes, scars, and wrinkles and addresses issues of self-esteem. Carnelian eliminates feelings of inadequacy and low self-worth. It works with amethyst to transmute with extreme negative states such as envy, fear, rage, and sorrow. This stone is especially good for recovery after an emotional disappointment. It transmutes sadness in your heart into the initiative to do something positive about the problem. This crystal encourages enthusiasm and is good for giving vibrancy to one's sexuality. Carnelian restores trust to spiritually jaded people and keeps the focus on a higher level rather than physical or emotional levels. Wear this crystal at the heart chakra or hold it in your hand during meditation.

celestite Provides openness and expansion of one's consciousness, giving you the ability to articulate messages from the higher realms. It facilitates the opening of the throat, third eye, and crown chakras; helps develop and heighten telepathic abilities; and provides a pathway for consciousness to enter the higher realms. It lets you speak authentically about spiritual matters. Celestite is said to be good to help those who fear heights and those with digestive disorders. Celestite keeps your crown chakra active for receiving messages from friends and family and from subtle spirit energies who use the dream state to teach us.

charoite This ray of purple light dispels fear and connects the third eye to the mental plane to help loosen the need for worldly attachments and to prepare for the vibration of giving and receiving unconditional love. It provides for deeper intellectual, creative, and analytical abilities. It is best worn at the heart chakra.

chrysocolla   Grounds emotional energy and eases extreme emotional mood swings. It provides emotional strength, balances expression and communication of emotions, and releases distress and guilt. It is best used at the solar plexus chakra. It is a very active crystal and can expel negative emotional states, sometimes rather dynamically, so use chrysocolla with a rose quartz or jade crystal to temper the effects.

chrysoprase   This lovely green crystal is used to alleviate alcoholism and to provide ease to feelings of depression. It allows you to take one day at a time, build on successes through small changes, and be patient with inner transformation. It is best used at the throat and third eye chakras.

citrine   This crystal increases a positive emotional influence and dispels negativity on the mental and emotional levels. It counters nonproductive energy and frees energy for spontaneous expression. The golden rays of citrine provide a complex energy structure that energizes the crown and sacral chakras. Citrine transmutes the grosser material and physical vibrations into higher spiritual aspects and provides protection for the aura. Use it at the heart chakra or hold it in your hand during meditation.

clear quartz   One of the Master Healers and a Universal Healer, clear quartz generates energy, brings energy in, or can send energy to someone else. It unblocks and transmutes negative energy and dispels negative disposition. It works as a translator for communication with all other forms of energy. It balances positive and negative electrical charges and provides clear thinking about issues and creating thoughts into reality. Clear quartz provides balance and harmony to all areas of your life, including love, health, and spirituality. The rainbow quartz neutralizes, dissolves grief and other sadness, and restores feelings of joy.

copper   A natural mineral necessary for the formation of hemoglobin to keep bones and nerves healthy, it is used for the treatment of arthritis. Copper is a conductive material and is able to pass electrical pulses along its matrix without interference. To that end, it also dispels complacency and lethargy and stimulates self-dependence.

coral   Although technically coral is not a crystal, it is semiprecious and often used in crystal healing for its blood purification properties. The common colors are red and white. Red is for physical ailments, and white is for accessing truth and higher communications. Coral quiets the emotions and dispels feelings of despair and despondency. It encourages a passionate energy and stimulates and strengthens female reproductive organs through tissue regeneration. This stone relates well to the spleen meridian for blood circulation and to purification of the kidneys and bladder. Red coral is considered to be the blood of Mother Earth by Amerindians and is considered particularly precious by Tibetan women for menstruation, fertility, and blood disorders.

diamond   Promotes trust and fidelity in relationships. Diamonds brighten and enliven your aura by clearing out stale energy. Diamonds provide spiritual confidence and activate the crown chakra. The brilliance of light from the diamonds dispels brain fog and gives clarity to meditation.

dioptase   This brilliant emerald-green crystal provides attunement for the third eye. Dioptase can provide a wake-up call for those still so attached to worldly problems that entering into higher states of consciousness is hardly possible. This crystal teaches one to live through her heart and to be in the moment. It can be used for easing pain, hypertension, and other physical ailments.

emerald   An ancient love stone, emerald helps to soften arrogance and promote cooperation. Emerald dispels negative thoughts and helps you hold onto what is practical. It cools an angry heart and promotes divine love and peace. This crystal is excellent for preserving love that is maturing into a long-term relationship. Emerald is an emotional heart soother. This crystal provides peace at the heart chakra, especially about matters that trigger anxiety. Instead of falling into a deep emotional pit, emerald will help focus and guide your action to stay centered on your life's purpose.

fluorite   Considered to be a crystal of high mental stimulation and creativity, blue fluorite relates to the throat chakra. Purple fluorite unblocks energy and opens the upper chakras, whereas red, orange, and yellow fluorite opens the lower chakras. Rainbow fluorite provides the full spectrum of healing that fluorite has to offer. All colors of fluorite calm the emotional body and stimulate intellectual certainty. Purple fluorite helps to break up blockages at all levels. This crystal holds intense white light and activates the third eye and crown chakras.

galena   Inhibits the growth of viruses (thus its use as kohl for eye makeup) and helps attune those to medicinal studies. It is used to reduce inflammations and stimulate the nervous system. It is best used at the root and solar plexus chakras. It's also a semiconductor material and was used in early crystal radio sets!

garnet   Effective for problems related to the second chakra and for correcting various gynecological issues, PMS, and infertility. It is best known for revitalizing the physical and emotional body. Garnet increases the life force and one's passion for life and regeneration. Garnet provides grounding for chaotic emotions and allows the release of love from within oneself. It is best used in the lower chakras.

gold   One of the purest of minerals on the planet, gold is the master of all metals. It gives a sense of power and connection to great strength, along with a sense of absolute purity. Gold has the ability to link with the matrix of other crystals and is an activator of their electrical circuitry. Gold also fortifies the energy fields to be more resilient to pain. As a refiner of energies, it has a role to play in purifying and balancing energy fields and to bring peace within one's self. Use it at the third eye and crown chakras.

halite   Also known as rock salt, its colors vary due to impurities. It has the ability to purify the environment. It clears chakras of negative imbalances and stimulates psychic abilities. If used externally for water retention, it can draw out excess fluids.

hematite   The natural magnetic quality of hematite makes it a perfect crystal to use instead of commercial magnets. Hematite is also a blood purifier and relates well to anger and other toxins stored in the liver. Hematite gives emotional support to new love and helps to ground love energy so it doesn't fly away when challenged. It protects the heart from small love wounds. Its shiny surface reflects back negativity and helps reduce stress to the whole body.

hemimorphite   Protects self-esteem and purifies one's intentions. It is effective to reduce anger and hostility toward others. Hemimorphite has some ability in being used for neurological reconnection in the brain after stroke or injury.

Herkimer diamond   An attunement tool, it provides expansion of consciousness and clears the channels to access higher spiritual levels for communication. It can sharpen your memory of dreams and provide healing at the mental and spiritual planes. It is best used at the third eye chakra.

howlite   Dyed sky blue to look like turquoise, it is named turquistite as an inexpensive alternative. Howlite dispels negative attitudes such as overcriticalness and selfishness. It is best used at the solar plexus and third eye chakras.

infinite   This opaque green crystal is also called the "healer's stone." It has a loving energy that seems to pull out pain, reduce stress, and cause relaxation. It can be used anywhere for reducing physical pain. Used at the heart chakra, it is a companion crystal for healers, providing insight to the ailments of others.

iolite   Provides an ability to open the third eye for clarity of visions and other intuitive work. It is a protector while entering higher states of consciousness and provides unconditional love. It promotes self-change. It is best used at the third eye chakra.

jade   Known as a crystal of tranquility and as the "sport stone," it promotes agility and swiftness. Some say jade is for good luck. It soothes the emotions and provides emotional detachment and restoration after various traumas such as minor surgery, divorce, funerals, or loss of a job. It promotes peace, family harmony, and tranquility. It provides a sense of self-worth, self-sufficiency, and capability in dealing with any situation. It is best worn in the upper chakras.

jasper   Makes it easier to use one's own power and to know that it cannot be taken away. It calms aggressive energy and facilitates safety and protection during recovery periods (for example, from stress, operations, and other life traumas). Red jasper provides lively fresh energy and reduces feelings of being victimized. Yellow jasper balances hormones and protects the wearer during travel. Green jasper restores energy and focus during recovery from burnout.

kunzite   This lovely pink crystal is used for the prevention of heart disorders, for pain in the heart, and for post-operative recovery after heart surgery. Kunzite opens the emotional heart to an inner dimension of divine love while dispelling negativity that would prevent the powerful connection. Because this gemstone has a high lithium content, emotional stress and behavioral disorders can be alleviated quickly. Just looking at kunzite provides a sense of peace and well-being and stimulates sensuality. It is best used at the heart and crown chakras.

kyanite   Clears mental illusions and helps you to see a situation for what it is. Kyanite helps align the chakra system.

lab-grown crystals   Also known as synthetics, these crystals are grown under extreme heat and steam using a hydrothermal process in a pressure cooker called an *autoclave*, which can produce over 20,000 psi (pounds per square inch).

labradorite   Helps to keep the aura clear and protects it from imbalances. It provides for access to other levels of consciousness. It is a crystal of leadership and is good for teachers to help others reach their potential. It is an excellent crystal for past life recall, improving inner vision, and helping with the perseverance of the spiritual journey. Labradorite relates best to the upper chakras, especially the crown.

lapis lazuli   A dark blue stone known to promote a clear mind and to provide spiritual protection, it unblocks and releases emotions from the heart for self-acceptance. Lapis lazuli has a third eye and crown connection to intensify inner visions and deeper connection through the crown chakra. Attunes the mental states of awareness and promotes self-acceptance of one's spiritual gifts. For intuitive people, lapis intensifies psychic power. The deep blue color stimulates expansion of consciousness in a supportive way, promoting purification and clarity of spiritual insight. This stone is highly prized for its protective powers and stimulation of all psychic senses.

lead crystal   Lead crystal is nothing more than glass containing up to 35 percent lead oxide to increase the sparkle. It does not contain the same crystal structure as a true crystal.

lepidolite   Reduces stress responses such as stiff shoulders and tight solar plexus and alleviates despondency. It provides grounding for "fly-away" emotions by providing detachment from situations so clarity of purpose can be seen. It can be very grounding when you don't know what else to do. Lepidolite operates on and unifies the upper chakras: heart, throat, third eye, and crown.

malachite   This deep forest-green stone clears the heart chakra of past experiences by unblocking and absorbing any negative energies. Malachite allows you to stay tolerant, loyal, and practical. It is a heavy releaser of negative emotions and is best used in conjunction with rose quartz to bring peace to emotions during deep releasing. It can aid in breaking down old patterns, whether emotional (stuck patterns of behavior) or physical (tumors, swollen joints, or muscular). The most important aspect of this crystal's healing ability, however, is for the preventive health of the physical heart and liver. If you are attracted to this crystal, chances are you have a family history of heart-related problems and probably need a heart check-up.

marble   Marble has the ability to absorb and retain energy and is soothing physically and mentally. It is best used in your hand during meditation to absorb the quiet qualities of each session.

Mexican lace agate   The multiple colors and crazy pattern of this agate can actually cause laughter. Used at the solar plexus, it can lighten the mood and provide an opening for happiness and joy to flow into and out of the heart chakra.

moldavite   A meteorite that is green and produces spacey prophetic, visionary dreams, moldavite is also a huge instigator of change or quickening. It is a major transformer and tool of consciousness and interdimensional communication.

mookite   This Australian dream crystal is a variety of jasper and is used to enhance dream time and to recall messages from the dream state. It is also said to be helpful in speeding the healing of wounds.

moonstone   Provides unconditional love and acceptance, as well as a sense of peace at emotional transition points (puberty, marriage, births, deaths, and menopause). Moonstone provides a depth of perception and discernment. It can increase creativity, intuition, and self-expression. It has physical rejuvenating qualities for the skin and hair and offers protection for travelers. It is best worn at the heart or solar plexus chakra.

moss agate   Soothes self-esteem and battered egos. It strengthens positive emotional traits and promotes communications with the plant devas. Because moss agate relates strongly to the earth's energy, it has a powerful influence on women's healing and nurturing. It is best used at the heart, solar plexus, and sacral chakras.

obsidian   This volcanic material is an important crystal used for grounding energies. When used at the solar plexus, it acts as a door opener and dispels negative emotions by releasing old energy patterns. Obsidian transmutes energy blockages into white light. It should be used in the lower chakras.

opal   The rainbow colors of opal provide a brightening of the aura. Opal helps to brighten a negative attitude and dispel a dark mood. It promotes spontaneity and is a tonic to uplift moodiness. It also helps to discern the truth and bring hope and happiness to the wearer. Opal is best worn at the heart and upper chakras.

pearl   Although not a gemstone, pearl is a natural material found worldwide from oysters. It stimulates purity and eases the pain associated with female physical issues, such as childbirth. The wearer and the pearl's energy integrate, and the luster of the pearl is a reflection of the inner spiritual glow of the person.

peridot   Peridot is often used as a dream stone and as a gemstone for physical regeneration and long life. It clears chakras and is best used after Reiki, crystal healing, and chiropractic and acupuncture treatments to maintain subtle body alignment. Peridot restores inner balance that is overpowered by egotistic drive and self-destruction. It is best used at the heart and solar plexus chakras.

petrified wood   A composite form of agate and jasper, it is calming to jittery types. It is especially good for calming fears when held to the solar plexus. It can be used to access past lives and the Akashic Record. It works on both the mental and emotional levels.

pyrite   Especially good for maintaining the purity of one's purpose and helping keep outside influences away, pyrite is like a small mirror—negative energy is reflected away and a protective shield of energy is created in the aura. It also provides a feeling of physical empowerment, that life in the physical form is perfect, and that love is abundant. Pyrite is all about perfection and flawlessness. It is best used for meditation and for feng shui to align the bagua to universal purpose.

quartz   *See* clear quartz.

rainbow moonstone   A form of colorless labradorite that looks like a miniature aurora borealis. *See* moonstone.

rhinestone   A jewel made from glass or acrylic and coated on the back with a reflective metallic coating to imitate diamonds and other gemstones.

rhodochrosite   This golden pink crystal with white banding provides renewal and a way to turn self-criticism, anger, and loathing into compassion, love, and self-acceptance. Rhodochrosite is a soothing emotional balancer for use after a period of intense emotional stress. It works well to dissolve and transmute feelings of guilt. It is best worn at the heart chakra.

rhodonite   This crystal is pink with black veins and provides excellent grounding for a heart chakra experiencing heartbreak. It can also stimulate the heart chakra and mental levels into a higher purpose for humanity. It relates to the root chakra but is best worn at the heart chakra so rhodonite's lessons can be absorbed at a more conscious level.

rock crystal   Rock crystal is composed of natural quartz crystal. *See* clear quartz.

rose quartz   A Master Healer and a heart chakra opener, rose quartz oozes compassion into all centers of the body. The wearer becomes aligned with a gracious and gentle energy where even tough emotional wounds can be soothed. It dispels negative emotional states, such as despondency and possessiveness, and promotes harmonious relationships. It also cools inflammations as well as emotional issues related to pain. It enhances one's ability to give and receive love by opening the heart chakra and stimulating greater flexibility in communications. It mellows out a reluctant heart and provides peace in relationships through harmony. Rose quartz is used for meditation, to still one's aggressive thoughts, and to provide mental tranquility. It is best used in the upper chakras but can be used elsewhere on the body as needed.

ruby   Encourages and preserves romantic love and promotes the ideal relationship. This crystal brings focus to the heart and releases disoriented and trapped love energy. It protects the heart from unnecessary love-suffering and promotes the attainment of love objectives: health, happiness, wealth, and spiritual knowledge. It is best worn at the heart chakra.

rutilated quartz   This Master Cleanser, with its fine "angel hairs," will unlock and unblock stagnant energy. This crystal breaks up old energy patterns and promotes clarity on issues. Rutilated quartz helps move you past out-dated thought patterns so you can embrace new values. It pulls apart complex emotional issues and unblocks chakras to allow negative energies to dissolve. Rutilated quartz can be used anywhere as needed to unblock energy.

sapphire   Very calming, it imparts patience and leadership abilities. It can amplify intuition and promotes emotional and mental maturity.

selenite   This frozen white light is a bridge between the crown chakra and the most subtle of energies. Selenite offers support and a sense of purpose from your higher self. It allows you to reach beyond your emotional state to the higher psycho-spiritual centers such as altruism, compassion, and love. It can provide teachings on various subjects by contacting the crystal deva. It is best used at the crown chakra overnight to provide attunement and refinement for the higher chakras.

silica   *See* clear quartz.

silver   When silver is worn, energy is retained and circulates throughout the subtle body. Silver also provides a balance when used with other crystals. It activates the upper chakras.

smoky quartz   Another Master Healer, its job is to clear and transmute negative emotions. It draws out pain and releases negative emotions that can be causing physical pain. This crystal is excellent for grounding all kinds of negative energy such as mood swings, aggressive actions, ill temper, and generally nasty thoughts. Smoky quartz is an excellent crystal to use in times of stress and to rebuild emotional burnout by offering protection during the healing period. It reduces the fear of failure, unblocks self-limitations, and lets you risk trying some new experiences. It is best used at the lower chakras but can be used elsewhere on the body for grounding energy as needed.

snakeskin agate   This agate almost instantly promotes inner peace and dispels worries. It promotes a cheerful disposition. It is best used in your hands for meditation.

sodalite   Calming emotions and numbing mental chatter caused by emotional stress, sodalite helps alleviate insomnia caused by overactive mental chatter. It helps to dispel irrelevant thoughts, provides mental focus, and maintains logical reasoning with regard to emotional upsets. Sodalite promotes issues of trust and enhances companionship and the commonality of goals with others. It is best used in the upper chakras.

spinel   Each color of spinel relates to a different chakra. It is a powerful detoxifier and rejuvenator.

sugilite   Sugilite helps you become more sensitive to higher spiritual values and will support your alignment with them as you develop more conscious awareness. Sugilite is a crystal that is spiritually inspiring and takes you into a contemplative space. It can also help dispel headaches. It is best used in the upper chakras or held in your hand during meditation.

Swarovski crystals   *See* lead crystal.

synthetic quartz   *See* lab-grown crystals.

tanzanite   Considered to be the crystal for the new millennium. Its qualities include opening your heart chakra to appreciate that your journey on the planet is a spiritual gift and remind you that you are guided by the wisdom of the heart. Tanzanite can be used at the third eye as an initiation to communicate with higher spiritual realms.

tiger eye   Provides mental and emotional discipline for people who are unable to appreciate self-responsibility. This stone is excellent for grounding psychic energy and providing security for opening up the psychic centers. This stone is useful as a grounder to put action to one's thoughts, especially if you are a dreamer or procrastinator. Tiger eye is about being practical. It is best used at the solar plexus or heart chakra.

topaz   A manifestation crystal that works well with the mental energies to create one's projections, golden topaz is known as a builder of faith and crown activator. It helps you recharge with golden light saturating your aura. Blue topaz opens and reconditions the third eye to see at a higher level. Use topaz in the upper chakras.

tourmaline   Tourmalines are very electrical and energetic. Green tourmaline is a major unblocker of emotional energy by keeping energy circuits open and energy flowing. Pink tourmaline activates and soothes the heart and provides feelings of intense beauty while preventing victimization. Tourmalines are initiators of access to higher levels of consciousness and are best worn in the upper chakras or used in meditation as part of a layout or held in your hand.

tumbled crystals   Stones that have been smoothed to a glossy finish using a physical process.

turquisite   *See* howlite.

turquoise   A Master Healer, detoxifier, and protector of the physical body, including during travel, turquoise aligns all subtle bodies and works with the meridians to unblock and promote the flow of chi. Turquoise is best known as a stone of communications, working enthusiastically with the throat chakra. It is a stone that provides for the expression of creativity, not only vocally through speech and singing, but also through activity. It provides emotional detachment and focus on self-accomplishment without entanglement with others. It can be used anywhere on the body.

unakite   The two colors of this crystal, pink and green, relate to the emotional (pink = movement) and the physical (green = grounding) parts of the heart chakra. This crystal helps you to move on after a disappointment.

yang crystals These include carnelian, diamond, fire opal, garnet, lapis lazuli, malachite, obsidian, rutilated quartz, smoky quartz, and sapphire.

yin crystals These include agates, amber, amethyst, aquamarine, calcite, clear quartz, fluorite, jade, moonstone, and rose quartz.

zircon As one of the crystals used in the Ayurvedic healing system, zircon provides access to higher levels of consciousness and integrates all energy levels. It gives the wearer joy and good luck and dispels nervousness. Zircon promotes the acquisition of wealth, wisdom, and nobility of heart. It protects the nerves, bones, muscles, and inner organs. It is best worn according to the Ayurvedic astrology system or at the heart chakra.

zoistite Used like malachite for the direct release of repressed emotions, it amplifies awareness about the issues. It connects the root and heart chakras for mutual release and integration of energies.

Glossary

affirmation   A statement used to counter a negative behavioral pattern with one that reflects a more positive outlook.

Akashic Record   Said to exist on another dimension and hold the information about yourself, your past lives, as well as all past events. The Record is like a huge library of energy!

astral travel   An event marked by your subconsciousness leaving the physical plane (also called an out-of-body experience) and traveling to a nonphysical astral realm where you can visit loved ones who have passed on, talk with spiritual teachers, and enjoy countless other freedoms.

attunement   The process of aligning your energy with that of a particular crystal.

aura   A reflection of the colors of the chakra system. Different colors can indicate which chakra and its associated systems are strongest in your body.

aurora borealis   Also known as the Northern Lights, this is the display of light energy in the northern hemisphere. Electrons from solar winds interact with the magnetic and electrical fields of our planet. The colorful display looks similar to the energy glow from the aura around the human body.

Ayurvedic   An ancient healing system from India based on natural methods and medicines.

Ayurvedic gemstones   Crystals that are believed to balance any cosmic energies that were out of balance when you were born.

bagua   A diagram of symbols used to represent different directions, yin/yang principles, seasons, and family members. Each section of a home or garden corresponds to one of the eight segments in the bagua.

blockage   A restriction in an energy pathway that prevents energy from being released and from passes through.

cabochon   A type of cut usually applied to opaque gemstones that leave an unfaceted convex-shaped top with a flat underside.

carat   The weight of a gemstone. 1 carat is equivalent to 200 milligrams.

catharsis   A dramatic and often sudden release of pent-up emotional energy. It is a purification process, a freeing of oneself from negative emotions that have contaminated the physical, mental, emotional, and psychic states of being.

chakra   Spinning wheels of energy that provide circulation of prana to the nadis and contain vital energies as well as spiritual energies. *See also* nadis.

chi   A Chinese word for air used to describe a person's vital life force. *See also* prana.

collective consciousness   A shared belief that unifies a social group.

crystal   A solid material comprised of two molecules of silicon dioxide and one molecule of oxygen. The different shapes of crystals are due to differences in molecular bonding. Crystals also have electrical properties as well as discrete light diffraction.

crystal energy therapist   A person trained both as a crystal healer and as a psychotherapist or life counselor.

crystal healer   A person who understands the crystalline complex and how to use crystal energy to create a curative transformation at the physical, emotional, and psycho-spiritual levels of being.

crystal initiation   A session during which one meditates and enters into the crystal matrix.

crystal layout   A geometric arrangement of crystals placed either around or on the body to create and augment crystal resonance for meditation and healing.

crystal structure   The unique arrangement of atoms in a crystal.

Crystal Therapy System (CTS)   A crystal healing methodology based on Tibetan energy medicine and dynamic techniques for opening, clearing, calming, rebuilding, and rebalancing energy using crystals. The training program consists of four levels of instruction on crystal healing.

crystalline   Also known as a crystal or crystalline solid. A repeating pattern of atoms, molecules, or ions extending in three spatial directions to form a structure.

crystallization   The process of forming a crystalline structure or crystal.

crystallography   The study of how crystals are actually formed, including their internal structures.

deva   A term used to convey contact with the awareness of a group of like-minded people or things.

diffraction   The parallel slits of light created when light passes through an obstacle in a crystal.

distance healing   The ability to influence healing at all levels—body, mind, and spirit—through focused healing intent.

empath   A person with psychic abilities and emotional intelligence allowing her to remotely sense or feel what another person feels.

energy medicine   A method of healing that restores an imbalance in the body's "energy field" to bring about health and wellness.

energy pathway   The unseen passageways that carry energy. These include prana or chi, meridians, and chakras. *See also* chakra, chi, meridian, prana.

energy vortex   The rotation of energy that swirls around its center. The speed of energy is faster at the center than at its outer boundaries.

ethereal   A subtle energy field that exists between the physical energy field of the body and the emotional energy field that provides a double of your physical body's configuration.

feng shui   Pronounced *fung shway*, it's an ancient art of placement based on the principle of an eight-spoke wheel in which each spoke represents a part of one's life and environment. Using "cures" for bad influences, objects and colors are placed in the areas of the home or building elements to restore balance and achieve harmony.

Gaia   A concept stating that the organisms of the biosphere (Earth) regulate the planet to the benefit of the whole. For example, rocks, soil, plants, and the atmosphere all work in harmony.

gem essence   A homeopathically prepared solution made by using sunlight to infuse spring water with the characteristics of specific crystals.

gemstone   A cut and polished mineral, crystal, or other material such as amber or pearl.

grounding   A method to transfer unwanted energies into the earth to minimize interference, damage, and build-up of harmful energy in the physical and emotional body.

guided meditation   A method of physical relaxation that stimulates various centers in the brain related to visual, auditory, or other sensory faculties. You are led through the stages of meditation by a calm, soothing speaker.

healing crisis   Physical, emotional, and/or mental symptoms and afflictions caused by repelling illness from the body.

holoenergetic healing   A holistic healing technique that uses energy, intention, imagery, and insight to influence and transform subtle energies.

hologram   An object whose image is recorded as light, is later reconstructed, and will appear as three-dimensional even though the object might no longer exist.

ida   One of two channels in the chakra system representing the sun or masculine element. *See also* pingala.

intent healing   The application of mental intent to cause a healing response.

intent medicine   The power of conscious mental intention; it can include prayer, meditation, or other like practices.

karma   The accumulation of positive or negative merit based on past action.

ki   A Japanese term to describe a person's life force.

lattice   A geometric arrangement or network of points.

lung   Subtle life force energies that flow through the body. *See also* chi, prana.

mandala   An ancient diagram of geometric patterns symbolizing the universe and the cosmic order of all things. By viewing the diagram, subtle energies are invoked.

manifestation crystal   A rare form of crystal that has another crystal growing inside it.

mantra   Repetition of a holy word to induce a state of peace and well-being or to call on spiritual powers.

matrix   The earthen structure in which the crystal actually grew.

meridian   An invisible pathway that energy travels along to provide health to major organs.

metaphysician   A philosopher who examines the nature of reality and the mind-body connection and sometimes will enter the border of the supernatural to seek explanations beyond established laws.

metaphysics   A philosophical inquiry into the nature of reality and the relationships between things.

miasm   A hereditary predisposition making one susceptible to various diseases that appear only if there is a trigger (such as food, the environment, trauma, or the introduction of chemicals).

mineralogy   The study of the structure, chemistry, and properties of minerals.

Mohs scale of hardness   A method used to determine the hardness and scratch-resistance of a rock. A lower number on the scale indicates a softer stone.

motif   An arrangement of atoms or molecules that repeat at each point in a lattice.

mysticism   The awareness of an absolute reality or spiritual truth through direct experience or communion with an ultimate source, such as God.

nadis   The network or pathways on which subtle pranic energy flows.

pendulum   A crystal or metal, charged with positive intent, suspended from a chain or string. It is used to answer your questions about the future or to hone your intuition.

piezoelectric effect   The ability to generate energy in response to pressure.

pingala   One of two channels in the chakra system representing the moon or feminine element.

prana   An Eastern Indian term to describe a person's vital life force. *See also* chi.

psi   Stands for pounds per square inch, a measurement of pressure.

psychoenergetics   A new field of science that investigates the meeting of consciousness, energy and matter, and the nature of reality.

quartz   A clear crystal comprised of two molecules of silicon dioxide and one molecule of oxygen.

quickening   A transformational process that speeds up spiritual awareness and development.

Reiki   A hands-on healing technique that increases the body's natural ability to heal physical ailments and release the causes of disease. The Reiki healing energy is focused and channeled by a Reiki healing therapist. Universal life force energy is gently absorbed into the body to heal at all levels.

sacred geometry   Formations used in the construction of sacred architecture and in the design of sacred art.

sacred healing   A term used for the processes that are not governed by conventional application of medicine or medical procedures. These can include all kinds of alternative therapies, such as working with crystals.

sacred trinity   The concept of three sacred elements, present in many major faiths.

scepter   A wand or staff used in ceremonies, sometimes decorative.

scrying   An ancient form of divination using a reflective surface such as water or a crystal ball to see images that can relate hidden or future events.

shiatsu   A treatment similar to pressure point massage that balances energy along the meridian lines.

siddhi   A spiritual power achieved through meditation, such as flying through the air, being in multiple places at once, moving objects with your mind, and manifesting one's wishes.

smudge   A method of fanning burning sage leaves, frankincense, myrhh, copal, or other incense substances over the body to purify it of negative influences and to clear the mind.

subtle body   The channels or pathways in the body that one's essential being (or chi, or prana) runs along.

subtle energy   One's essential energy that travels along pathways in the body.

sushumna   The central channel in the chakra system to which the chakras are joined.

tigle   The seeds of energy that are considered to be more subtle than lung or prana. The mind is dependent on the tigle flowing freely. *See also* lung, prana.

toning   A method of singing or playing a tone to resonate, rebalance, and harmonize a chakra.

transcendent   Moving beyond the limitations of personal reality and ordinary experience.

transpersonal   The transcendence of the ego's psychological limitations to search for and move beyond the rational realm and into the mystical realm.

tsa   The channels or pathways on which subtle energy flows. *See also* nadis.

tumbled crystals   Stones that have been smoothed to a glossy finish using a rotary tumbler as part of a physical process. It takes several days of continuous rotation to transform a jagged rock into a highly polished stone.

x-ray crystallography   A method of studying the basic molecular structure of a crystal by looking at the light patterns created when x-rays are shone through it.

x-ray diffraction   Instrumentation used for the identification of crystals' crystalline structures.

yang   The male component embodying the concept of strength, aggression, creativity, the sun, and positive polarity.

yin   The female component embodying the concept of nurturing, openness, receptivity, the moon, and negative polarity.

Appendix C

Further Reading

Andrews, Ted. *Crystal Balls and Crystal Bowls: Tools for Ancient Scrying for Modern Seership.* Woodbury, MN: Llewellyn Publications, 2005.

Andrews, Synthia, and Colin Andrews. *The Complete Idiot's Guide to the Akashic Record.* Indianapolis: Alpha Books, 2010.

Baer, Randall N., and Vicki Vittitow-Baer. *The Crystal Connection: A Guidebook for Personal and Planetary Ascension.* San Francisco: Harper and Row, 1986.

Brennan, Barbara Ann. *Hands of Light: A Guide to Healing Through the Human Energy Field.* New York: Bantam Books, 1987.

Chase, Pamela Loiuse, and Jonathan Pawlik. *The Newcastle Guide to Healing with Gemstones: How to Use Over 70 Different Gemstone Energies.* North Hollywood, CA: Newcastle Publishing Co., Inc., 1989.

Chokyi Nyima Rinpoche, with David R. Shlim, M.D. *Medicine and Compassion: A Tibetan Lama's Guidance for Caregivers.* Boston: Wisdom Publications, 2006.

Edison, Deborah. *Vibrational Healing: Revealing the Essence of Nature Through Aromatherapy's Use of Essential Oils.* Berkeley, CA: Frog Ltd., 2000.

Gardner, Joy. *Color and Crystals: A Journey Through the Chakras.* Freedom, CA: The Crossing Press, 1988.

Johari, Haroish. *Chakras: Energy Centers of Transformation.* Rochester, VT: Destiny Books, 2000.

———. *The Healing Power of Gemstones in Tantra, Ayuveda and Astrology.* Rochester, VT: Destiny Books, 1988.

Judith, Anodea. *Wheels of Life: A User's Guide to the Chakra System.* Woodbury, MN: Llewellyn Publications, 1999.

Laskow, Leonard. *Healing with Love: A Physician's Breakthrough Mind/Body Medical Guide for Healing Yourself and Others: The Art of Holoenergetic Healing.* San Francisco: Harper, 1992.

Mason, Henry M. *The Seven Secrets of Crystal Talismans: How to Use Their Power for Attraction, Protection and Transformation.* Woodbury, MN: Llewellyn Publications, 2008.

Masunaga, Shizuto, with Wataru Ohashi. *Zen Shaitsu: How to Harmonize Yin and Yang for Better Health.* New York: Japan Publications, Inc., 1989.

Melody. *Love Is in the Earth: A Kaleidoscope of Crystals.* Richland, WA: Earth-Love Publishing House, 1991.

———. *Love Is in the Earth: Laying-on-of-stones: The Journey Continues.* Richland, WA: Earth-Love Publishing House, 1992.

Pawlik, Jonathan, and Pamela Chase. *The Newcastle Guide to Healing with Crystals: Balancing the Human Energy Field for Physical and Spiritual Well-Being.* North Hollywood, CA: Newcastle Publishing Co., Inc., 1988.

Rafael, Katrina. *Crystal Enlightenment: The Transforming Properties of Crystals and Healing Stones, Vol. 1.* Santa Fe, NM: Aurora Press, 1985.

———. *Crystal Healing: Applying the Therapeutic Properties of Crystals and Stones, Vol. 2.* Santa Fe, NM: Aurora Press, 1987.

———. *The Crystalline Transmission: A Synthesis of Light, Vol. 3.* Santa Fe, NM: Aurora Press, 1990.

Rippentrop, Betsy, and Eve Adamson. *The Complete Idiot's Guide to Chakras.* Indianapolis: Alpha Books, 2009.

Ryan, Karen. *How to Use Your Pyramid.* Mississauga, ON, Canada: The Crystal Tiger, 1998.

———. *Spiritual Aromatherapy: The Subtle Effects of Essential Oils on the Human Spirit.* Mississauga, ON, Canada: The Crystal Tiger, 1997.

Scheffer, Methchild. *Bach Flower Therapy*. Rochester, NY: Thorson's Publishing, 1986.

Sheldrake, Marianna. *The Crystal Healer: A Guide to Understanding Crystals and Their Healing Gifts*. Saffron Walden, Essex, UK: C.W. Daniel Company Limited, 1999.

Sibley, Uma. *Crystal Ball Gazing: The Complete Guide to Choosing and Reading Your Crystal Ball*. New York: Fireside, 1998.

———. *The Complete Crystal Guidebook: A Practical Path to Self Development, Empowerment and Healing for the Beginner to the Advanced*. San Francisco: U-Read Publications, 1986.

Tulku Thondrup Rinpoche. *The Healing Power of Mind: Simple Meditation Exercises for Health, Well-Being and Enlightenment*. Boston: Shambala Publications, Inc., 1996.

Wilde, Stuart. *Affirmations*. Taos, NM: White Dove International, 1987.

———. *The Quickening*. Carlsbad, CA: Hay House, 1988.

Index

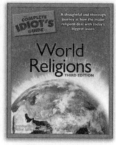

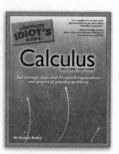

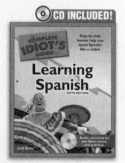

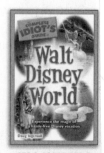